KINGS IN CONFLICT

KINGS IN CONFLICT

The Revolutionary War in Ireland

and its Aftermath

1689-1750

edited by W.A.Maguire

THE
BLACKSTAFF
PRESS

BELFAST

First published in 1990 by
The Blackstaff Press Limited
3 Galway Park, Dundonald, Belfast BT16 0AN, Northern Ireland
in association with
the Ulster Museum

Typeset by Textflow Services Limited

Printed by the Bath Press
British Library Cataloguing in Publication Data
Kings in conflict : the revolutionary war in Ireland and its aftermath, 1689–1750.
1. Ireland, 1603–1799
I. Maguire, W. A. (William Alexander), 1932–
941.506
ISBN 0-85640-435-7

CONTENTS

SOURCES OF ILLUSTRATIONS

BLACK-AND-WHITE ILLUSTRATIONS

COLOUR ILLUSTRATIONS

MAPS

ACKNOWLEDGEMENTS

The thanks of the editor and contributors are due first to the bodies that provided the financial support without which this volume could not have been published. The Northern Ireland Bankers' Association and the Northern Ireland Tourist Board were particularly generous, but substantial assistance was also given by the Esmé Mitchell Trust, Bord Fáilte (the Irish tourist board), and the Trustee Savings Bank. The editor is also grateful for useful help and advice from Rosemary Evans, Sir Desmond Lorimer, Dr Anthony Malcomson and Rafton Pounder.

Thanks are also due to the Director and Trustees of the Ulster Museum, which provided many of the illustrations, and to a number of the editor's colleagues in the museum: Heather White for making available the maps she drew for the tercentenary exhibition; Bill Anderson-Porter, Michael McKeown and Gerry Watters for photographic work; and Pauline Dickson, who did all the work on the typescript with her usual efficiency and cheerfulness. The sources of the illustrations are separately acknowledged elsewhere; all who provided prints or gave permission are gratefully, if collectively, thanked here.

Lastly, the editor would like to thank the contributors. Though only one or two were as prompt in submitting their scripts as an anxious editor (is there any other kind?) would have wished, all did so before the real deadline was reached and all submitted without complaint to the minor changes that were thought necessary. It has been a pleasure to deal with them.

CHRONOLOGY
1660–1766

NOTE

Dates of days and months are given here according to the calendar used in the British Isles before 1752, which was ten days behind the present reckoning in the years preceding 1700 and eleven days behind in the years 1700–52.

14 May 1660	Charles II is proclaimed king in Dublin.
31 July 1662	Act of Settlement establishes the ownership of disputed Irish land in favour of existing Cromwellian proprietors.
21 August 1663	Court of claims, appointed under the Act of Settlement, closes after issuing 566 decrees of innocence to Catholics, but leaving thousands of claims unheard.
1665	Act of Explanation modifies the Act of Settlement by requiring most of the Cromwellians to give up one-third of their holdings to provide land for restored Catholics.
1672	Louis XIV of France invades Dutch Republic (United Provinces). William of Orange is appointed captain-general of the Dutch Republic and stadtholder in Holland and Zeeland.
1677	William of Orange marries Princess Mary, elder daughter of the duke of York (later James II).
1678	Peace of Nijmegen ends the Dutch war with France, to the advantage of the Dutch. Titus Oates uncovers the so-called Popish Plot in England.
15 May 1679	Exclusion Bill is introduced in English House of Commons to bar the duke of York from the throne.
1680	Louis begins extending France's north-eastern frontier towards the Rhine.
1682	War (not concluded till 1699) breaks out between the Ottoman Turkish empire and the Austrian Habsburgs.
1683	Vienna is besieged by the Turks.
6 February 1685	James II becomes king of England, Scotland and Ireland on the death of Charles II.
20 June 1685	Richard Talbot, Irish Catholic champion, is created earl of Tyrconnell.
July 1685	The rebellions of Monmouth and Argyll against James are crushed.
January 1686	Second earl of Clarendon is sworn in as lord lieutenant of Ireland.
5 June 1686	Tyrconnell is appointed to command the Irish army.
July 1686	The league of Augsburg (Habsburgs, Sweden and various German states) is formed to resist Louis.

12 February 1687	Tyrconnell is sworn in as lord deputy of Ireland.
10 June 1688	James's queen, Mary of Modena, gives birth to a son (the Old Pretender).
30 June 1688	The 'seven bishops', arrested by James for refusing to promulgate his Declaration of Indulgence, are acquitted in London. Leading Whigs and Tories invite William of Orange to invade England.
September 1688	Following the refusal of Pope Innocent XI to appoint the French candidate archbishop of Cologne, Louis invades the Rhineland, thus clearing the way for William's invasion of England.
5 November 1688	William lands in Devon.
16 November 1688	Louis declares war on the Dutch Republic.
7 December 1688	The gates of Derry are shut against the earl of Antrim's regiment.
23 December 1688	James escapes to France, at the second attempt.
8 January 1689	Richard Hamilton, sent by William to negotiate Tyrconnell's submission, arrives in Dublin and joins Tyrconnell.
13 February 1689	William and Mary accept the Bill of Rights and are declared joint sovereigns of England, Scotland and Ireland.
12 March 1689	James lands at Kinsale, Co. Cork.
14 March 1689	The Ulster Protestants are routed at the 'break of Dromore', Co. Down.
21 March 1689	James Hamilton arrives at Derry with money and supplies. William appoints Lundy commander of the city.
18 April 1689	James is refused entry to Derry; the siege begins.
1 May 1689	Inconclusive battle in Bantry Bay between English and French fleets.
7 May–18 July 1689	James's Irish parliament.
7 May 1689	England declares war on France.
18 June 1689	James issues a proclamation providing for the circulation of 'brass money'.
22 June 1689	Irish parliament repeals the Restoration land settlement.
27 July 1689	The Jacobite leader in Scotland, Viscount Dundee, is killed at the battle of Killiecrankie.
28 July 1689	Williamite ships break the boom at Derry and relieve the city.
31 July 1689	Jacobite army under Justin MacCarthy, Viscount Mountcashel, is defeated by the Enniskilleners at Newtownbutler, Co. Fermanagh.
13 August 1689	Williamite army under Schomberg lands near Bangor, Co. Down.
12 March 1690	French regiments under the comte de Lauzun land at Cork.
13 March 1690	Danish army under the duke of Wurtemberg, hired by William, arrives in Belfast Lough.

18 April 1690	Irish regiments under Justin MacCarthy leave Cork for France.
14 May 1690	Charlemont, Co. Armagh, surrenders to Schomberg.
14 June 1690	William lands near Carrickfergus, Co. Antrim.
30 June 1690	French fleet defeats the English and Dutch off Beachy Head.
1 July 1690	William's army defeats James's at the River Boyne.
4 July 1690	James sails from Kinsale for France.
6 July 1690	William enters Dublin.
17–24 July 1690	Williamite siege of Athlone fails.
9–30 August 1690	First siege of Limerick, directed by William, fails.
5 September 1690	William returns to England.
12 September 1690	French army, with Lauzun and Tyrconnell, sails from Galway for France.
28 September 1690	Cork surrenders to the earl of Marlborough.
14 January 1691	Tyrconnell arrives back in Ireland, landing at Limerick.
9 May 1691	Marquis de St Ruth, French general, lands at Limerick.
21–30 June 1691	William's commander in Ireland, Ginkel, besieges and takes Athlone.
12 July 1691	Ginkel defeats the Jacobite army with great slaughter at Aughrim.
21 July 1691	Galway surrenders on terms to Ginkel.
25 August 1691	Second siege of Limerick is begun by Ginkel.
14 September 1691	Sligo surrenders to the Williamites.
3 October 1691	Treaty of Limerick is signed, ending the war in Ireland.
22 December 1691	Sarsfield sails to France with 12,000 Jacobite soldiers.
6 April 1692	Irish privy council begins hearing claims under the articles of Limerick.
24 May 1692	French invasion fleet is defeated off the coast of France at La Hogue.
28 December 1694	Mary II dies.
7 September 1695	Irish parliament passes acts disarming Catholics and forbidding them to send their children abroad for education.
15 February 1696	Jacobite plot to assassinate William is foiled in London.
10 September 1697	Peace of Ryswick between France and the Allies (England, Holland, Spain) brings the Nine Years War to an end. Louis recognises William as legitimate king of England and promises to withdraw support from James.
20 October 1697	Emperor Leopold I makes peace with Louis.
January 1699	Irish parliament passes 'An Act to prevent papists being solicitors'.

11 April 1700	Act of Resumption in England cancels William's grants of forfeited land and appoints trustees to sell estates.
27 August 1701	Grand Alliance (England, Dutch Republic, Habsburg emperor) is formed against France, following the death of Charles II of Spain and Louis XIV's acceptance of the throne of Spain for his grandson.
6 September 1701	James dies at Saint-Germain; Louis recognises his son (the Old Pretender) as James III.
8 March 1702	William dies and is succeeded by Queen Anne.
4 May 1702	War of the Spanish Succession begins.
4 March 1704	Irish parliament passes an 'Act to prevent the further growth of popery', and an act requiring Catholic clergy to register with the authorities.
March 1708	Jacobites attempt to invade Scotland.
30 August 1709	Irish parliament strengthens the popery act of 1704.
31 March 1713	Treaty of Utrecht ends the War of the Spanish Succession. Protestant succession in England is confirmed, Old Pretender has to leave France. Orange becomes part of France. Louis's grandson keeps Spain but France and Spain are never to unite. The emperor gets the Spanish Netherlands. England makes important colonial gains at the expense of France.
1 August 1714	Queen Anne dies and is succeeded by George I.
21 August 1715	Louis dies and is succeeded by his grandson Louis XV.
6 September 1715	Jacobite rising in Scotland begins.
22 December 1715	Old Pretender lands in Scotland.
4 February 1716	Old Pretender leaves Scotland for France.
2 November 1719	Toleration act for Irish Protestant dissenters is passed.
25 July 1745	Charles Edward Stuart, the Young Pretender, lands in Scotland.
16 April 1746	Jacobite army is finally defeated at Culloden.
1 January 1766	James III, the Old Pretender, dies. Thereafter the pope ceases to accept Stuart nominations of Catholic bishops for Ireland.

INTRODUCTION

Many events in the past are hard for us to apprehend because they have become obscure and neglected; a few, on the contrary, because they have never ceased to be famous. The events of the Irish Jacobite war, 1689–91, are in the latter category. Their use as symbols of triumph and disaster by successive generations of Irish people has made it even more difficult than is usually the case to appreciate them as historical events in their own right. This book is intended to assist the process of understanding those events in the context of their time, by putting before the general reader, in an easily accessible form, the results of recent work by scholars of the period.

The book has its origins in an Ulster Museum exhibition, also entitled *Kings in Conflict*, which was planned to mark the tercentenary in 1990 of the battle of the Boyne. The year 1690 is to Irish history what 1066 is to the history of England: every schoolchild is supposed to know what happened then. But whereas *1066 and All That* could safely be employed as the title of a comic history of England, '1690 and All That' seemed altogether too facetious a title for an exhibition illustrating events that can still stir powerful emotions. At the same time, 'all that' was just what needed explaining: the background to the events of three hundred years ago, and their immediate consequences, required to be dealt with as well as the war itself. This consideration determined the shape of the exhibition and, when it was decided to produce a volume on the same theme, the contents of this book.

There would have been no Jacobite war in Ireland if there had been no Glorious Revolution in England; and there would have been no Revolution (at least of the kind that happened) if William of Orange had not needed to ensure the participation of England in his crusade against Louis XIV. In the first chapter Graham Gibbs, in dealing with the complex European origins of the Glorious Revolution, emphasises both the dominating position of Louis and the messianic nature of William's determination to thwart the French king's ambitions. Given the chancy chain of circumstances that enabled William to complete his English venture successfully, it is little wonder he believed that divine providence was on his side. John Miller's chapter on the Glorious Revolution analyses the causes of James II's downfall, the mixed feelings that William's invasion and the flight of James created for his subjects, and the reasons for William's decision to go to Ireland. In Chapter 3 James McGuire argues convincingly that James's headlong policy in Ireland, which created enormous alarm among the Protestants there, as well as greatly adding to fears of 'popery' and arbitrary government in England, was really the policy of his domineering friend and lord deputy, Tyrconnell. At any rate Tyrconnell created a base from which James – his nerve recovered and his hand strengthened by Louis – could attempt to recover his lost thrones; with his arrival in 1689, Ireland became part of the theatre of operations in a European war.

The next four chapters deal with aspects of that conflict. Its Irish name, *Cogadh an Dá Rí*, which translates as the 'war of the two kings', reflects the Irish perception of it as a struggle for power between James and William. From a European point of view, however, the two kings in conflict were William and Louis; this view was shared by some English observers too, such as the author of a 1689 pamphlet entitled *K. William or K. Lewis*, 'written out of Cheshire by a Gentleman lately arrived there from Ireland'.[1]

Perhaps, as Harman Murtagh suggests in his chapter on the war in Ireland, it would be appropriate to call the struggle 'the war of the three kings'. Louis's military aid to James, however, after Lauzun's expedition in 1690, was never sufficient to do anything more than prolong the war and divert William. That a great deal more could have been done is amply demonstrated by Alan Pearsall in Chapter 5. Able to come and go without serious challenge apart from the single sea fight off Bantry Bay in 1689, the French dominated the sea between the battles of Beachy Head in 1690 and La Hogue two years later. Analysis of this vital but comparatively neglected aspect of the war shows how it too was affected, on both sides, by the imperatives of a much wider strategy, and how it affected in turn the wider ambitions of William. The nature and importance of propaganda, used by both sides but with conspicuously greater success by the Williamites, is the subject of a wide-ranging chapter by David Hayton. As he says, in Ireland itself there was little scope for changing hearts and minds by such means, but propaganda had other uses and the struggle for Ireland spawned a great deal of it. Lastly, in this section, Robert Heslip explores the complicated question of James's emergency Irish coinage, the 'brass money' of Williamite demonology.

Chapters 8 and 9 deal with the two major consequences in Ireland of the war of 1689–91. My own contribution on the land settlement is inevitably based to a large extent on J. G. Simms's masterly work on the Williamite confiscation, which has provided a reliable framework for the detailed analysis that remains to be done. The significant points are that the Williamite land settlement confirmed and extended the Restoration settlement; and that it was much less sweeping in the matter of confiscations than has often been supposed.

As Sean Connolly points out in his chapter on the penal laws, however, the transfer of wealth and power from Catholic to Protestant was already far advanced by 1689; the application of the penal laws merely completed the process, once the attempted counter-revolution had failed. The new-found importance of the Irish parliament (after 1690 an entirely Protestant body), which was a consequence of the Revolution, limited the ability of English monarchs to mitigate the intolerance of its members even when consideration for the feelings of Catholic allies might have inclined them to do so. The volume ends, appropriately enough for a book that revolves around military events, with Thomas Bartlett's chapter on the army and society in eighteenth-century Ireland. The picture he reveals is a great deal more complicated, and more interesting, than the generally accepted one of a colonial territory occupied by an English army.

One aspect not dealt with here, except in passing, is the cost of the war in Ireland. In terms of money, it cost William's government more than six million pounds, far more than even the most optimistic calculation of the value of what might be forfeited by the defeated, not to mention the cost to the French treasury. The cost in blood was also considerable, though not so great as it might have been. Contemporary warfare in Europe, conducted by professional armies according to generally recognised rules, seldom sought to annihilate the enemy and did not usually seek to destroy the territory in which both sides operated (hence the shock when occasionally the brutality of the soldiery was deliberately used as an instrument of terror, as by Louis in the Palatinate in 1688, rather than checked). Things were rather less tidy than that in Ireland, especially in areas held firmly by neither side and therefore plundered by both. Nevertheless, considering the length of the war and the size of the armies engaged, the number of soldiers killed in battle was not enormous – probably less than twenty-five thousand, two-fifths of whom died in one day at Aughrim. Thousands more, of course, died of disease, most notably in Schomberg's army in 1689.

The effects on the civilian population are more difficult to estimate. Serious physical destruction was worst at Londonderry, where the long bombardment severely damaged most of the houses. Limerick, though heavily bombarded during the second siege, suffered much less in this respect. Cork endured only a brief siege. Smaller places, such as Athlone, in County Westmeath, and Carrickfergus, in County Antrim, fared worse in proportion to their size. Dublin, however, by far the largest centre of population, was entirely saved from destruction. The breakdown of normal government in the countryside no doubt led to a good deal of damage to the houses of those active on one side or the other and to the plunder of their contents, such as is described in the diary of that long-suffering, if not uncomplaining, Englishwoman Elizabeth Freke. Returning to Rathbarry, County Cork, in November 1692, she found her

> House quit Burntt downe, Only two little Rooms, & neither A Bed, Table or Chair or Stool fitt for a christian to sett on – dish or plat to eatte outte of . . . and on the Land . . . only Two sheep And Two Lambs & three or 4 Garron horses, worth aboutt Ten shillings A piece.[2]

Sometimes property was destroyed by the owners themselves, as the fighting caused panic among civilians fearful of a traditional enemy. After the defeat of the northern Williamites at the 'break of Dromore', we are told:

> the Irish proceeded towards Colerain, and found no opposition till they came thither; but for the first 15 or 16 miles found nothing but ruin'd Houses, and the Ditches full of Houshold-goods, Meal and Corn, thrown away by the

Protestants to prevent its falling into the hands of the merciless devouring Enemy.[3]

There are harrowing descriptions, by the Williamite historian George Story and other eyewitnesses, of the misery of a civilian population affected by shortages of food in a land devoured by soldiers as by locusts. Official proclamations from both sides prohibiting the plunder and destruction of crops and fodder only confirm that such behaviour was common wherever the soldiers passed. Other, more fortunate, areas appear to have continued almost as in peacetime: in his diary the Williamite officer Thomas Bellingham mentions the corn growing at Gernonstown, his property in County Louth, and notes visiting it on his way to the Boyne in 1690 and finding 'severall of the tenants with theyr cattle'.[4]

There is ample evidence from similar sources that that most moveable kind of property – livestock – was requisitioned, confiscated or simply stolen in enormous numbers, to the ruin of land-holders great and small. Those who profited from such plunder included some prominent people: the report of the forfeiture commissioners in 1699 accuses Coningsby, William's paymaster-general, of having 'seized a great many Black Cattle, to the number of 300, or thereabouts, besides Horses, which were left in The Park after the Battel of the Boyne, and which we do not find were ever accounted for to his Majesty'.[5] Some estates lost most of their tenants, and found it hard to replace them during the lean years that followed. The evidence of the hearth tax suggests that the number of households able to pay it declined by one-third between 1687 and 1694, the worst-affected counties being in north Munster, south-west Ulster and the north Midlands.[6] At the same time it is worth remembering that normal life in some other parts of the British Isles could be bad enough to make even Ireland seem attractive: a series of disastrous harvests in Scotland led to heavy emigration to Ulster in the late 1690s, to the well-publicised alarm of the episcopalian clergy there.

Reviewing the events of this momentous period in Irish history prompts one final reflection. While historians generally consider it unprofitable, indeed unprofessional, to speculate on what might have happened if things had not turned out as they did, one justification for considering alternative outcomes is that they help to remind us that what actually happened was not inevitable. Of course nothing can change the past, but one of the chief obstacles to understanding how things were at the time is the difficulty of imagining how their outcome could have been different. Yet chance, or providence, plays a large part in human life, and never more obviously than in war and battle.

Whatever general theory one may hold about the importance of individuals in history, as opposed to impersonal forces, no one can doubt that at this particular juncture in the history of England and Ireland, as also of Europe, William of Orange occupied a crucial place and exercised a crucial influence. In 1690 he could easily have been killed, and in fact had several narrow escapes at the Boyne, at a time when his deposed father-in-law still occupied most of Ireland and would have been conveniently placed to negotiate his own restoration. It would indeed be idle to speculate in any detail as to what difference William's removal from the scene might have made, but there can be little doubt that it would have made an immediate difference to the campaign in Ireland, if not to the outcome of the war. George Story was quite certain about that. After describing William's injury by a Jacobite cannon ball on the eve of the Boyne, he writes:

> I cannot but take notice of a signal piece of Providence in the preservation of the Kings Person, for whatever ill effects it might have had for the future, it would have been of fatal consequence to the Army at the time, if he had fallen, since instead of our going to them, the Irish would have been ready to come to us next morning, and how we would have received them there's none can tell.[7]

W. A. Maguire
Department of Local History
Ulster Museum, Belfast
January 1990

PART ONE

THE CONTEXT

KONSTE VAN
KINING-WILLEM
IN HOLLAND.

In den Haegh
by Arnout Leers 1691.

THE EUROPEAN ORIGINS
OF THE GLORIOUS REVOLUTION

G.C. GIBBS

On 10 October 1688 William of Orange published a Declaration setting out his reasons for deciding to proceed with the invasion of England. Although initiated in England, the Declaration was completed in the Dutch Republic after consultation with a number of English Whig exiles and after redrafting by Gaspar Fagel, grand pensionary of Holland and one of William's most trusted advisers, and Gilbert Burnet. It appeared in English, Dutch, French and German, and was published in The Hague, Amsterdam, Edinburgh, London, York, Hamburg and Magdeburg. Around fifty thousand copies were shipped to England, and copies were also handed to all the foreign representatives at The Hague except those of England and France.[1]

The circumstances in which the Declaration was formulated, published and distributed serve as a reminder that the Glorious Revolution was an unusual conspiracy, which combined great secrecy with enormous publicity. More to the point here, it was as much an event in European as in British history and its European significance extended far beyond the Dutch Republic. Indeed the need for the Revolution, its timing and its aims were all firmly rooted in, and mainly determined by, European politics – in particular, by William's perception of his role, and the role of Britain, in European politics. The fact that the Glorious Revolution brought to the throne of England an international statesman whose grasp of international relations was rivalled only by one other contemporary, Louis XIV, and for whom European considerations outweighed all others, contributed powerfully to the speed with which the major changes of the Revolution were enacted in England and ensured that the Revolution would be European in its consequences as well as in its origins and establishment.

The European aspect of the Revolution is the subject of this chapter; in particular, the role played by European factors in making it necessary, possible and successful. One does not need to replace 'the persuasive reality of a Dutch invasion' with 'the more comfortable vision of international co-operation', even less to echo G.M. Trevelyan's characterisation of that

Allegorical representation of the triumph of William II, by Romeyn de Hooghe, title page of *Komste van Koning Willem in Holland*, published to record the returning hero's welcome to The Hague in 1691.

9

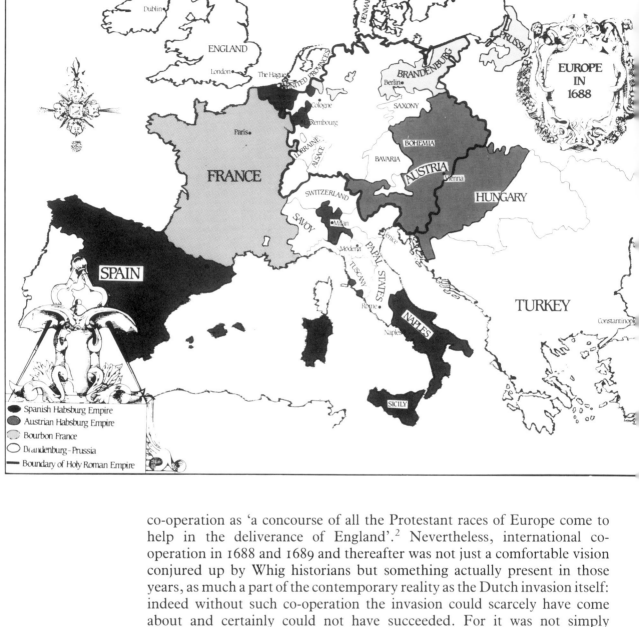

co-operation as 'a concourse of all the Protestant races of Europe come to help in the deliverance of England'.[2] Nevertheless, international co-operation in 1688 and 1689 and thereafter was not just a comfortable vision conjured up by Whig historians but something actually present in those years, as much a part of the contemporary reality as the Dutch invasion itself: indeed without such co-operation the invasion could scarcely have come about and certainly could not have succeeded. For it was not simply William's response to events in England, or even the response of the Dutch Republic: it grew out of a particular conjunction of European events, forces and alignments. Those involved were concerned fundamentally not with the deliverance of England from James II but with England's deliverance into a European coalition against the France of Louis XIV – a move that proved impossible without replacing James. In terms of European history, the Glorious Revolution has an order of importance which places it alongside the defeat of the Ottoman Turks before Vienna in 1683 and the revocation of the Edict of Nantes in 1685, as one of the three most important international events in European history in the last quarter of the seventeenth century; and

not simply alongside them chronologically, but linked in a chain with them.

The beginning, however, must be with William of Orange himself, the principal of principals in the Glorious Revolution and the main architect of the European coalition against Louis. William was a complex person, but in one respect he was, after 1672, a man of clear insight, single-minded purpose and determination. In 1672 the Dutch Republic had come near to destruction at the hands of France and England. Henceforth William's dominating lifelong purpose was to curb French aggression and so prevent a recurrence of the terrible events of that year. It seemed obvious to him that the Dutch alone could not successfully resist and contain France, and equally obvious that France would attack again if allowed to grow more powerful. The remedy was to unite those powers threatened by France, and this meant persuading others of their common interest and, in the first place, persuading the Dutch themselves. For although in 1672 William had become what he was to remain, the national leader of the Dutch, his position in the United Provinces was peculiar and difficult. Many Dutchmen were attached to the House of Orange and most Dutchmen probably admired William, but practically all of them wanted their country to remain a republic. That republic was a loose confederation of provinces, in which unanimity was required for common action, even if its absence did not always prevent common action. Prompt and effective action depended fundamentally on two things; a general determination that the constitution must work, and the preponderance of the province of Holland, which paid over half the taxes of the republic. When William and Holland agreed, the other provinces usually fell into line.

William and his friends among the oligarchs could often manage Holland,

William received as a ward of state, 1666, a mark of his growing importance in Dutch affairs.

The people of Orange pledging loyalty to Prince William, 7 May 1665. William had to agree to appoint a Catholic governor before Louis XIV would restore the principality. After further occupations, it finally became part of France in 1713.

but they could not attempt to coerce it. The great city of Amsterdam, in particular, did not always see eye to eye with William. Amsterdam was traditionally suspicious of the House of Orange, and since it was one of the world's great ports, it was always reluctant to support a war, or a policy that might result in war, till convinced that national security depended on it. In 1672 William had become captain-general, or commander-in-chief, of the United Provinces for life; after 1674 he was also the chief civil magistrate (stadtholder) in five of the provinces, including Holland. These positions enhanced his prestige and influence, which varied from one province to another, and therefore his power. But, though powerful, William lacked the power to command the republic to take any decision. Fundamentally his power depended on his capacity to persuade his countrymen that his policy was in the interest of the common weal. A formidable task in persuasion confronted him in the 1680s, in the first place and most urgently in regard to Amsterdam.

The peace of Nijmegen in 1678, ending the Dutch War, not only preserved intact the territorial integrity of the Dutch Republic but also caused Louis to moderate significantly his economic war against the Dutch. Given the threat to the republic's very survival in the early years of the war, this represented a considerable victory. William himself, however, drew very different inferences from the republic's performance in the war and achievements at the peace. To William the peace was not a victory, and was more a moral failure than a disappointment. He accepted it not merely reluctantly but, after needless and costly procrastination, as falling short not only of what further military effort might have achieved but of God's expectations. The dramatic turnaround in Dutch fortunes seemed to him a miracle, which strengthened his faith in divine providence and his conviction that he had been chosen by God as His instrument in a mission to humble Louis's pride and to make him see reason. The struggle against Louis therefore became something at once personal – more personal after 1682, when French troops occupied William's principality of Orange in south-east France – and universal, even cosmic.

For the next two decades this struggle locked both William and Louis in a world of monstrous fantasies: William was seen by Louis as totally irrational in his opposition to France, and Louis was seen by William as the unrelenting protagonist of a design to impose upon Europe a 'universal monarchy', even a 'universal religion'.[3] For William the struggle meant running risks and not counting the costs or, what amounted to the same thing, being prepared to pay all the costs in the certainty that in God's grand design for him and the Dutch Republic all would come right in the end. Thus in March 1682, when a French invasion of the Spanish Netherlands was imminent, he argued before the States of Holland[4] for honouring immediately the republic's treaty obligations to help Spain defend her territories against an actual attack by France, even if this necessitated acting alone in support of

The signing of the peace of Nijmegen, 1678, which ended the war begun by Louis XIV's invasion of the Dutch Republic in 1672.

French envoys at the peace of Nijmegen, 1678: (seated from left) d'Estrades, Colbert and d'Avaux.

Spain. The best security against a war with France, he insisted, the best means of enlisting allies if such a war occurred, and the surest guarantee of the maintenance of Dutch interests, was for the Dutch Republic to set an example and to live up to its mission.[5]

This was less an argument than a declaration of faith, and it did not commend itself to the States of Holland or to the city of Amsterdam, which saw in William's policies not only unacceptable risks and crippling burdens but also a renewed Orangeist threat to use the war to advance the powers of the stadtholder – as had happened in past wars, including the most recent.[6] There was, however, a more principled and more solidly based case for opposition. For if it was true, as William asserted, that the security of Dutch trade depended on the security of the Dutch Republic and its will to resist French territorial expansion,[7] it was also true, as was argued by Amsterdam, that the ruin of Dutch trade would seriously impair, and might fatally weaken, the capacity of the republic to defend itself.

Lack of trust and good will between William and the regents of Amsterdam, and the absence of a threat from France which both sides could recognise as requiring their common action, delayed reconciliation of these opposing views in the early 1680s. When reconciliation came in 1685, it came as a result of a great wave of anti-French feeling generated by Louis's treatment of French Protestants, the Huguenots, which reached a momentous climax in October 1685 with the revocation of the Edict of Nantes, abolishing what remained of the civil rights and religious freedoms granted to the Huguenots in 1598.

The first results of the revocation in the Dutch Republic, and in the towns of the province of Holland in particular, were a sharp increase in arrivals of Huguenot refugees. In Amsterdam, which already had a community of nearly thirty-five hundred, more refugees arrived in 1685 than had arrived in the three previous years combined, and more than five times as many as had arrived in 1684. Even this dramatic increase was dwarfed by arrivals in the following years: in 1686, the peak year of the decade, refugees are held to have numbered 1,246; to have exceeded 1,000 in 1687; and to have come close to 1,000 in 1688. In the course of the four years 1685 to 1688 inclusive, nearly four thousand refugees arrived in Amsterdam and the size of the French community there almost doubled. Even so, as a proportion of the total population of the city, the community remained small, hovering around the figure of 3 per cent at its peak: a smaller proportion of the city's population than was the case with the Huguenot population of London.[8] But numbers were less important than the economic importance attached to Huguenots as potential energisers of a failing economy and by their remarkable articulateness: more than 40 per cent of the seven hundred or so Huguenot ministers who fled France after 1680 settled permanently in the Dutch Republic, and a fifth of those who settled permanently and died there were domiciled in Amsterdam.[9] As in England, in the 1680s the Huguenots in the Dutch Republic constituted a highly vocal, influential and increasingly visible presence. As in England, their standing helped to bring about decisive changes in the climate of opinion and the balance of political forces, both domestically and in terms of attitudes and policies towards France, which opened the way for the Glorious Revolution.

Louis's treatment of the Huguenots made it increasingly difficult, and ultimately impossible, to hold Amsterdam to its opposition to William's policies, and for Francophiles in the republic to retain a belief in the benevolence of Louis's intentions, which was a main thrust of the diplomatic endeavours of the comte d'Avaux, the French ambassador at The Hague in the 1680s. It also provided William and his many Orangeist and Huguenot publicists in the republic with easy and eagerly seized opportunities to mobilise the Dutch in support of William's policies and to represent him as the saviour of European Protestantism. The revocation of the Edict of Nantes was followed almost immediately in the republic by the formal reconciliation of William and the city of Amsterdam. According to d'Avaux,

William and Mary receiving Huguenot refugees and providing them with money and food; detail from 'Tyrannies towards the Protestants in France' by Romeyn de Hooghe, 1686.

TIRANNIEN TEGEN DE GEREFORMEERDEN IN VRANKRYK

Caricature of the Sun King as persecutor. Louis XIV's savage treatment of the Huguenots shocked European Protestants, especially the Dutch.

French religious affairs had become a consuming Dutch interest. Also, again according to d'Avaux, Amsterdammers were scarcely less sensible to the economic repercussions of Louis's persecution of his Protestant subjects upon Dutch trade with France than they were with the threat to Protestantism.[10] A consuming interest in French religious affairs, then, was accompanied by a panic about Dutch trade with France.

It is somewhat surprising, therefore, that after providing reassurances in 1686 that the revocation was not intended to prevent or impede normal trading contact between foreign Protestants and France, or to reduce their customary liberties in France, Louis should have resumed in the second half of 1687 large-scale economic warfare against the republic.[11] The consequence of this among the Dutch was a renewed and intensified panic about French trade. When it became clear that Louis was not disposed to abate his mercantilistic assault, despite diplomatic representations and the threat of Dutch economic retaliation, there seemed no alternative but to fight it out.[12] Withdrawal of opposition to William's policies, which had been the extent of reconciliation achieved in 1685, was transformed into active support for them, and for his English venture.

Unquestionably, economic factors of the kind indicated were an important element in the general context. One tribute to their importance was William's view that although there was no intention on the part of the Dutch towns to proceed with retaliatory economic measures, such deliberations at least served the purpose of heightening political awareness in the republic; they also brought to the fore the need to take diplomatic and military measures for Dutch defence in the event of French attack, and to facilitate the military enterprise upon England.[13] In other words, if William's reading of the balance of priorities in the Dutch towns in August 1688 is correct, trade was not only important to them but so important as still to constitute a restraint upon action against France, even economic action.

That certainly seems to have been the case with Amsterdam, where as late as 24 September 1688 – the very day on which William made his formal request to the States of Holland for support in his expedition to England – the regents apparently still hoped that the threat of economic retaliation would prove sufficient to cause Louis to beat an economic retreat.[14] Yet five days later, on 29 September 1688, the States of Holland with the unanimous concurrence of Amsterdam pledged military and naval support to William in his expedition to England. It seems too simple to ascribe this dramatic turnaround on the part of Amsterdammers in particular, and of the mercantile interest more generally, merely to a careful consideration of trading interests, which led them to the conclusion that the situation could not get worse. In fact the situation did worsen once war against France had begun, and the Dutch found themselves involved in what has been described very recently as the most relentless economic war in the mercantilist era, a war in which the Dutch had to struggle not only against France but also against an English preference for total economic warfare, which they did not share.[15]

William III (1650–1702) on
horseback, c.1690, a pose
that has become traditional

Mary II (1662–94) as
Princess of Orange

Leaving aside that miscalculation, it may be suggested that the crucial effect of William's request for support in his English enterprise was to oblige the Dutch to concentrate their minds, and that there was more for them to concentrate upon in September 1688 than the economic warfare waged by France.

There was first of all the return of a nightmare, recurrent since the accession of James II, namely the existence or imminent re-creation of a second union between England and France such as had been formed in 1670 and had so nearly extinguished the republic in the following years. Fears of its revival had acted as a spur to the reconciliation of 1685 and had been strengthened in 1687 and 1688 when James demanded the return of English troops in the service of the republic. These fears were very much alive in August 1688 when Hans Willem Bentinck (in the course of a European mission to the Protestant princes of Germany designed to drum up sufficient military force to replace those Dutch troops that would be required to be taken out of the republic for William's expedition to England) confided to a former Brandenburg diplomatic representative in the republic that William attached the greatest importance to the dangers threatened from England and France.[16]

The spectre of combined Anglo-French action against the republic walked again when, on 9 September 1688, d'Avaux asked the States-General for an explanation of the military preparations in the republic, adding that Louis suspected that they were directed against England and warning that the Dutch should take account of the treaties that existed between England and France. The existence of any such treaties was speedily denied by the English ambassador at The Hague, and by James himself to the Dutch representative in London.[17] But the damage had been done and the denials were not believed. When, on 28 October 1688, the States-General of the republic published its reasons for assisting William in his English venture, pro-minence was given to the good understanding and friendship that existed between Louis and James, and reference was made specifically to their near and strict alliance, after which the resolution of the States-General continued:

> The French king having often, yea, upon all occasions, showed the ill-will he bore to this Republick, it is to be feared that if the King of Great Britain reach his mark, to wit, ane absolute power over his people, then will both these kings, partly out of maxime of state, and partly out of hatred and zeale against the Protestant religion, endeavour to ruine, and, if possible, to extirpate this republick.[18]

William's invasion of England therefore possessed for the Dutch Republic something of the nature of a pre-emptive strike directed against an Anglo-French alliance simply waiting to be activated. Nor did its activation seem to depend necessarily upon the co-operation of Louis and James: the reference in the resolution of the States-General to the ruin of the Dutch Republic as

Maximilian II Emmanuel, elector of Bavaria (1622–1726). Son-in-law of Emperor Leopold I (and like him a Catholic), Maximilian was regarded as a valuable ally by William III.

being a maxim of state for both England and France – something rooted in the very nature of these states – points to that. That being so, if the Dutch did not act and if England then rose and expelled James in a purely domestic rebellion, a new British republic might follow the tradition of the first and make war against the Dutch in alliance with France. That was likely to happen, according to Edward Russell, envoy of a party of influential Englishmen who opposed James's policies, when he visited Holland in 1688.[19] The only certain security against that eventuality was Dutch intervention and William on the English throne.

There was another reason in 1688 for the Dutch to remember the terrible events of the 1670s. In January 1688 William Egon von Fürstenberg, bishop of Strasbourg, was elected coadjutor to the sickly archbishop–elector of Cologne and, upon the latter's death in June 1688, was elected archbishop in July 1688. Fürstenberg's brother had been the architect of an offensive alliance concluded between Cologne and Louis in 1672 under which the archbishop of Cologne, who was also prince–bishop of Liège, had provided French armies with free passage, quartering and provisioning facilities through his lands, and thus access for France to invade the republic without the need to invade first the Spanish Netherlands. In the war of 1672 troops

Leopold I, Holy Roman
Emperor (1640–1705)

from Cologne, in whose army Fürstenberg himself had served, had helped to overrun and devastate the provinces of Gelderland, Twente and Overijssel and partially to re-Catholicise them.[20] Fürstenberg's elections as coadjutor and archbishop and the fact that he was the protégé of Louis (Louis had invested both money and reputation in getting him elected) were matters of the greatest concern to the republic – especially when it became evident that France would support Fürstenberg's election as archbishop of Cologne by force if necessary.[21]

The use of force by France came palpably nearer after the archiepiscopal election. The election required papal confirmation and imperial investiture. Pope Innocent XI, deeply and bitterly involved in a long-standing dispute with Louis, supported the rival candidature of Prince Joseph-Clement of Bavaria, younger brother of the elector Maximilian, son-in-law of Emperor Leopold I and commander of the imperial forces against the Ottoman Turks. Joseph-Clement had the support not only of the pope and the emperor but also of the Dutch Republic and the Protestant powers of the Holy Roman Empire. By the end of August 1688 war was held to be inevitable, and there was a general belief that Louis would launch an attack on the Lower Rhine, occupy Liège and besiege Maastricht. This belief in a repetition of 1672 became stronger in September 1688 when James made clear his strong support for Fürstenberg. This added force to an already firm conviction among the Dutch that the English king and Louis were coupled in a design to destroy the republic; and its moment of realisation hurried ever nearer when in the same month the pope conferred the archbishopric upon Joseph-Clement.[22] While these developments strengthened William's position in the republic, they at first seemed likely to imperil, or at any rate delay, his English venture. A French attack on the Lower Rhine might make it impossible for him to leave the republic, and might cause the Protestant princes of the empire to backtrack upon the promises of military assistance to the republic, which William's personal diplomacy had secured from them in the summer months of 1688 and upon which the launching of the English expedition depended.[23]

In the event there was no backtracking on the part of the German princes, and on 22 September 1688 the States-General agreed to foot the bill for their military assistance.[24] Above all, and this too was crucial to the speedy implementation of William's English plans, there was no French attack upon the Lower Rhine. Instead, on 24 September 1688, the day on which William formally requested support from the States of Holland for his English expedition, French troops entered the Rhineland and three days later settled down to the siege of Philippsburg, a fortress – key to Alsace and long a focus for dispute between Leopold and Louis. Once again, as had happened previously in 1685 with the revocation of the Edict of Nantes, Louis had come to the aid of William, this time at a moment, and in a manner, of decisive importance to the launching and the success of William's English enterprise. Indeed it might well be argued that apart from Louis's longevity, achieved in the face of the best attentions that contemporary medicine could provide or inflict, the greatest achievement of the French king was his contribution to the success of his arch-rival in taking into his possession the English crown. It is to the policies of Louis in the months immediately preceding that attention must now be turned.

Right: pikeman in a regiment of the province of Zeeland, 1672; *far right:* pikeman in a Gelderland regiment, 1672

20

In the course of an exceptionally long reign the priorities of Louis's foreign policy changed as circumstances changed, even if certain concerns were always present. In the 1680s – one of several turning points – the overriding concern of French foreign policy was relations with the Vienna Habsburgs.[25] Relations had been transformed since 1684 when, at the truce of Ratisbon, Leopold I and Charles II of Spain had been forced to recognise (for a period of twenty years) the territorial gains made by Louis since the conclusion of the treaty of Nijmegen in 1678. By September 1688 the paramountcy achieved by Louis in 1684 in the empire, and more generally in Europe, had disappeared. The revocation of the Edict of Nantes in 1685 had angered the German Protestant princes and had turned permanently against Louis his former fitful ally, Frederick William, the elector of Brandenburg. After 1685 Louis never again acquired a Protestant ally. With the succession in May 1688 as elector of Brandenburg of the strongly anti-French Frederick III, who soon acquired a reputation as 'ye Pr. of O's Vicar in ye Empire',[26] Brandenburg became a pivot of the European coalition William was fashioning against Louis, and of the diplomatic and military moves William judged necessary to the launching and success of his English venture.

Moreover, if in revoking the Edict of Nantes, or at least in doing so at that time, Louis had hoped to pose as a Catholic crusader and so attract the Catholic princes of the empire back into the field of French influence, that hope was not realised.[27] As a crusader for Catholicism, or at least as a persecutor of Protestants, Leopold rivalled Louis. More importantly, in the European struggle against the Ottoman Turks, from which Louis had distanced himself, Leopold had acquired the much more dazzling image of a ruler fighting and winning on behalf of all Christendom. The enormous collective European relief experienced in 1684 with the raising of the siege of

Right: musketeer in a regiment of the province of Holland, 1672: *far right:* sergeant in a regiment of the province of Holland, 1672

21

Frederick III, elector of
Brandenburg (1657–1713),
William of Orange's cousin
and heir, painted in 1688.

Vienna was followed by the exhilaration of the capture of Buda in 1686, the decisive defeat of the Turkish army near Mohacs in August 1687, and the capture of Belgrade on 6 September 1688. The power and prestige of the emperor had grown so spectacularly as a result of these victories that in 1688 it seemed to Louis only a question of time before a triumphant Leopold forced the Ottoman Turks to peace, and then turned upon France to try and recover the gains made by Louis since 1678.

Louis's obsession with Cologne in 1688, therefore, is to be seen as an expression of his larger obsession with a Habsburg threat that had grown, was growing, and had to be diminished. More specifically, in pressing the Fürstenberg candidature, Louis hoped to win back by intimidation, and by force if necessary, some of the ground lost in Germany to the Vienna Habsburgs. The attack upon Philippsburg in September 1688 was rooted in the same concerns. Its conquest was intended to make more complete Vauban's 'Maginot Line' of fortresses covering France's northern and eastern frontiers, while the war it might unleash was expected by France to be localised, short, and sufficient to encourage the Ottoman Turks to persist in their struggle against the emperor.

In retrospect, Louis's preoccupation with Cologne, and his expectation that his invasion of the Rhineland would result in a limited war, proved not merely miscalculations but major and irretrievable blunders. The war that ensued was full scale and it lasted until 1697. In that war Louis found ranged against him not only the emperor (who proved capable of fighting a war on two fronts), the Dutch Republic, Spain, and the majority of German princes but also England. Louis's attack on the Rhineland gave William the opportunity to invade England and to bring her into the European coalition already formed against France.

Yet at the time of Louis's fateful decision to accord priority to the Habsburg problem there was much to be said in defence of it, more than the undoubted fact of greatly increased Habsburg power and the certainty that such power would eventually be turned against France. There was also the fact that though Louis did not suffer from a lack of intelligence about William's military and naval preparations, he did suffer from uncertain, confused and contradictory intelligence about their purpose. In the late winter and spring of 1687–8 d'Avaux thought that they were intended for some Baltic enterprise, against Sweden or Denmark; then that they pointed to action against Cologne. In May and June 1688, it is true, d'Avaux noted reports that an invasion of England was being mounted, only to express doubts as to their credibility. Even when his doubts had been removed, he remained uncertain about its timing, and his uncertainty on that score increased as autumn and bad weather approached.

Louis experienced the same doubts, and held them for longer. If by August 1688 he seems to have been convinced that William's preparations were directed against James, and sufficiently convinced to dispatch the diplomat Bonrepaus to England to try to persuade a somewhat somnambulant James of this fact, he still remained uncertain as to the timing of the attempt. Bonrepaus not only failed to stir James but added to Louis's uncertainty by sending a dispatch from London, dated 8 September, reporting intelligence from Amsterdam that a postponement was likely until the next spring. That was also the opinion of the French minister of marine, the marquis de Seignelay, at the beginning of September 1688. In any case, by that time the French fleet had been dispatched to the Mediterranean and Louis found himself unable to blockade the English Channel and powerless to act.[28] He was perhaps still hopeful that William would be caught up in a long civil war.[29] If so, it proved another hope dashed, another major miscalculation.

Relations with the Vienna Habsburgs were not only in the forefront of Louis's diplomatic and military considerations in 1688, they were also crucial to William's international preparations for his English venture. In May 1688, in another exercise in personal diplomacy, William sent to Vienna a German nobleman from Hesse-Cassel, Baron Johann von Goertz. Goertz's mission was to attempt to persuade the emperor that they shared a common concern in re-establishing harmony between James and his parliament, in preventing James from falling into the hands of Louis, and to move from the acceptance of this shared concern to a closer alliance. No specific mention seems to have been made in the memorandum containing these propositions of any armed undertaking on William's part, but it is difficult to see how discussion of such an agenda could have taken place without account being taken at some level of how the desired result might be brought about. Negotiations were conducted in conditions 'of all imaginable privacy' and on 4 September 1688, unbeknown to the official representative of the States-General at Vienna, a provisional, personal understanding was reached with the emperor under which he agreed not only to stand by existing treaty obligations to the Dutch Republic but expressed his readiness to move towards a stricter alliance.[30] It was the embryo of the Grand Alliance of May 1688, implanted before French troops had crossed into the empire. Bringing it to maturity posed problems, however, for both Leopold and William.

In broad terms the essential problem for Leopold, and for other Catholic princes of Europe, was how to square maxims of state with the demands of religious conscience and religious duty. Leopold and his court had no cause in 1688 to look upon James kindly, nor did they. James's support for Fürstenberg rankled at Vienna as it did at Rome, and it was condemned by the emperor as interference in a matter in which England was in no way concerned, 'meerly to pleasure France'.[31] After hearing on 7 November 1688 of William's intended voyage to England, it seemed to the emperor and his ministers 'in the interest of the state . . . to wish for a change in English affairs . . . to see the affairs of England upon another footing'.[32] It was one thing, however, to regard James as almost Louis's harlot, to wish for a change of footing in English affairs, which would place England in the anti-French camp, and to see William's expedition as the only means of bringing that about quickly. It was quite another to assist and sanction James's dethronement in favour of William. Such actions challenged the deepest convictions of Europe's rulers and seemed subversive of the principles upon which lawful government was generally held to depend.

Moreover, in addition to this concern not to do anything prejudicial to the principle of hereditary right in England, Leopold was also mindful of the possible repercussions upon England's Catholic population of William's invasion and reordering of English affairs. William recognised the force of these concerns, and the fact that they were concerns shared more widely in Europe. He addressed himself specifically to them in the Resolution of the States-General of 28 October 1688. He did not have, he said, any design of dethroning James or of rendering himself master in England; neither had he any thoughts of 'prejudgeing or inverting the lawfull succession, nor yet of banishing or persecuting the Papists'.[33]

There is no difficulty in accepting William's repudiation of any intention to be a persecutor of English Catholics. Whether or not it was his early education that set him on the path of religious tolerance, or at least directed him away from a state-enforced religious uniformity, he did take that path and strove steadily to keep on it. As the ruler of the principality of Orange, he left Catholics free to exercise their religion, though Protestantism was the official religion of the state: doubtless he was mindful of the fact that Orange

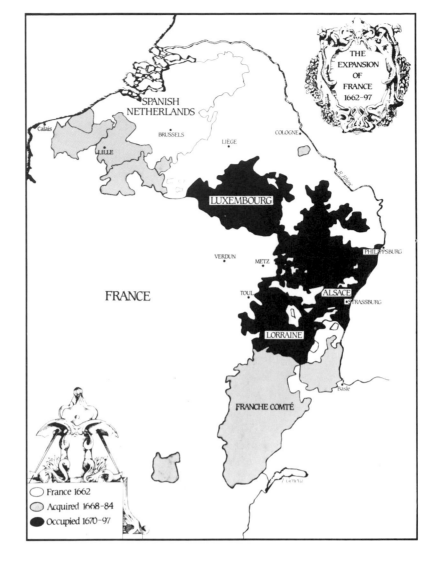

The map shows:
- THE EXPANSION OF FRANCE 1662-97
- SPANISH NETHERLANDS
- Calais
- BRUSSELS
- LIÈGE
- COLOGNE
- LILLE
- R. Rhine
- LUXEMBOURG
- VERDUN
- METZ
- PHILIPPSBURG
- TOUL
- ALSACE
- STRASSBURG
- FRANCE
- LORRAINE
- FRANCHE COMTÉ
- Basle
- France 1662
- Acquired 1668-84
- Occupied 1670-97

was a threatened Protestant enclave in a hostile France swept by Counter-Reformation fervour. Yet as stadtholder in the Dutch Republic, he followed similar policies and exhibited similar attitudes in both his private and his public life. Even at the height of the Huguenot influx and of a strong anti-Catholic tide in the republic, William remained loyal to the many Catholic friends and servants in his conspicuously cosmopolitan entourage; he opposed demands for the repression of the liberties enjoyed by Catholics in the republic at large; and he continued to proclaim that a man's conscience was his own affair and God's. So far as the position of Catholics in England was concerned, his position remained consistent, and by the standards of a generally intolerant age, tolerant. Thus there should be no persecution for conscience' sake; he was ready to accept the repeal of the penal laws, provided that had the approval of a free parliament, though the Test Acts (which excluded Catholics from parliament and from public office) must remain; and where laws could not be repealed they would be enforced softly, as softly as in the Dutch Republic.

In these circumstances to designate William *tout court* the champion of

25

Protestantism is not only to misrepresent him but to demean him. It is also to flatter him, for though ready enough when it suited his political purposes to see himself represented as a latter-day Protestant David come to slay a latter-day Catholic Goliath, he showed no enthusiasm for heading a denominational religious war: indeed he always feared and resisted tendencies and pressures in that direction.[34]

There is some difficulty, however, in accepting without gloss or qualification William's statements in the October Resolution about his political aims in invading England. If by 'design to dethrone' is meant a preconceived plan to depose James and take his place, then there is no evidence that William possessed such a plan prior to his invasion; though in the nature of things it has to be admitted that if he had possessed such a plan he would scarcely have shouted it around. His original aim seems to have been what he and his English supporters professed it to be: to secure the calling of a free parliament in the hope that this would prevent James from continuing in his allegedly illegal ways and force him to declare war upon France. English Protestant sentiment and desire to prevent France from cornering the Spanish Netherlands and the Dutch Republic gave grounds for this hope. However, what lends most force to the argument that William's original aims were limited in the way suggested is the fact that neither he nor his English supporters expected that events would take the course they did, and that James would cut and run. When James did succeed in escaping to France on

The palace of Het Loo, c.1700. Begun in 1685, it took nine years to complete. The formal gardens were laid out, in the style of those at Versailles, by the Huguenot Daniel Marot.

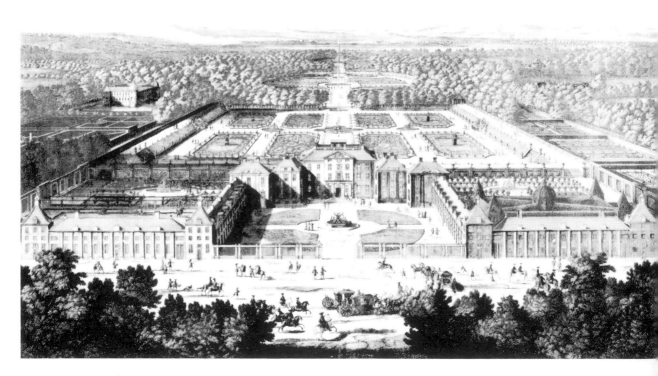

Coronation of William III and Mary II, 11 April 1689, by P. Pickaert. William, reared as a Calvinist, asked the burgomaster of Amsterdam what he thought of 'those foolish old Popish ceremonies'.

23 December 1688, the situation was altered; new possibilities and needs opened up for William and for parliament. The choice came to be seen as a choice between making terms with William and making terms with James.

Even before James's flight, however, William had made it clear to Leopold that in declaring his intention not to attempt anything prejudicial to the lawful succession in England, he did not mean that he accepted the Prince of Wales's right to succession; indeed since in William's view the Prince of Wales was not the son of the queen of England, the reference was a reference to Mary's claims and his determination to protect them.[35] Repudiation of the Pretender proved the great stumbling block in subsequent relations with Leopold, his successors, and other European powers. Rulers who became William's allies because they needed England's assistance in the war against France could not avoid recognising William as king of England, however little they liked doing so. Admitting the legitimacy of the Revolution settlement and the Protestant succession was a much more bitter pill for the powers of Europe to swallow. Its full achievement still eluded William at his death, and constituted the main concern of British foreign policy in the reigns of his two successors.[36] But if that prize was not finally and securely won until long after the Glorious Revolution, the prize upon which above all William had set his heart in 1688 – and to which so much of his endeavour

27

had been devoted since 1672 – was achieved in May 1689 when as king of England he declared war upon France. He is supposed to have remarked that the day on which parliament pledged its support for the war was for him the true beginning of his reign.[37]

Identifying the decisive consideration in a complex historical situation is always difficult and can often become something of a will-o'-the-wisp, since very often *the* decisive consideration turns out to be no more than yet another decisive consideration. William's reasons for intervening in English affairs were certainly complex: personal and dynastic, religious and economic, national and international. Yet his basic reason seems obvious, as obvious as it seemed to one of his contemporaries, the marquis of Halifax, who wrote: 'He hath such a mind to France that it would incline one to think, he took England only in his way.'[38] Bringing England into a European war against France may have been for William the beginning of his reign, but it was also the end of a long political odyssey.

2

THE GLORIOUS REVOLUTION

JOHN MILLER

The war in Ireland in 1689–91 was repeatedly, and often decisively, influenced by events elsewhere. The Glorious Revolution of 1688–9 – James II's flight to France and his replacement by William III – had a profound impact on the history of both Britain and Europe. It also had major repercussions in Ireland, although the leading protagonists were rarely influenced by specifically Irish considerations. Ireland's strategic position and relationship with England drew it into a complex web of events in which it became a battleground for foreign forces and its fate was decided by other powers with greatly superior resources.

When James succeeded his brother Charles II in February 1685, his accession was acclaimed throughout his three kingdoms of England, Scotland and Ireland. Such acclaim was in many ways surprising. Between 1679 and 1681 there had been repeated attempts in the English parliament to exclude him from the succession on the grounds that he was a Catholic. For many Englishmen Catholicism was inseparable from 'arbitrary government' or royal absolutism. They feared that a Catholic king would destroy the balance between the king's powers and the subject's rights, which lay at the heart of the English constitution. If James became king, it was argued, liberty, property and religion would be in peril: 'When he (as all other Popish kings do) governs by an army, what will your laws signify?' asked one pamphleteer. 'You will not then have Parliaments to appeal to; he and his council will levy his arbitrary taxes and his army will gather them for him.'[1]

Ireland played only a peripheral part in the Exclusion Crisis. The immediate occasion for the movement for James's exclusion was Titus Oates's fanciful tale of a Popish Plot to murder Charles II; a few disreputable Irish 'witnesses' were brought over to England to add credence to his story (and were well paid for their pains). Overall, however, Ireland remained quiet. Lord Lieutenant Ormond wrote that the Dublin government had more to fear from the Ulster Presbyterians than from the native Irish, apart from a few 'tories'.[2] Indeed Ireland's most lasting contribution to the crisis was the word 'tory': its association with Catholicism, banditry, and the Irish made it an all-embracing term of abuse, to be used against those who supported James's claim to the throne. It was a term that members of the Tory party at first deeply resented, but it was typical of the way in which the proponents of exclusion, the Whigs, used the rhetoric of anti-Catholicism increasingly indiscriminately against members of the Established Church of England as well as against Catholics. The Tories remembered a similar exploitation of anti-popery, as well as talk of popish plots, in the years 1640–2,[3] and became convinced that the Whigs were bent on starting another civil war. The Tories therefore rallied to Charles and his brother James. Charles gave them a near-monopoly of administrative and judicial power in the localities. In the counties he ensured that most justices of the peace and sheriffs were now Tories. In the boroughs, magistrates were nominally elected (rather than being appointed by Charles) so the king and the Tories 'persuaded' many boroughs to surrender their charters and to receive new ones, under which the king could remove borough officials at will. In county and town the Tories used their power to harass the Whigs and their political allies – Protestant nonconformists or dissenters (Presbyterians, Baptists, Quakers, and the like). A few Whigs (notably Lord Russell and Algernon Sidney) were convicted on questionable charges of treason and executed; others were sentenced to huge fines that they could not possibly pay, and so languished in gaol for nonpayment. Dissenters were persecuted more systematically than at any time in Charles's reign. The four years of the 'Tory reaction' (1681–5) left the Whigs divided and demoralised: many crept to make their peace with the Crown.

In rallying to James's defence, the Tories were not acting out of unthinking loyalty. On the one hand, they saw Whiggery and dissent as posing a serious threat to their interests: they had no wish to see the 'world turned upside down' as it had been in the civil wars of the 1640s and 1650s. On the other hand, they assumed that their interests and the Crown's were essentially the same: it seemed only common sense that the king should place his trust in, and give his full backing to, his natural supporters. The Tories' political principles were founded on loyalty to the king. They denied that subjects had any right to resist the king on any pretext whatever, but that did not mean that they believed that the king had to be obeyed in all things. If his commands were unjust, his subjects could refuse to obey, but they had then to suffer passively the consequences of their disobedience. This philosophy was expounded particularly forcefully by the Anglican clergy. Their Church, with its hierarchical and authoritarian form of government, provided a natural buttress for monarchy, a point emphasised by the overthrow of both Church and monarchy in the civil wars. The clergy therefore assumed that the interests of 'Church and king' were one and indivisible. James was to show them that they were not.

Soon after his accession, James called a parliament in England. The general election produced an overwhelmingly Tory House of Commons, which voted him enough revenue (for life) to support the Government in peacetime, with an additional grant to pay for putting down the 1685 rebellions of Monmouth (in England) and Argyll (in Scotland). James was even able to afford a standing army of around twenty thousand men – much larger than that of any of his predecessors. He was thus unique among the Stuarts in having no financial problems and no need to fear invasion or insurrection. Had he been content merely to keep the Government ticking over and to avoid contentious policies, James would doubtless have lived out his days in peace. Inactivity, however, did not come naturally to him. After twenty-five years as his brother's heir presumptive, he was determined to make the most of his position as king. Moreover, his conversion to Catholicism gave him a cause far nobler than personal gratification. He believed strongly that God's providence determined everything that happened on earth. As God had preserved him against the malice of his enemies – in the civil wars, in the Exclusion crisis, against the rebellions of 1685 – then clearly God had some great work that He wished James to do. And that task, in James's eyes, could only be the advancement of Catholicism.

As an Englishman, his primary concern was to promote Catholicism in England, the largest and richest of his kingdoms. Catholics, however, made up only a minute percentage of England's population – and James probably knew it.[4] They were, moreover, heavily discriminated against in law: a wide range of penal laws prohibited Catholic worship and all other aspects of Catholic activity; the Test Acts excluded Catholics from parliament and from public office. Yet if those laws constituted a great barrier to the promotion of Catholicism, they also gave James grounds for hope. Could it be that the paucity of Catholics was essentially a product of these laws? If it was, then it

Dutch print of the capture of the earl of Argyll, who led an unsuccessful rebellion against James II in Scotland in 1685.

followed that if the laws were taken away, far more people would declare themselves Catholics. Like many converts, James assumed that the arguments for the rightness of Catholicism that had convinced him would prove equally convincing to others: 'Did others enquire into the religion as I have done,' he wrote, 'without prejudice or prepossession or partial affection, they would be of same mind in point of religion as I am.'[5] He had found the transition from the Church of England to the Church of Rome so easy and natural that he assumed others would too: the Anglicans, he said, were Roman Catholics without knowing it.[6]

In order to induce converts to come forward James had first to remove the legal penalties and disabilities which Catholics faced. He was particularly concerned to remove the Test Acts, as he believed that 'the possibility of holding offices and employments will make more Catholics than permission to say Mass publicly'.[7] Removing laws, however, was not easy. Acts of parliament could, legally, be repealed only by parliament, and it was improbable that many would openly embrace Catholicism unless they could do so without fear of punishment. By the end of 1685 James realised that his first Tory parliament was unlikely to repeal these laws: Tories might be staunch monarchists, but they were also staunch Anglicans – and strongly anti-Catholic. James was therefore forced to embark upon an alternative strategy. Catholics were only one of several denominations persecuted by the

Dutch print of the execution of the duke of Monmouth, 15 July 1685. The incompetent executioner took five strokes of the axe.

32

James II (1633–1701). The original of this portrait was painted in 1684, when James was Lord High Admiral, hence the ships in the background; the royal regalia were added later.

Louis XIV (1638–1715) in
royal robes. The original of
the portrait was painted
in 1701.

Church of England and debarred by law from worshipping freely or holding offices. James had hitherto done nothing to end the vigorous persecution of dissenters, but now he expressed his commitment to a general toleration of all denominations, Catholic and Protestant. In April 1687 he issued a Declaration of Indulgence, in which he suspended all the laws against non-Anglican religious worship and stated his intention to enable persons of all religions to hold offices, by dispensing them from the penalties of the Test Acts.[8]

The sincerity or otherwise of James's sudden conversion to toleration need not detain us here.[9] Its immediate and avowed purpose was to secure a parliament that would repeal the penal laws and Test Acts; given Anglicans' hostility to toleration, such a parliament would have to consist mainly of dissenters. But dissenters were far less numerous than Anglicans and of less social and political weight. They were divided among themselves and most were strongly anti-Catholic. In order to allow them to hold the offices that would enhance their electoral influence, James had to interfere grossly with the enforcement of laws designed to prevent just that. He secured a judicial ruling that he could dispense with the penalties of law in individual cases as he thought fit – but only after dismissing judges who thought otherwise. He proceeded to interpret this 'dispensing power' more widely than most of the judges had anticipated, extending it to a point where he used it to suspend laws altogether. Meanwhile, as it became clear that few electors wished to repeal the penal laws and Test Acts, James interfered increasingly blatantly in the affairs of the parliamentary boroughs, turning out members of corporations and installing others in their places. In many boroughs the electorate, already small, was further reduced, and the few remaining electors were subjected to a barrage of propaganda and a variety of threats and inducements to vote as the king wished.

Thus in his quest for a parliament that would do his bidding, James suspended whole categories of laws and threatened to reduce parliament to a rubber stamp prepared to repeal laws that the great majority of the political nation wished to retain. In so doing, he did much to confirm the Whigs' dire prophecies about the likely behaviour of a popish king. By 1688 many Tories were profoundly disillusioned with James. Not only had he abused his prerogatives but he was openly vindictive towards the Church of England. As early as March 1685 he had warned the bishops that he would not tolerate anti-Catholic preaching from their clergy. His support for the Church had been based solely on political calculation. When it failed to live up to what he saw as its principles (he habitually confused nonresistance with unconditional obedience), he had no qualms about turning his favour elsewhere. He set up an ecclesiastical commission to silence parsons who preached against Rome, and he expelled the fellows of Magdalen College, Oxford, for refusing to elect a Catholic as president (an attack on academic tenure that was seen as both spiteful and illegal). Finally he required the bishops to order their clergy to read the Declaration of Indulgence in their churches, thus publicising and implicitly endorsing the demotion of the Established Church to the status of one denomination among several. Seven of the bishops refused and James had them prosecuted for seditious libel. 'Is this what I have deserved,' he stormed, 'who have supported the Church of England and will support it?' (Men less deferential than the bishops might have replied that with 'supporters' like James they hardly needed enemies.) The trial, from James's point of view, was a fiasco. One of the judges roundly condemned the dispensing power, and the jury found the bishops not guilty.[10]

Clearly then, by 1688 both Whigs and Tories had a wide range of purely English reasons to be dissatisfied with James. They were not, however, oblivious to what was happening in Ireland. Lord Deputy Tyrconnell's determination to put all civil and military offices into Catholic hands raised the prospect that Ireland might seek to shake off English rule when James died. Still more alarming was the fear that what was happening in Ireland could be a blueprint of James's plans for England. With Catholics gaining a monopoly of office in Ireland, many found it hard to believe James's professed intention (which was anyway not borne out by his conduct in England) to appoint men to office regardless of their religion. Could it be, people wondered, that only a shortage of Catholics was preventing James from giving them a monopoly of English offices as well?[11]

The fact that there were few Catholics in the English army posed problems

The Seven Bishops on their way to imprisonment in the Tower, 8 June 1689; from a Dutch print.

The Portsmouth
CAPTAINS.

The Hon:ble Coll:John Beamont.

The Hon:ble Capt:Tho:Paston.

Capt:Simon Pack.

Capt:Thomas Orme.

Capt:John Port.

Pro Latria Patria, Atria.

Capt:William Cook.

Engraven by R.White and Sold at his house in Bloomsbury Market 1688.

The 'Portsmouth captains' of the duke of Berwick's regiment, who refused to accept Catholic Irish recruits when ordered to do so in September 1688.

for James. In an attempt to redress the balance, in March 1688, he created an Irish regiment under Colonel MacElligott, made up of soldiers newly returned from the Dutch service. As too many returned, some Catholic soldiers were added to the regiment of which James's illegitimate son, the duke of Berwick, had been appointed colonel; several of the officers refused to receive them and were cashiered. This led to wild rumours that James planned to bring over hordes of bloodthirsty Irish Catholics to cut English throats. James in fact hesitated to bring over reinforcements from Ireland, even when faced with the prospect of invasion, because he feared a hostile political reaction in England. Only in September did he finally order four Irish regiments to be brought over.[12]

Thus events in Ireland and the coming of Irish troops played only an

Mary Beatrice d'Este of Modena, whom James II married as his second wife in 1673 when she was fifteen. Louis XIV helped to negotiate the marriage and contributed to the bride's dowry.

incidental role in the growth of dissatisfaction in England. As yet, however, that dissatisfaction posed no real threat to James. English nobles could no longer raise large numbers of armed men, and James's army was more than capable of suppressing localised disorders. Such an army, indeed, could realistically be challenged only by another professional army from outside the British Isles; and from the summer of 1688 just such an army was being prepared. James's nephew and son-in-law, William of Orange, had become alarmed at James's conduct. William was married to James's elder daughter Mary, and (as James had no sons) William expected her to inherit the English throne when James died. William would then be able to bring England's resources (especially the navy) into his lifelong struggle against Louis XIV's France. William was therefore highly perturbed by rumours (almost certainly unfounded) that James planned to cut Mary out of the succession in favour of a Catholic. Later, William became worried that James might provoke another civil war: if, like the last, this led to a republic, there would be no crown to which Mary could succeed. Finally, late in 1687 it was announced that James's queen, Mary of Modena, was pregnant. His Catholic courtiers seemed unnaturally confident that she would have a son. As the

The birth of the Prince of Wales (the Old Pretender), 10 June 1688; engraving by P. Pickaert. Father Petre, James II's Jesuit confessor, is shown displaying the child.

queen had not conceived for five years and had, in fourteen years of marriage, failed to produce a child who lived beyond infancy, their confidence gave rise to suspicions that whatever happened, the papists would produce a 'Prince of Wales'. Such malevolent suspicions seemed to be confirmed when the queen did indeed give birth to a healthy son on 10 June 1688.

By the time the child was born, William had already decided to invade England. Like many Dutchmen he feared that James and Louis were planning to attack the Dutch Republic, so it was possible to portray the invasion as a pre-emptive strike. The projected invasion was attended with great risks and uncertainties. Not until mid-September did William hear that Louis had attacked Philippsburg and so would be unlikely to attack the republic that year. William's huge fleet – much larger than the Spanish Armada – contained many unarmed transports and so was vulnerable to attack by the English fleet. When he first sailed, a storm drove him back into port. The second time he was luckier. Strong easterly winds pinned James's fleet against the Essex coast, while William's sailed unopposed down the English Channel, landing at Brixham on 5 November.

William's motives for invading were essentially European. While he probably hoped to drive James out, he could not admit this openly: his allies (notably Charles II of Spain and Emperor Leopold I) would not welcome his displacing a fellow-monarch (and fellow-Catholic); nor would he have won much English support had he declared his wish to become king. William

37

William's departure from Hellevoetsluys, 3 November 1688, by the calendar used in England; from a Dutch print.

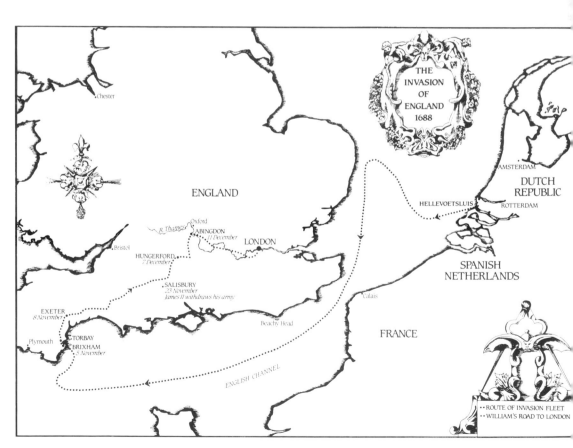

The English convention parliament of 1689. William (A) stands to the left, the Speaker (C) is on a dais to the right.

would, however, have settled for less than the Crown. If he could secure Mary's claim (by having James's son set aside as 'supposititious'), he could then wait for her to succeed her father. Moreover, with a great war breaking out on the Continent, he expected the English parliament to demand that England should join the coalition against France. William had little interest in England as such, or in the rights and liberties of Englishmen: it was remarked later that he took England on his way to France. About Ireland, he knew and cared still less. The Declaration in which he justified his invasion concentrated on English grievances – the breaking of laws, the rigging of elections, the maltreatment of the Church, and the queen's 'pretended bigness'. William claimed that he had been invited by many spiritual and temporal lords and others of all ranks (in fact, a grand total of seven men). The remedy which he offered for all England's ills was a 'free parliament'.[13]

William's Declaration was designed to appeal to the widest possible spectrum of English opinion: many items appealed more to Tories than to Whigs and it said nothing of the Tory reaction of the early 1680s, mention of which would have revived earlier partisan hostilities. It was also intended to justify William's conduct in the eyes of the European public: it was printed in Dutch, German and French, as well as in English. Within England, it capitalised on the breadth and diversity of disillusionment with James. The Tories' principles would not allow most of them to appear in arms against their king, but did not prevent them from doing nothing to oppose an

39

invader pledged to secure a free parliament, a prospect welcomed by most. They could expect to do well in a general election and a Tory House of Commons could then reverse all that James had done since 1685 and make the world safe for people like themselves. Bishops and Tory peers pressed James to cut the ground from under William's feet by calling a free parliament: 'And then,' wrote one, 'I can't see what the Prince has to do.'[14]

James, however, refused to call a free parliament that would presumably undo all that he had done and, worse still, disinherit his son. He resolved to fight – his army was larger than William's – but then lost his nerve. Until the summer of 1688 everything had seemed to go right: the birth of his son, after so many years of waiting, reinforced his belief that God was with him. But then everything fell apart. His people – even his own daughters – refused to believe that the child was his. Louis, instead of coming to his aid, became embroiled in a bloody war on the Rhine. Even the wind turned against him, and when William landed, James's subjects, instead of resisting the invader, urged their king to concede his demands. Anti-Catholic riots erupted in London; Protestant nobles appeared in arms in the north; ugly rumours proliferated that James planned to bring over French or Irish troops to butcher his Protestant subjects. Everywhere there were signs that his subjects hated him. A few army officers deserted to the enemy, including men with more reason than most to remain loyal, such as his nephew, Lord Cornbury, and his protégé John Churchill. Even his younger daughter, Anne, fled from his court. Worn out by nervous tension, overwork and lack of sleep, James fell prey to debilitating nosebleeds. As his world collapsed

James II refuses to call a free parliament until persuaded by his friends to do so; Dutch engraving by P. Pickaert. Note the portraits of the pope and Louis XIV, representing the twin phobias of most Englishmen – popery and arbitrary power.

around him he could no longer believe that God was with him; he refused to risk a battle and agreed to negotiate.

Had James been prepared to negotiate in good faith he would have kept his throne, but his heart was not in it. He feared that, at best, he would have to make humiliating concessions to his subjects; at worst, he would follow his father Charles I to the Tower of London and to the block. Having sent his wife and son to France, he fled. Most of his army promptly submitted to William, but the Irish contingent could expect no welcome from the prince, who had declared forthrightly against the employment of Catholics, contrary to law. As they tried to find their way home, these 'poor naked timorous and hated Irish . . . with scarce a knife to cut their victuals' sparked off a nationwide panic. Rumours of a huge force of Irish papists, putting towns to fire and sword and sparing neither woman nor child, swept the country from Cornwall to Berwick.[15] The rumours did little to affect the course of events, except to make people 'wish for the Prince of Orange's coming to quiet things'.[16] When James was stopped in Kent and brought back to London, William's plans suffered a slight hiccup. However, James proved more than willing to escape again and William was eager to let him do so: once James had gone, there was no real alternative to William's being made king.

James's conduct as king had united against him Tory and Whig, Anglican and dissenter; but this unity was negative and fragile. Men who agreed on the need for a free parliament soon disagreed about what that parliament should do. Even before James fled, there was much jockeying for position. Whigs sought to discredit Tories in William's eyes by pressing them to subscribe the 'association' – a promise to adhere to William against his enemies (and the

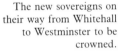

The new sovereigns on their way from Whitehall to Westminster to be crowned.

James II leaving Rochester, his second and successful attempt to escape; a Dutch print.

papists). Some Tories refused, claiming that it was incompatible with their oath of allegiance to James. With James's flight, any prospect of consensus disappeared. Tories complained that James had been driven out by force – he had left London the second time with an escort of Dutch troops – and that William had duped them: he had never really, they claimed, intended to call a free parliament and had always aimed at the Crown. Thus the Tories, despite their principles of nonresistance, had been tricked into aiding and abetting a military coup against their lawful king. To make matters worse, William made clear his dislike of the Established Church and his sympathy for dissenters. The Tories responded by doing all they could to prevent William being made king in his own right. William, however, let it be known that he would not be satisfied with the position of his wife's consort. If he did not receive satisfaction, he added, he would go home and leave the English to extricate themselves from the ensuing confusion as best they could. Given the condition of Ireland, the bitter divisions of Whig and Tory, and the mutinous state of what remained of James's army, it seemed probable that William's departure would be followed by severe disorder, perhaps civil war. In these circumstances the Tories bowed to the inevitable: both houses of parliament agreed that James had abdicated and that the Crown should be offered jointly to William and Mary. As the marquis of Halifax drily remarked, if they did not know what to do with William, nor did they know what to do without him.[17]

In all these complex manoeuvres the condition of Ireland figured (at most) as one of several reasons for a speedy settlement. On 18 February 1689, five days after the offer of the Crown, William stressed to parliament the need to support England's new continental allies and to secure Ireland. As James had fled to France, it seemed inevitable that England would have to join in the war against France, if only to prevent James's return as a French puppet: this was to be, among other things, the war of the English succession. Moreover, as Tyrconnell extended his control over Ireland it was clear that swift action was needed there to maintain English Protestant rule. The Commons, not surprisingly, responded to William's appeal with a promise to assist him with their lives and fortunes; but they did little else until news came in March that James had landed in Ireland with French troops and munitions, thus making Ireland a major theatre in the European war. ''Tis more than an Irish war,' declared one MP, 'I think 'tis a French war. The French king has carried King James into Ireland; and there is no way possible to bear that great force but by securing Ireland.' 'If Ireland be lost,' said another, more succinctly, 'England will follow.'[18]

Until they heard of James's arrival in Ireland the Commons had been more generous with words than with money. 'I am well pleased we should consider the relief of Ireland,' said one MP, 'but our affairs at home fright us more than those abroad.'[19] Now they voted over £700,000 for the reduction of Ireland, but the ensuing campaign was hamstrung by military and administrative incompetence, exacerbated by partisan recriminations at home. The mutual hatred of Whig and Tory had been slurred over by a common resentment of James's conduct. Now the Whigs called for inquiries into the deaths of the Whig 'martyrs' of the early 1680s and denounced the Tories for abetting the 'tyranny' of James and his brother. Seeking revenge for their exclusion from office during the Tory reaction, many Whigs demanded a monopoly of office, claiming that they alone were truly loyal to William. They eagerly reopened old wounds – even seeking to reverse Oates's conviction for perjury – and tried to add a clause to the indemnity bill (the 'Sacheverell clause'), excluding most Tories from municipal office for seven years. William saw clearly the self-seeking motivation that underlay the Whigs' conduct and regarded many of them as closet republicans, no friends to monarchy. He therefore employed Tories as well as Whigs, notably the earl of Nottingham as secretary of state. The Whigs responded by blaming the lack of success in the Irish campaign on Tory treachery and argued that it would be foolish to vote more money until William chose better (in other words Whig) ministers. William seemed alone in being less eager to apportion blame than to get things done. He even offered, in exasperation, to let the Commons take over the running of the war; they responded that they would not presume to meddle in the affairs of the executive: their role was simply to give advice.[20]

William was not unused to such disunity and disarray, thanks to his experience of the Dutch States-General; and he had long since realised that the way to ensure that something was done properly was to do it himself. By the end of 1689 it was clear that Jacobite resistance in Ireland would not easily be overcome and that it would be unwise to let the war drag on: Ireland could well become the starting point for a French descent on England. It was probably in December that William decided to go to Ireland in person: in January 1690 he told one of his confidants that it was essential to concentrate on Ireland that summer. When rumours of his intentions leaked out, some

Louis XIV receiving James II on his arrival at the French court; from a Dutch print.

43

Whigs argued that only traitors could have advised him to leave England, and there was a motion in the Lords that he should be asked not to go; in the Commons, Whig MPs threatened to hold up the money promised for Ireland unless the Sacheverell clause went through. William had had enough. He dissolved parliament and called another, which promptly voted £1,200,000 for the war. At last William was ready and able to depart.[21]

Throughout this period, Irish considerations had only a limited impact on developments within England. William's view of events was broad and European; that of most English politicians was narrow and English. The Glorious Revolution in England happened for European and English (but not Irish) reasons. Englishmen expressed alarm at Tyrconnell's conduct, but only when James's arrival in Ireland posed a direct threat to England did the Commons act decisively to facilitate the reduction of Ireland. Even then, English politicians were easily sidetracked into feuds and recriminations. Ironically it was William, with less interest than his English subjects in maintaining English rule over Ireland, who resolved that a decisive move was necessary; and in his view, Ireland was just another theatre – like Flanders or the Rhineland – in the great struggle against France. For William the troubles in Ireland were an irritant, a running sore that needed to be healed quickly, so that he could get back to the real centre of events, on the Continent.

William and Mary proclaimed king and queen in England; from a Dutch print.

JAMES II AND IRELAND
1685–90

JAMES MCGUIRE

In 1691 Protestants in Ireland were convinced that the defeat of James II and his army had freed them from the threat of popish absolutism and economic desolation. For William King, the newly appointed bishop of Derry, the deliverance was substantial since, in his view, James had 'designed and endeavoured to destroy and utterly ruin the Protestant religion and English interest in Ireland and to alter the very frame and constitution of the government'. James's 'fondness of France', his 'affecting to imitate' Louis XIV, his 'prosecuting the same, if not worse methods towards the Protestants in Ireland, that the king of France did with Huguenots in his dominions', all amounted to 'a clear and full proof of both kings being in the same design, to root out not only the Protestants of these kingdoms, but likewise of Europe'.[1] This judgement on James's purposes in Ireland was commonplace among the bishop's contemporaries and was matched by similar views among many Englishmen of what the deposed king had had in store for England: arbitrary government on the French model and the imposition of Catholicism on an unwilling nation. Whig historians subsequently elaborated this view of James's aims, and though Whig history has long ceased to be fashionable, Whig assumptions about James's intentions in England and Ireland have proved remarkably durable.[2] Are such views justified?

As king, James clearly bore responsibility for policies pursued throughout his dominions; so far as Ireland was concerned, he was responsible for the Catholic ascendancy which was all but established by 1689. This is not to say, however, that he intended it or wanted it, at least in the form it took. Protestant propagandists naturally made no distinction between the king's intentions and the policies carried out in his name, and once the war was over, contemporaries, and after them Whig historians, interpreted James's policies from his accession in 1685 as an intended and co-ordinated overturning of the Protestant and English interest in Ireland. They did so in the light of what happened in the 1689 Jacobite parliament, especially the repeal of the Restoration land settlement and the act attainting over two thousand Protestant landowners. But the evidence does not support so coherent a view;

rather it suggests that the policies pursued under James were in part an extension to Ireland of policies designed for England, in part the work of James's Catholic lord deputy, Tyrconnell, to which the king gave his reluctant approval under pressure, and in part responses to events (especially after 1688).[3] What can be said with some certainty is that James had one consistent objective from 1685 to 1690, and that was to better the lot of his Catholic co-religionists throughout his dominions by obtaining for them a legal toleration that would endure after his death. What changed during his reign were the means by which he tried to achieve his objective.

The Protestant case against James rested on the content and impact of government policy over a wide area: central government appointments, the army, the judiciary, the magistracy and commission of the peace, the parliamentary boroughs, the Churches, the land settlement. In fact no feature of the Restoration settlement in Church and state seemed immune from the Catholic revolution of the 1680s. On James's accession in 1685 the settlement was intact and the political nation was Protestant. Three years later, and before the cataclysmic events of the Jacobite–Williamite conflict, few Irish Protestants could fail to feel anxious for their future prospects in Ireland should James's reign continue for much longer; the events of 1689, especially the legislation of the Jacobite parliament, merely confirmed what had become increasingly apparent between 1685 and 1688.

The first significant break with the status quo was the appointment of Catholics to the army, an initiative with modest enough results in 1685 but which turned a Protestant army at the beginning of James's reign into a predominantly Catholic army within eighteen months.[4] Early in March 1685 the new king ordered that regiments be given to two Catholic officers, Richard Talbot and Justin MacCarthy, though this involved dispensing with the oath of supremacy. Soon after, the Protestant lords justices in Dublin Castle had orders to grant twelve further dispensations from the oath and to take advice on army matters from Colonel Talbot (recently raised to the peerage as earl of Tyrconnell), who was to inspect the army in Ireland during the summer months.[5] By the end of 1685, as a result of Tyrconnell's efforts, there were over eight hundred Catholic soldiers, a figure that increased sixfold when Tyrconnell returned to Ireland the following year as lord general of the army. This change in the army's religious composition was especially noticeable among the rank and file, of whom 67 per cent were Catholic by the end of 1686. It took longer to find Catholic officers, though by 1688 only a minority of Protestant officers remained.[6] All these changes aroused growing dismay in Protestant Ireland, since they involved the commissioning of many whose forebears had fought in the Irish confederate armies of the 1640s, the dispensing with statutory requirements for taking the oath of supremacy, and the widespread dismissal of Protestant officers and soldiers.

Closely linked with these army dispositions was the resolute action taken in 1685 to disarm the disaffected and potentially rebellious in Ulster, for the

'Cruelty of King James and comte d'Avaux to the Irish Protestants'; a Dutch propaganda print. Though some Protestants certainly suffered under Jacobite rule, there was no official persecution of the kind suggested here. The publisher of the engraving simply adapted part of an existing plate illustrating the siege of Bonn.

most part dissenting Protestants with strong Scottish connections. At the same time James ordered the Dublin government to call in arms issued to the militia during the English Popish Plot scare of the late 1670s, effectively disarming the Protestant nation at a time when the admission of Catholics to the army was beginning to gather pace.[7]

Tyrconnell's role in transforming and enlarging the army anticipated his appointment as viceroy in 1687, the first Catholic to hold the post since the Reformation. His immediate predecessors as chief governors had been manifestly ineffective in their attempts to thwart his growing influence. In 1685, when the viceroyalty was put into commission, the Protestant lords justices, Archbishop Michael Boyle and Lord Granard, had meekly acquiesced in the appointment of Catholics to the army, and the following year the English Tory lord lieutenant, the second earl of Clarendon (James's brother-in-law by his first marriage), had allowed himself to be humiliated in the face of Tyrconnell's growing political ascendancy, even to the extent of seeing the viceroy's traditional mandate as commander-in-chief go instead to Tyrconnell. When James appointed Tyrconnell as lord deputy, the enthusiasm with which the news was greeted by Catholics in Ireland was matched only by the fear it generated among Protestants. As a Dublin Protestant recorded in his diary: 'the king sends earl of Tyrconnell lord deputy of Ireland, the news of

47

KNAVE

48

Tyrconel arming ỹ Papists in Ireland.

Propaganda playing card, one of a set dealing with events in 1688.

which put the city into great consternation and very many families prepared to return for England'.[8]

Responsibility for Tyrconnell's appointment as viceroy was James's alone. It is clear that he had recognised the danger involved in appointing his domineering and longstanding Irish friend and for the first eighteen months of his reign he had resisted Tyrconnell's own importuning and the requests of the Catholic clergy.[9] Tyrconnell might be the ideal man to reform, Catholicise and enlarge the Irish army but his appointment as chief governor was quite another matter. He had long been associated with attempts to reopen the Irish land question on behalf of dispossessed proprietors, and he was regarded with the deepest suspicion in England and positive loathing in Protestant Ireland. Even the king's Catholic advisers in England strongly advised the king not to appoint Tyrconnell, since they feared that this Irish Catholic with Irish interests and objectives might place in jeopardy what had been so far achieved under the Catholic king.[10] So why was he appointed?[11]

The explanation of James's volte-face on Tyrconnell's appointment must focus primarily on the personalities of both men. Tyrconnell's ability to dominate James, whom he had known since the mid-1650s, and the integrity of his determination to achieve power were eventually more than a match for the king, who withstood for as long as he could the pressure to appoint him, but who ultimately gave in to Tyrconnell's relentless appeal to his Catholic convictions and to Tyrconnell's portrayal of how Catholics had suffered in Ireland since the Cromwellian settlement of the 1650s.[12] James's only concession to English opinion, which would obviously be disturbed at the appointment of an Irishman and a Catholic to the viceroyalty, was to give Tyrconnell the lesser title of lord deputy. But whatever about the title, Tyrconnell's appointment put into Dublin Castle a chief governor with his own policy priorities.

In the year preceding Tyrconnell's appointment Catholics were appointed to a number of important civil posts, against Clarendon's advice and by dispensing with the oath of supremacy (as with the army). Three Catholic lawyers, Thomas Nugent, Denis Daly and Stephen Rice, were appointed to the bench. Once Tyrconnell took over, more Catholic judges were appointed, so that by the end of 1687 a majority of judges were Catholic, as were the attorney-general, Richard Nagle, and the lord chancellor, Sir Alexander Fitton (an English Catholic). It was a similar story with the privy council, to which eleven Catholics were appointed under Clarendon in 1686 and which had a Catholic majority the following year. The end result was that Catholic appointees dominated the central administration just two years after James's accession.[13]

The pattern in the provinces was similar and just as important. Protestant magistrates and justices of the peace were dismissed and Catholics appointed in their stead. In 1686 Clarendon was instructed to send circulars to the borough corporations requiring them to admit Catholics as freemen and not to enforce the oath of supremacy. A few months before his recall he received

TYRCONEL, Vice-Roy in Irlande

A German engraving of
Tyrconnell, published in
Hamburg in 1691.

THE
JOURNAL
OF THE
PROCEEDINGS
OF THE
PARLIAMENT
IN
IRELAND.
WITH
The Eſtabliſhment of their FORCES there.

Licenſed and Entred according to Order.

LONDON:
Printed for *Robert Clavell*, at the Peacock in St. *Paul's*
Church-Yard. MDCLXXXIX.

positive instructions not to appoint sheriffs for 1687 and to leave the task to his successor. Predictably Tyrconnell appointed Catholic sheriffs, a crucial development not just for local administration but for the future composition of an Irish parliament, since sheriffs acted as returning officers at parliamentary elections. Soon after, on formal instructions from James, Tyrconnell instituted quo warranto proceedings against the parliamentary boroughs. Inevitably this led to the recall of borough charters and the issuing of new ones in their place. The Protestant domination of local government was thereby broken and, more significantly, the election of a majority of Catholic members to a future Irish parliament was guaranteed.

James seems to have raised no objection to the quickening pace of Catholic appointments to the judiciary, the privy council, and in local government. In the case of quo warranto proceedings he positively encouraged Tyrconnell's activities.[14] There is nothing surprising in this, since all these policies were already being implemented in England as well. Indeed from James's perspective it could be seen as the application to Ireland of policies intended primarily for England. What James seems not to have fully appreciated was the extent to which Irish conditions differed from English conditions, and the impact that the remodelling of the borough charters and parliamentary representation would have on the composition of the Irish parliament he intended to summon. The priorities of its members would not be James's. A Catholic parliament could not be prevented from seeking a substantial alteration to the land settlement.

In 1691 Bishop King accused James of having designed the destruction not only of the Protestant religion but of the 'English interest'. The grounds for this charge were in the statute book of the 1689 parliament: the repeal of the Restoration land settlement and the act attainting over two thousand Protestant landowners.[15] But the blame is misplaced, for James never intended or designed the overthrow of the land settlement, the bedrock of the English interest in Ireland. After his accession, James strove to resist lay and clerical pressure for repeal or substantial modification, much to Tyrconnell's disappointment. When Clarendon arrived in Dublin in January 1686, at a time when Tyrconnell's influence at court was increasing perceptibly, he was able to reassure the privy council: 'I have the king's commands to declare on all occasions that whatever apprehensions any men may have, his majesty hath no intention of altering the acts of settlement.'[16] James, of course, had no love for the beneficiaries of the Cromwellian and Restoration settlement, but he accepted the conventional wisdom that the Anglo-Irish connection depended on its being maintained. Catholics in Ireland should enjoy the restoration of political, civil and religious rights, but full-scale restoration of the dispossessed proprietors was not a practical political option. Individuals might be facilitated with restoration, but even here James was reluctant to see the settlement's terms raised in the law courts.

James's opposition to substantial modification of the settlement remained constant until the autumn of 1686. It was only with the return to Whitehall of

Anthony Dopping, bishop of Meath (1643–97), by an unknown artist. Though an outspoken Protestant, Dopping stayed in Ireland and was one of the four Church of Ireland bishops who attended James II's Irish parliament in 1689.

Tyrconnell, after his successful purge of the Irish army, that the king countenanced discussion of measures to alleviate the position of the former Catholic proprietors. Clearly Tyrconnell's persistent lobbying, supported by Richard Nagle, was proving too strong for the king's desire to uphold the status quo, and once Tyrconnell was installed in Dublin Castle he was well placed to prepare the political groundwork for a new land act. Nevertheless, the king continued to hope for a minimalist solution, and it was not until he and Tyrconnell met at Chester in August 1687 that the lord deputy was authorised to prepare draft legislation in the form of alternative bills for consideration at Whitehall.[17]

The draft land bill, which the king subsequently approved, was Tyrconnell's own preferred compromise solution and one which fell far short of repealing the Restoration land settlement. What Tyrconnell proposed, and the king accepted in the spring of 1688, was the division on an equal basis between the existing Protestant proprietors and the former Catholic land-owners of all estates possessed by the beneficiaries of the Cromwellian settlement; where improvements had been carried out, the Protestant proprietors would continue to reap the benefit.[18] In accepting Tyrconnell's proposal, the king was in effect repudiating his blanket undertaking of two years earlier not to interfere with the settlement. He was able to do so because Tyrconnell had so studiously avoided recommending total repeal. With Protestant landowners keeping half their estates, the Protestant and English interest would have been weakened but not destroyed. As a solution to the land question, it obviously went further than James would have wished and fell far short of what Tyrconnell might have hoped for; it none the less represented a reasonable compromise between the king's English perspective and the lord deputy's Irish expectations.

Twelve months later, when the Jacobite parliament met in Dublin, the spirit of compromise was no longer apparent. An attempt to introduce a measure similar to Tyrconnell's moderate draft was rejected, which suggests that Tyrconnell enjoyed comparatively diminished political authority in the parliament whose Catholic composition he had so carefully prepared. The king did what he could to have the repeal bill rejected, even asking the Protestant bishop of Meath, Anthony Dopping, to oppose it in the Lords, but nothing could stop its inexorable progress onto the statute book.[19] The royal assent was inevitable and tells us nothing about the king's intentions towards the English and Protestant interest in Ireland; rather it underlines his political vulnerability in the only kingdom which still acknowledged him as king after the Glorious Revolution. In the circumstances of 1689 James could do little to protect the 'English interest' in Ireland.

What of Bishop King's charge that James intended the destruction of the 'Protestant religion'? No positive attempt was made to disestablish the Church of Ireland in James's reign but little official favour was shown it either, especially after Clarendon's departure early in 1687. Even while Clarendon was viceroy the Church's position looked increasingly uncertain: his recommendations for improving its finances and administration were generally ignored, episcopal vacancies were left unfilled (with serious implications for the survival of the Protestant episcopate in Ireland), and the rents that traditionally accrued to the Crown from diocesan vacancies were used, in part at least, to pay modest pensions to the Catholic hierarchy, illegal rivals of the Church of Ireland bishops.[20] Furthermore, Clarendon was told to intimate to magistrates that the Catholic clergy were not to be molested and to report complaints about Catholic priests to their own bishops before involving the civil authorities.

Official favours to the Catholic Church continued apace when Tyrconnell became lord deputy: the chapels at Dublin Castle and the Royal Hospital, Kilmainham, were reconsecrated for Catholic use; a dispensation to continue as dean of Derry was granted to the recently converted Peter Manby; Jesuits were to fill all vacancies in schools under royal control.[21] Perhaps the most remarkable sign of royal favour to the Catholic clergy (and one little mentioned by historians) was the king's decision to make the Catholic archbishop of Armagh, Dominick Maguire, chaplain-general of the army in Ireland – the most senior Catholic bishop was thereby given an official position under royal authority.[22] The net result of these favours was a

dramatic rise in the official standing of the Catholic Church from a position of relative persecution at the beginning of the 1680s, and a consequential decline in the authority and standing of the Established Protestant Church.

The extent of Catholic revival was enthusiastically described in a report to the Vatican by the Catholic archbishop of Cashel, John Brenan. The king, 'who publicly professes the Catholic and apostolic faith', had appointed as viceroy the earl of Tyrconnell, 'a sincere and zealous Catholic, very intent to promote the glory of God and the splendour of the Holy faith and to advance the Catholic lords and nobility of the kingdom in position and fortune'. Tyrconnell had made 'a good beginning':

> He has now made the army nearly all Catholics, as well commanders and officials as ordinary soldiers. The royal council in Dublin is for the greater part Catholic. The civil officials, both judges and magistrates, are for a great part Catholic. The bishops and priests may appear in public and private in their clerical dress. The religious, particularly those of St Francis and St Dominic, go about in the religious habit.

Well might Archbishop Brenan conclude on a note of cheerful optimism:

> Catholics of this kingdom . . . hope for an increase of consolation every day . . . during the life of this glorious king and during the government of this his zealous minister in this kingdom.[23]

Operations during a siege, supposedly that of Charlemont, Co. Armagh, in 1690.

The archbishop's exuberant words bear substantial testimony to Catholic satisfaction with recent policy, but they also provide ample support for the Protestant case against James's government by November 1687, more than a year before the dramatic polarisation of attitudes in Ireland (with the harassment of Protestant clergy and the seizure of Protestant churches) following the Glorious Revolution in England.[24]

That James was ultimately responsible for what happened (with official approval or connivance) to Protestants and the Church of Ireland is undeniable, but the charge that he himself designed the destruction of Protestantism is difficult to sustain. John Miller's depiction of James as fundamentally tolerant seems closer to the truth.[25] Pious Catholic though he was, he did not accept contemporary wisdom about the necessity of religious uniformity in the state. As he himself put it: 'our blessed Saviour whipt people out of the temple, but I never heard he commanded any should be forced into it'.[26] In the 1680s he certainly hoped for conversions on a large scale to Catholicism in England, but there is no evidence to suggest that he planned to establish Catholicism in Ireland, where it was in fact the majority religion. Indeed all James's personal interventions on religious matters seem tolerant: from strict instructions to Tyrconnell in 1687 not to interfere with Protestant dissenters in Ulster to a strong plea for toleration at the opening of the 1689 parliament.[27] The writs for the lords spiritual in that parliament were sent to the Church of Ireland bishops and four of them actually took their seats. James's recommendation of religious toleration might not have pleased them in normal times, but it must have appeared mildly, if temporarily, reassuring in the religiously charged circumstances of 1689. The subsequent passage of a toleration act set the seal on James's determination to uphold the principle. In this matter at least he had his way.

James himself had no intention of destroying Protestantism or establishing Catholicism in 1689, that much seems clear, but whether the episcopalian Protestantism of the Church of Ireland would have survived many more years under James's government is highly doubtful, for the king's good intentions were no guarantee for an Established Church in a kingdom where Catholics had gained a political ascendancy in parliament, the administration and the courts. The only Protestants likely to thrive, or at least survive, under Jacobite toleration, were the closely knit and densely concentrated Presbyterians of Ulster.

Do the policies pursued in James's name suggest that the king was bent on establishing arbitrary government and an absolute monarchy? Most Irish Protestants thought so at the time, and considering the policies and the threat to the Restoration settlement, that perception is understandable. Bishop King wrote of James's 'fondness of France', his 'affecting to imitate' Louis, his endeavouring 'to alter the very frame and constitution of the government'. Historians, too, have long since made a case for the 'absolutist' interpretation of James's intentions by linking developments and policies in England with those in Ireland, Scotland and the colonies: the appointment of

Sir Neil O'Neill of Killelagh (?1658–91) as an Irish chieftain, by J.M. Wright. Painted in 1680, the picture is a nostalgic and idealised portrayal of a Gaelic aristocracy that had lost its power. The Japanese armour (bottom left) is probably a covert reference to the persecution of Catholics in England; the Jesuits were undergoing persecution in Japan at this time.

Catholic army officers, Catholic judges, Catholic sheriffs in the counties; the instigation of quo warranto proceedings and the granting of new charters to cities and boroughs; preparations for a packed parliament.[28] These policies were not just bad in themselves but the methods used to implement them were illegal and arbitrary.[29]

The 'absolutist' interpretation of these developments looks less convincing, however, if each area of Tyrconnell's intervention, in James's name and often with James's approval, is examined. In the case of the army, his dispensing with the oath of supremacy had many precedents; the appointment of Catholic lawyers to the bench and as sheriffs involved a similar use of the prerogative to dispense with the oath. What was unusual was the scale on which the royal prerogative to dispense was used, not the dispensing itself. As for the quo warranto proceedings against the boroughs and the granting of new charters admitting Catholics to the corporations, the 1672 rules for the government of the boroughs (which had the force of law) obliged members of corporations to take the oath of supremacy but also empowered the viceroy to dispense with the oath at his own discretion.[30] In this case, therefore, the viceroy was not even using prerogative powers in dispensing but activating a statutory right.

The one area of substantial doubt about James's absolutist pretensions lies in Tyrconnell's remodelling of the Irish army: the dismissal of Protestants, the appointment of Catholics and the substantial enlargement of the army's size. The methods Tyrconnell used to accomplish this feat may or may not have involved an arbitrary use of prerogative power, but the purposes for which he did it, and which clearly had James's wholehearted endorsement, suggest that the intention was the same as Wentworth's in the 1630s – to provide the king with a ready means of military support in the event of internal dissension in England. Certainly James accepted readily enough Tyrconnell's suggestion that Irish troops be dispatched to England in the gathering crisis of late 1688 (with disastrous results, as it turned out, because of English hostility to the very idea of an Irish Catholic army). The fact of a large standing army in Ireland is not, however, proof of an intention on the king's part to establish absolute monarchy in Ireland or England. Such a conclusion is possible and may be inferred, but it has not been proven.

An epilogue to the reign is provided by the king himself. In 1692, in the third year of his final exile, he wrote a memorandum of advice 'for my son the prince of Wales' on how his dominions should be governed after the hoped-for restoration of the Stuart monarchy. The pages devoted to Ireland[32] are especially revealing since they were written in the light of James's own experience of the country (apart from William, he was unique among English monarchs between the fifteenth and eighteenth centuries in having visited Ireland). Starting from the principle that it was in the Crown's interest to improve the country, he recommended that the New English, that is, the Protestants, 'must be supported for the good of trade and the improvement of that kingdom'. But clearly his experiences in 1689–90 had done nothing to diminish the adverse view of them that Tyrconnell had so assiduously sown in his mind, for he warned his son that they were not to be trusted too far, since they were 'generally ill principled and republicans'.

James's view of the 'natives' (the term he used to describe both Old English and native Irish Catholics) was more benign. They must be given 'especial care' for two reasons: the great loyalty they had demonstrated, and James's own desire 'to keep up a Catholic interest there, that at least in one of the kingdoms there may be a superiority of those of that persuasion'. However, there was a need to civilise the native Gaelic Irish, to see that they were 'weaned from their natural hatred against the English'. This would be achieved by having 'the sons of the chief of them bred up in England', and by the Crown establishing schools to teach the children of the 'old natives' the English language, and 'by degrees wear out the Irish language'. This theme of anglicisation is continued in his comments on the Catholic clergy when he recommends the appointment of English clerics to Irish sees and the establishment of colleges in Ireland so that priests need no longer be educated abroad.

James's most telling advice concerns the appointment of a lord lieutenant. He should not be a native, nor an Englishman with an estate or 'great relations' in Ireland, nor should he buy land or hold office for more than three years. In other words, the lord lieutenant should be a disinterested Englishman capable of ruling the country in the interests of the Crown and unattached to any particular interest group in Ireland. A clearer statement of regret at having appointed Tyrconnell could hardly be imagined.

What James learned in Ireland in 1689–90 was that he had little understood the country when he embarked on policy initiatives that were designed for English purposes and when he listened too credulously to the partisan advice of Tyrconnell. He found in Ireland a Catholic body politic loyal to the Crown but not to the Crown's wider English interests. Only in exile could he begin to formulate a coherent strategy for an English Catholic king to follow in the governance of Ireland.

James II and Mary of Modena, with the Prince of Wales (the Old Pretender); from a Dutch print

PART TWO

THE CONFLICT

4
THE WAR IN IRELAND
1689–91

HARMAN MURTAGH

From 1689 to 1691 Ireland was engulfed by war on a major scale.[1] For three years a series of pitched battles, sieges, and other military operations was conducted by two regularly organised armies, comprising many nationalities and commanded by generals of international repute. In Irish, the conflict is called *Cogadh an Dá Rí*, 'the war of the two kings', from its most obvious cause, namely the attempt of the deposed James II to recover the throne of England that he had lost to his Dutch son-in-law, William of Orange, in 1688. The conflict might with equal justification be called the war of the three kings, for it made Ireland an important theatre in the wider international struggle between Louis XIV of France and an alliance of powers headed by William. So far as the inhabitants of Ireland were concerned, however, local issues and old loyalties were predominant; for them the war was the climax of a long struggle for supremacy between Protestant settlers, who supported William, and an older, Catholic population, which remained loyal to James. The war was therefore a major crisis in Irish history; after three hundred years, the shock waves released by it have still not fully subsided.

James's accession had brought improvements to the position of the Irish Catholic majority. Their leading spokesman, Richard Talbot, was made earl of Tyrconnell and appointed lord deputy in Dublin. But the Glorious Revolution was a severe blow to Catholic hopes of reversing the Restoration land settlement, and Tyrconnell would probably have submitted to an early show of strength by William. Instead, it was Louis who took the initiative and encouraged the Irish to resist. The English Revolution had upset his plans; the most effective way he could retaliate was to intervene in Ireland on the side of the Jacobites. This policy had the backing of Seignelay, Louis's minister of marine. The French navy was strong and there was a favourable report from one of its officers, the sieur de Pointis, who had been sent to Ireland at the beginning of 1689. For Tyrconnell and the Irish, Louis's support was crucial, but in France the Irish war was primarily viewed as an irritant to William. The marquis de Louvois, the powerful war minister, disapproved of the venture, and there was little real faith in an ultimate Jacobite victory. Most of the French who came found Ireland an uncomfortable country in which to campaign and despised the Irish as allies.

The Revolution had undermined the effectiveness of the English navy. It kept control of the Irish Sea but could not prevent a succession of eight major French convoys sailing to the south and west of Ireland with support for the Jacobites. Only the second convoy of 1689 was attacked as it unloaded in Bantry Bay in May, and on that occasion the French came off best in an inconclusive six-hour engagement.[2]

Under pressure from Louis, James travelled on the first of the French convoys, disembarking at Kinsale, County Cork, in March 1689. He hoped that Ireland would be a stepping stone to the recovery of power on the British mainland. Reluctantly he agreed to the repeal of the land settlement by the patriot parliament as the price of Irish support for his cause. Tyrconnell, who was now made a duke, had previously transformed the hitherto exclusively Protestant Irish standing army into an overwhelmingly Catholic force, about eight thousand strong.[3] However, some of the best units had been sacrificed in England in 1688 in a futile bid to support James. Tyrconnell reacted to the Glorious Revolution by expanding his diminished forces to a massive forty-five thousand men. But with an empty treasury he could neither pay nor clothe the new troops, and there was a lack of weapons, ammunition and other military equipment. Most serious of all, the long exclusion of Catholics from military life left a severe shortage of skilled officers to provide leadership, discipline and training.

The help sent from France was intended to remedy these deficiencies.[4] In 1689 Louis's convoys brought 16,000 sabres, 3,000 swords, 5,000 muskets, 1,000 pairs of pistols, 500 carbines, 500 flintlocks and 100,000 pounds of powder. More arms and ammunition, together with hospital supplies, tents, flags, clothing, carts, harness, tools, and flour, were shipped the following year. The convoys also carried Irish, English and Scottish Jacobite officers, together with French generals, engineers, artillerymen, commissaries and, in 1690, troops. To some extent this influx of personnel helped to make good the Jacobite army's lack of military expertise, but much of its leadership at battalion and company level remained mediocre: although the infantry, for example, undoubtedly improved with experience, they never achieved reliability in the open on a battlefield.

The problem of pay was temporarily resolved by minting coins of brass, copper and pewter at Dublin and Limerick with a face value of £1.5 million to £2 million.[5] This emergency coinage was later called 'gunmoney' because some of the metal used in the mints came from melting down old brass cannon. It was much derided by James's opponents but it certainly retained some value until the Jacobite defeat at the Boyne in 1690, after which it became virtually worthless. Thereafter, except for small sums received from France, the Irish army seems to have been unpaid.

Conrad von Rosen, the senior French general, took charge of the Jacobite

IRELAND
1689-1691

LONDONDERRY
SIEGE

CARRICKFERGUS
Siege

Bangor

Belfast

CHARLEMONT
Siege

ENNISKILLEN
Siege

Sligo

L.Erne

NEWTOWNBUTLER

Dundalk

Drogheda

R. Boyne

BOYNE

Dublin

AUGHRIM

ATHLONE
Siege

Galway

R. Shannon

LIMERICK
SIEGE

Wexford

Waterford

CORK
Siege

KINSALE
Siege

BANTRY BAY
Sea Battle
May 1689

	BATTLE
Sib-Lit.	MAJOR
Siege	MINOR

army in 1689. He came originally from the Baltic province of Livonia and was a competent professional soldier, but his blunt speech and rough ways soon antagonised James. The army was reorganised and its strength reduced to about thirty-five thousand men by the disbandment of regiments and companies surplus to its needs.[6] The final establishment for the 1689 campaign was forty-five regiments of infantry, eight of dragoons, seven of cavalry and two troops of Life Guards. Regiments, excluding the guards, were named after their colonels, who were drawn from the wealthier and more influential Jacobites, more than a third being peers or their sons. Most had only entered military life in the wake of Tyrconnell's purge of the old army, or later. A minority was more experienced: Patrick Sarsfield of Lucan, for example, who commanded a cavalry regiment, was a professional soldier who had served in England and on the Continent.[7] Many of the regimental officers were kinsmen, connections or neighbours of their colonel.

The infantry battalions, in particular, had strong regional associations: in the regiment of foot raised by the third earl of Antrim, fully a quarter of the officers were Macdonnells, and most of the remainder bore familiar Ulster names such as O'Neill, O'Donnell, MacSweeny, O'Cahan and Magill.[8] The heads of families impoverished by earlier wars and plantations frequently retained enough influence to raise a company from their traditional followers, and the Catholic clergy helped with recruiting. A commission in the army was a potentially valuable asset and a regiment resembled a business venture, headed by the colonel, in which the other officers were sharehol-ders. (There were complaints of financial ruin from those who lost commands in the reorganisation of 1689.) Although Tyrconnell was known to favour the Old English, the necessity of recruiting large numbers of the Os and Macs meant that the Jacobite forces were essentially a national Catholic army.[9]

The infantry regiments were generally single battalions of thirteen com-panies. At full strength a battalion would have mustered close to eight hundred officers and men, but this figure was seldom achieved in wartime. A few regiments, such as the élite Footguards, were of two-battalion strength. The standard infantry weapon was the matchlock musket, or in some cases, the more modern flintlock. There were no bayonets but up to a third of the troops were pikemen, whose role was to protect the musketeers from cavalry attack. Each regiment included a company of shock troops, known as grenadiers because they carried hand grenades. Some of the muskets sent from France were of poor quality and swords were in short supply. There are references to Jacobite troops armed only with sticks and scythes. Dragoons rode small horses to where their service was needed, but then dismounted to fight. Still regarded as infantry, they were armed and organised accordingly. The cavalry regiments were the army's social élite. Well-mounted and well-led, they won the respect of their opponents in the early stages of the war, but their morale deteriorated as the likelihood of victory receded. They were equipped to fight on horseback, with sabres, carbines, and pistols. Each cavalry regiment was divided into troops, but in battle they fought in squadrons of 120 to 150 troopers. The royal Stuart livery of red was the preferred colour for the uniforms of the Irish Jacobite army, but shortages of supply meant that homespuns, leather, and grey and white French cloth

Friedrich Herman, duke of
Schomberg (1615–90). This
portrait of the great soldier
was painted about 1675.

Antonin Nompar de Caumont, comte (later duc) de Lauzun (1632–1723). He is shown wearing the insignia of the Order of the Garter, bestowed on him by James II for his services in escorting the queen and the Prince of Wales (the Old Pretender) to France in 1688.

Richard Talbot, earl of Tyrconnell (1630–91)

were also used. The infantry wore broad-brimmed hats, full-skirted coats, breeches, stockings, and shoes. Cavalry and dragoons wore boots.

The Glorious Revolution encouraged Irish Protestants to come together in armed associations, especially in the north where they were soon in control of wide areas. A 'supreme council' was set up at Hillsborough, in County Down, under Lord Mount-Alexander, a local peer, and contact was made with William. However, Jacobite authority was restored in east Ulster when the Irish army routed Mount-Alexander's forces at the 'break of Dromore' in March 1689.

Only Londonderry and Enniskillen then remained as significant centres of resistance to James. Both had refused to admit Catholic garrisons in December 1688, but Derry had subsequently accepted some Protestant companies of the Irish army, and their commander, Lieutenant-Colonel Robert Lundy, who was of Scottish origin, became governor. William and Mary were proclaimed in the city in March, and Lundy reluctantly accepted a commission from William, who supplied arms and money for Derry's defence.[10] Plenty of manpower was available, but there was a lack of military experience and the hastily improvised Protestant forces retreated in disorder before the Jacobites at the Clady and Lifford river crossings on 15 April. Lundy was defeatist and others in Derry shared his pessimism. Two regiments that had come as reinforcements from England were sent away and negotiations opened with the Jacobites. Meanwhile, the Irish army had been joined by James. Apparently he believed that Derry would not defy him in person, but when he rode towards the city with some of his troops, he was met by a hail of

View of Londonderry from the north-east, c.1685, by Thomas Phillips

LONDONDERRY,

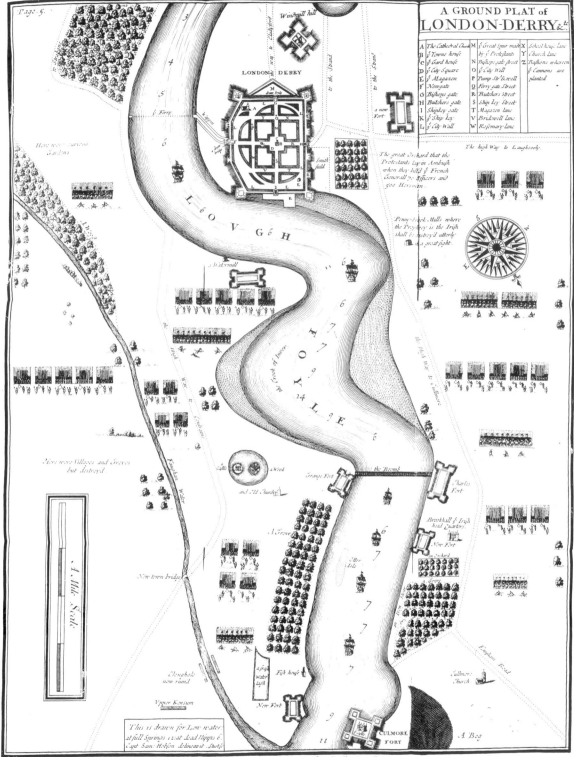

'A Ground Plat of London-Derry etc.' in 1689, by Samuel Hobson, from Story's *Continuation of the Impartial History* . . . (1693)

gunfire and forced to retire. This incident was associated with a change of leadership within the city. A militant faction, with wide popular support, ousted those in favour of peace. Lundy was accused of treachery and fled

Title page of the German
translation of Walker's
Account (1689)

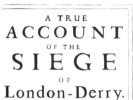

Title page of Walker's
Account (1689)

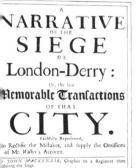

Title page of Mackenzie's
Narrative (1690), written
from a Presbyterian point
of view and criticising
Walker's *Account*.

from Derry in disguise. Subsequently interned in the Tower of London, he was later rehabilitated and sent to Portugal on English pay.

The new joint governors of Derry were Major Henry Baker, a professional soldier from County Louth, and the Reverend George Walker, a Church of Ireland rector from County Tyrone. In June, after Baker died of fever, he was succeeded by John Mitchelburne, another soldier. Common adversity temporarily obliged Episcopalians and Scots Presbyterians to sink their differences, but an ugly controversy afterwards broke out when the Presbyterians accused Walker of undervaluing their contribution and exaggerating his own role in his published account of the siege. The defenders were organised into seven regiments of infantry and one of horse, a total of about 7,500 officers and men. Derry's fortifications were comparatively strong: the ramparts were in good condition; there were numerous bastions, four fortified gateways, and twenty guns. The River Foyle guarded the north and east sides, and marshy ground was an impediment to trenchworks on the west. However, Windmill Hill – about five hundred yards south of the city wall – was an obvious danger point and there was high ground east of the river from which the city could be bombarded. The main problem for the defenders was a shortage of food, made more acute by the need to provide for thirty thousand refugees crowded into the city.

Outside the walls, the besieging Jacobite army was beset with problems. Two French generals, Maumont and Pusignan, were unluckily killed in sallies by the garrison on Pennyburn village. Richard Hamilton, the Jacobite general who then took charge of operations, understood little of the art of siege warfare. At first he had only four thousand men, which was less than the strength of the garrison, and when he was sent reinforcements they were poorly armed and trained. Desertion and sickness were rife. There was a lack of siege equipment and the few pieces of artillery available made little impact on the fortifications.

Actual fighting was spasmodic. After the early Pennyburn clashes, the garrison showed little inclination to sally beyond the defences. The Jacobites seized Windmill Hill on 5 May, but the defenders retook it in a counterattack the next morning. Further assaults on it in June and July were repulsed. On 28 June the earl of Clancarty's regiment was driven off after an attempt on a bastion beside the Butcher Gate. It was increasingly clear that the capture of Derry by assault was beyond the resources of the Jacobites. Their main hope lay in the maintenance of a blockade, which would eventually starve the defenders into submission.

In England, as soon as it was realised that Derry was holding out, a relief expedition was organised at Chester. It comprised three battalions of foot, together with much-needed supplies, and was under the command of the veteran Major-General Percy Kirke. The Jacobites were aware of this development and the French naval officer, Pointis, constructed a boom across the Foyle in an effort to thwart it. Kirke's force reached the Foyle on 11 June and subsequently sailed round to Lough Swilly, where a bridgehead

Dutch print of the siege of Derry, 1689. Though not very accurate topographically, it shows some lively details of siege bombardment, particularly the huge mortar.

Seventeenth-century siege guns in use: (from top) firing; cooling the barrel; cooling the breech with sheepskins soaked in water

'Victory of the Enniskillen garrison over the Irish', a Dutch print that probably refers to the complete defeat of the Jacobite army under Justin MacCarthy (Viscount Mountcashel) near Newtownbutler in July 1689.

ashore was established on Inch Island. It was extraordinary, however, that for six weeks he made no attempt to come to Derry's relief. Conditions in the city were deteriorating, with food and ammunition desperately short and disease widespread. At last, on 28 July, some of the provision ships broke through the boom and were towed up to Derry's quay. The final ration of horse meat had been issued to the garrison that morning; an officer noted in his diary that not a dog was to be seen in the city, as they had all been killed and eaten.[11] The arrival of the relief ships ended Jacobite hopes of forcing the city to surrender and the siege was raised. It had lasted 105 days.

There was a contrast between the dogged resistance of Derry and the lively aggression of the Enniskillen Williamites.[12] Secure amongst the lakes and marshes of Fermanagh, Enniskillen was the refuge of the Protestants of south Ulster and north Connacht. It was supplied with arms and ammunition through Ballyshannon. Gustavus Hamilton, a local landlord with a military background, was appointed governor, but a more enterprising leader was Thomas Lloyd, of Roscommon, soon nicknamed 'Little Cromwell'. He made the most of the Enniskilleners' cavalry strength to raid Jacobite positions and harass communications between Dublin and the besiegers of Derry. Successive Jacobite attempts to deal with Enniskillen all ended in failure. The worst setback was at Newtownbutler in July 1689 when the Enniskilleners routed a force of three thousand troops under Justin Mac-Carthy, the leading Irish general, who was made prisoner, but subsequently escaped.[13]

The failure to subdue Derry and Enniskillen robbed James of the military

69

initiative. The Jacobite army was badly demoralised, and except for a few strongholds, it abandoned Ulster. Simultaneously, the Jacobite cause in Scotland collapsed with the death of its leader, Viscount Dundee, at the battle of Killiecrankie. All hope of mounting an expedition to the British mainland was at an end; instead, it was William who sent a major force to subdue Jacobite Ireland.

Command of the Williamite expedition went to the duke of Schomberg who, as a Protestant, had resigned from Louis's service at the time of the revocation of the Edict of Nantes and subsequently joined William. He possessed a great reputation but was now over seventy and, it transpired, well past his military prime.[14] The first troops disembarked at Belfast Lough on 12 August and by mid-September the Williamite strength in Ireland, including the Ulster forces, exceeded twenty thousand men. In all, twenty-two infantry battalions, two regiments of dragoons and eight of cavalry were sent to Ireland in 1689. The Williamite army was of rather uneven quality. The bulk of the troops were newly raised in England. Schomberg formed a low opinion of the officers: many were Anglo-Irish, whom William regarded as more trustworthy than their English counterparts. A stiffening of professionalism and experience was provided by two battalions of Dutch infantry and four regiments of Huguenots. These French, Schomberg claimed, were worth twice the number of any other troops.[15] The initial impression created by the Derry and Enniskillen forces was unfavourable. One observer compared them to a horde of Tartars; Schomberg described the officers as peasants, and the men, on account of their fondness for plunder, as 'so many Croats'. In time, however, they won his respect and eventually six thousand Ulster troops were taken on to the establishment in nine regiments; of these, six were from Enniskillen and three from Derry.

Schomberg's campaign opened with the capture of Carrickfergus, County Antrim, which capitulated after a week's siege. The defenders, on their way to the nearest Jacobite garrison after the surrender, were so roughly handled by the Scots-Irish that Schomberg had to intervene personally – pistol in hand – to prevent them from being murdered.[16] With his rear secure, Schomberg next turned towards Leinster and the Jacobite capital, Dublin. The march south was through countryside devastated by the retiring Jacobites and an inadequate commissariat left the Williamite army with a growing shortage of supplies. Schomberg called a halt at Dundalk, County Louth, to await the arrival of provisions by sea. The weather was wet, and the main camp site poorly located on marshy ground. There the army was struck by a serious outbreak of disease, thought to have been either dysentery, typhus or pneumonia. Soon the casualties ran into thousands, Schomberg himself suffering from '*une fluxeon sur la potrine*'. He felt unable to resume the advance and instead took up a defensive position behind trenches.

Schomberg's expedition greatly alarmed the Jacobite leadership in Dublin (the French advice was to burn the capital and withdraw to Connacht). The Jacobite army was in poor shape after Derry and Enniskillen, but eventually twenty thousand men were led northwards into County Louth by James himself.[17] Towards the end of September, when the Jacobite forces approached the Williamite camp at Dundalk and arrayed for battle, Schomberg made no response. The two armies remained in close proximity for a fortnight. James then fell back on Ardee before returning to Dublin with the bulk of his troops in November. Soon afterwards, Schomberg's army also retired, unopposed, to winter quarters in Ulster. His troops continued to die during the winter; as much as half the expeditionary force was estimated to have perished.

The military pendulum had swung back and forth in 1689. The professional generals had been unable to evoke much more than amateurish performances from either army. The major offences were unsuccessful and the campaign ended with the position of both sides not very different from when it commenced. Although the Williamites had consolidated their position in the north, the failure of Schomberg's offensive was a boost to Jacobite morale, and they had more good news from the north-west, where Sarsfield recaptured Sligo from the Enniskilleners at the end of October.[18] In England there was criticism of the mismanagement of the Irish expedition. The official scapegoat was John Shales, the commissary-general, who was dismissed from his position and then arrested. Privately William blamed Schomberg, and reluctantly concluded that his own presence was essential if the subjugation of Ireland in 1690 was to be speedily completed.

There was a great build-up of troops for the campaign.[19] Five of the weakest battalions in Schomberg's depleted army were broken and six thousand recruits brought over from England to fill up the ranks of the remainder. Reinforcements for the Huguenot units came from Switzerland. A major addition was seven thousand Danish troops rented by William from King Christian V.[20] The Dutch contingent was about the same size. Other units from England and Germany, together with the Ulstermen and some Scots, brought the army's strength up to about thirty-seven thousand men. It was easily the most cosmopolitan and professional force ever to take the field in Ireland. In regimental organisation and style of dress there was little to distinguish the Williamite troops from their Jacobite counterparts. The English regiments were mostly dressed in red; the Dutch Guards wore blue with orange facings; the Danish infantry, green, blue and grey uniforms and their Guards 'an orange-coloured livery faced with crimson velvet'. On campaign the soldiers of both armies would have grown increasingly ragged and unkempt. William's men had a good supply of up-to-date firelock muskets, and the Dutch and Danes, at least, were equipped with bayonets.

Every effort was made to overcome the logistical and other difficulties that had beset Schomberg. More efficient management of the commissariat was provided by Sir William Robinson, the architect of the Royal Hospital at Kilmainham. He shared the responsibility with Bartholomew van Homrigh, a Dutch merchant, who later became lord mayor of Dublin. The supply of bread was entrusted to the Pereira brothers, the Amsterdam Jews who had the contract for the Dutch army. Large quantities of stores were ferried across the Irish Sea, together with 550 wagons and 2,500 draught horses to meet the army's transport needs. An artillery train was brought from Holland. The medical services were improved by the establishment of a fixed hospital and a marching hospital, the latter under the direction of Sir Patrick Dun, an eminent Dublin physican. William's personal accommodation needs in the field were met by a portable wooden house, to the design, it is said, of Sir Christopher Wren.

The Jacobite army's preparations for the 1690 campaign were on a more modest scale. Tyrconnell made every effort to supply the troops with uniforms, and organised the manufacture of muskets in Dublin. Some new regiments were added to the army, but there were complaints of neglect of duty by the officers who spent their meagre pay in 'revels, gaming and other debauches'.[21] The most significant development was the arrival of a major French convoy at Cork in March. It brought a wide range of military supplies and technical personnel, together with six infantry battalions from the French army. These reinforcements totalled 6,666 men, about half of whom were Germans and Walloons. In exchange, 5,387 Irish troops were sent to France under the command of Justin MacCarthy, whom James had created Viscount Mountcashel. They were organised into three regiments on their arrival and became part of the French army, serving first in Savoy and Catalonia. Mountcashel's men proved excellent soldiers and were the forerunners of the large numbers of Irish who served in France after 1691. The comte de Lauzun replaced Marshal Rosen as the French commander in Ireland. Although possessed of some military background, he was chiefly a courtier and quite unfitted for high command. The impact of the French reinforcements was substantially lessened by Lauzun's overriding concern for their preservation. These were his orders from Louis's war minister, the marquis de Louvois, whom he greatly feared, and whose misgivings about the Irish venture had been increased by Lauzun's appointment.

The principal action during the winter was the investment of the Jacobite stronghold of Charlemont on the Armagh–Tyrone border, which finally capitulated in May 1690. William arrived at Carrickfergus in mid-June accompanied by an impressive fleet of three hundred ships. English politics had delayed him and he declared on landing that he had not come to let the grass grow under his feet. The army was speedily mustered and inspected, and after a week, the march south commenced.

Meanwhile, the Jacobite army moved north as far as Dundalk. The French advice was to retire west, but James was reluctant to abandon Dublin and the rich provinces of Leinster and Munster without a fight. His army was in good heart and many in its ranks must have shared his view, especially those from the Pale. There was a skirmish at the Moyry Pass, between Dundalk and Newry, after which the Jacobites withdrew to the south and took up a position behind the River Boyne, the only defensible physical obstacle that remained between William and Dublin.[22] Drogheda, a few

miles downstream, was garrisoned. On the river, at the centre of the Jacobite position, stood the village of Oldbridge. Despite its name, there was no bridge, but the Boyne was fordable there and at several other locations nearby, especially at low tide. Lauzun thought that the fords made the position untenable but James considered it 'an indifferent good one'. The most serious weakness was the location of Oldbridge in a loop of the river. Immediately to the west the Boyne swung south for about four miles to Rosnaree, before turning north again to Slane. This meant that James's forces in the loop at Oldbridge would be automatically outflanked if their opponents proceeded upstream. Furthermore, if the Williamites then got across the river, the whole Jacobite army would be imperilled, for almost any point west of Oldbridge was closer to Duleek, a few miles to the south. The bridge there, across the Nanny river, which flows parallel to the Boyne, was the only practicable line of retreat for the Jacobites. If the Williamites gained it first, the Irish army would be in danger of annihilation. To a large extent these topographical realities dictated the course of the battle of the Boyne.

The Williamite army pitched camp at Tullyallen, on the high ground north of the river, on 30 June. William declined to attack that day because it was a Monday and considered unlucky. Later, he had a narrow escape when a ricochet shot from a Jacobite cannon grazed his shoulder as he reconnoitred the river crossings. The Williamites regarded the Boyne as a formidable obstacle. In the evening, at a council of war, Schomberg, supported by some of the other generals, advocated an attack across the river at Oldbridge as a

73

Romeyn de Hooghe's view
of the battle of the Boyne,
1 July 1690 (11 July by the
calendar used in Holland).
The print depicts the
crossing of the river at
Oldbridge, where
Schomberg (11) and
Walker (10) were killed.

diversion, while the main army was concentrated upstream against the
Jacobite left flank. Against this, Count Solms, the dour commander of the
Dutch Guards who was also general of the infantry, urged that everything
should be thrown into a frontal assault on Oldbridge. Schomberg's plan was
the more daring but William was not a great general and, in the wake of the
1689 débâcle, little inclined to heed the old marshal's advice. Instead, he
opted for a compromise: the main assault would be at Oldbridge, but a flank

OVERWINNING VAN
KON. WILLEM DE
door het volkomen Slaan van Jacob de II. in Ie
den 11. July 1690.

attack upstream by a third of the army would precede it.

The battle was fought on 1 July. The day started misty but soon cleared and brightened. Shortly after dawn the Williamite flank attack got under way when Meinhard Schomberg, the marshal's son, and Douglas, the Scottish lieutenant-general, set off upstream to the west with ten thousand men. The Irish had broken the bridge at Slane, but a few miles downstream the Williamites found a ford at Rosnaree. The crossing was vigorously defended

VICTOIRE REMPORTÉE
LE ROY GUILLAUME III
defaite entiere de l'Armée de Jaques II
en Irlande. l'11.e de Juillet 1690

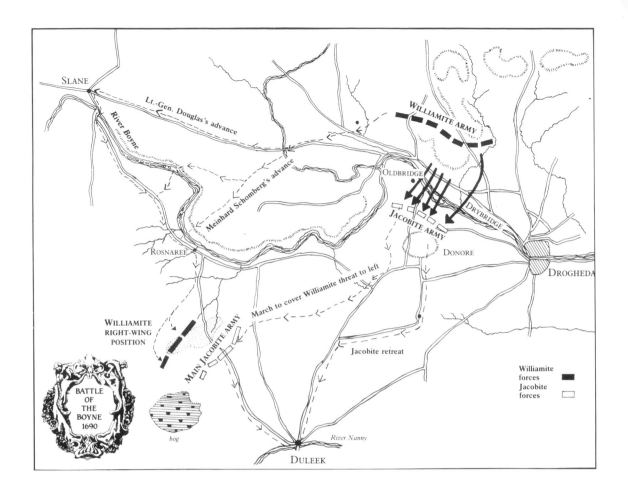

by a party of Jacobite dragoons, but they fell back when their leader, Sir Neil O'Neill, was mortally wounded. Observing the movement of the enemy upstream, James drew the conclusion that the whole Williamite army was about to follow. Accordingly, with the bulk of his own troops, including Lauzun and the French, he too moved across towards Rosnaree. This disposition halted the developing threat from the Williamite right. The two forces confronted each other, but there was no combat because a steep ravine with a boggy bottom kept them apart. A smaller Jacobite presence on the left wing might have been equally effective.

The transfer of troops left less than half the Jacobite forces to face the bulk of William's larger army in the Oldbridge sector. The infantry attack, under Solms, commenced at 10 a.m. when the three battalions of Dutch Guards entered the river ten abreast and waded, waist-deep, across the ford. They were followed by the Huguenots and some of the English battalions. The Danes, who crossed downstream about an hour later, had the water up to their armpits: they held their powder and muskets above their heads and two grenadiers carried their commander, the duke of Würtemberg, on their shoulders. Most accounts of the battle are critical of the Irish infantry. However, the regiments at Oldbridge met the Williamites with a brisk fire and the Irish Guards engaged their Dutch counterparts with spirit. There was general praise for the performance of the Irish cavalry. The Williamites attributed their courage to a generous ration of brandy, but ever afterwards treated them with considerable respect. The corpulent duke of Tyrconnell in person, together with the English Jacobite, Dominic Sheldon, and the young duke of Berwick, James's bastard son, led the squadrons in repeated charges on William's infantry as they struggled to deploy on the south bank. For two hours there was hot fighting. The disciplined Dutch Guards fixed bayonets and held their ground. The Huguenots wavered but were rallied by old Marshal Schomberg, who was then killed. Another casualty was George Walker, the former governor of Derry. Later in the day the Williamites captured Richard Hamilton, the city's besieger.

William forded the Boyne further downstream near Drybridge, and placing himself at the head of a substantial force of cavalry, charged the Jacobite right flank. The Irish horse had already taken heavy losses; now, at last, they fell back from Oldbridge across the Hill of Donore. The fighting at this stage became very confused: the Enniskilleners engaged the Huguenot cavalry regiment for a time before it was realised both were on the same side. It was not easy to distinguish friend from foe, the only mark of difference

James II's departure from Ireland after his defeat at the Boyne; a German adaptation of a Dutch print

William III's entry into
Dublin, 6 July 1690; a
Dutch print of an
imaginary scene

being that the Irish wore pieces of paper on their hats and the Williamites a green bough or sprig.

Upstream, on the Jacobite left, news of the retreat from Oldbridge came when there were already worrying signs of a fresh probe south by Meinhard Schomberg. There was a growing danger of the Irish being caught in a pincers movement, or even surrounded. A general withdrawal commenced, which soon degenerated into a rout as both wings of the Jacobite army converged in confusion on the bridge of Duleek. Weapons and baggage were abandoned; discipline disintegrated. Only the French infantry maintained their order, twice turning to face the pursuing Williamites and save the fleeing Irish from worse disaster. James was first into Dublin. His hopes were shattered and he was totally disenchanted with the Irish, as they were with him. He fled to the south coast, where a squadron of French frigates was waiting to escort him to France. He never saw Ireland (or any of his three kingdoms) again.

The Boyne is the most famous battle in Irish history but its military significance is sometimes exaggerated. The actual fighting was on a limited scale and the casualties – about one thousand Jacobites and five hundred Williamites – correspondingly light. William had certainly won a dramatic victory over James, which gave him Dublin and most of eastern Ireland. But he had failed to destroy the Jacobite army, which retreated in disorder to Limerick, where it regrouped. Anxiety over the French naval victory off

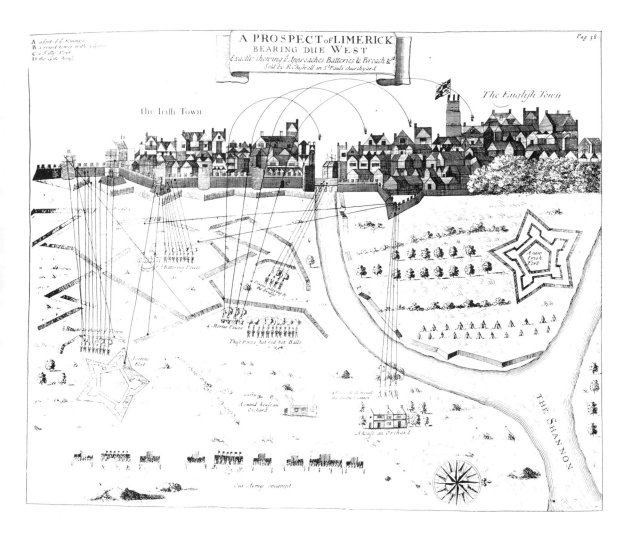

A PROSPECT of LIMERICK
BEARING DUE WEST
Exactly shewing ye Approaches Batteries & Breach &c.
Sold by R Chifwell in St Pauls churchyard

The Irish Town

The English Town

The New Irish Fort

THE SHANNON

'A Prospect of Limerick'
during the first siege
(1690), from Story's
*Continuation of the Impartial
History . . .* (1693)

Beachy Head slowed William's advance westwards. The remaining Jacobite garrisons in the east put up little resistance. The first setback was at Athlone; the principal mid-crossing on the River Shannon, where Colonel Richard Grace, the governor, broke down the bridge and from the castle, west of the river, defied Douglas and ten thousand Williamite troops.[23]

William's own failure to take Limerick in August was a major reverse.[24] Limerick's fortifications were old-fashioned and its chief strength was the location of the main town on an island in the Shannon. William made no attempt to invest the city from the west. Instead, he directed his attack on the Irish town part of the city, which extended south-east on to the mainland. He had twenty-five thousand men, against fourteen thousand Irish infantry available for the defence. The Irish cavalry, under Patrick Sarsfield, were in County Clare and staged a spectacular raid across the Shannon on the Williamite siege train, which was encamped overnight at Ballyneety en route from Dublin. The guns were dismounted and most of the ammunition destroyed, severely disrupting the subsequent siege operations at Limerick.

Only a small breach had been made in the wall near St John's Gate when

Cork as imagined in a
German print of 1691.

William impatiently attempted to storm the Irish town on 27 August. The
marquis de Boisseleau, the French major-general who was governor of
Limerick, led the defenders in person. There was furious fighting in the
breach as the Irish resisted the Williamite assault. Even the women of the city
contributed to the defence by hurling stones and broken bottles at the
attackers. The Brandenburg regiment was decimated when its gunpowder
exploded. The Williamites could make no progress, and after four hours they
broke off the attack. They had suffered over two thousand casualties. Bad
weather soon obliged William to lift the siege, and he returned to England
disappointed at having failed to bring the war to a conclusion.

After the Boyne, both Lauzun and Tyrconnell had favoured negotiations.
But when William demanded unconditional surrender, power on the Jacobite side shifted to some of the more militant senior army officers committed
to continued resistance behind the line of the Shannon.[25] The most prominent of this group was Sarsfield, 'the darling of the army' after his Ballyneety
exploit. Lauzun and the French troops had taken no part in the defence of
Limerick; in September they embarked for home aboard a French fleet that
had put in to Galway. They were accompanied by Tyrconnell, to whom the
Jacobite militants were openly hostile. Although he retained the confidence
of James and Louis and adopted a more warlike stance after his return to
Ireland in January 1691, Tyrconnell never regained his old authority. In his
absence the young duke of Berwick was in nominal command of Jacobite
Ireland but real power rested with Sarsfield and the militants, who were
discreetly opposed by an unofficial peace party favouring negotiations.

In September Cork and Kinsale fell to the Williamites in an efficient
three-week campaign conducted by John Churchill, earl of Marlborough.[26]
He brought over five thousand fresh troops, including marines, and a train of
artillery from England, and was joined by a contingent of similar size –
chiefly Dutch, Danes and Huguenots – from the army in Ireland. Although
Cork's location on an island in the River Lee was advantageous to its defence,

The battle of the Boyne,
1 July 1690, by Jan Wyck

A cavalry skirmish, *c*.1690,
by Jan Wyck

it was dominated by high ground. Berwick's order to abandon the city was ignored by the governor, Colonel Roger MacElligott, an experienced officer with three thousand to four thousand men under his command. A Williamite bombardment from the high ground soon breached the wall and the Jacobite outworks were overrun. The defenders were short of ammunition, and with the city about to be stormed, MacElligott surrendered and the garrison were made prisoners of war.

At Kinsale Marlborough first attacked James Fort, an earthen defence work on the western side of the approach to the harbour. It was captured after a short resistance in which the governor and half the garrison were casualties. Charles Fort, on the eastern shore, was a more formidable obstacle and defied Marlborough for a fortnight until his artillery arrived from Cork. The wall was then breached on the landward side, which was vulnerable to assault, and the governor capitulated on terms that allowed the garrison to retire to Limerick. This ended Marlborough's intervention in the Irish war and he returned to England. The Munster campaign, his first independent command, gave a preview of the qualities that later made him the leading general in Europe. Cork and Kinsale had been the chief ports used by the French convoys and their capture was a gain in terms of Williamite naval strategy, as well as a further reduction in the territory under Jacobite control.

The Jacobites were distracted from any attempt to relieve the Munster ports by the problem of preserving their army through the coming winter.[27]

View of Charles Fort (right) and the harbour of Kinsale, Co. Cork, in 1685, by Thomas Phillips

The immense pressure on the meagre resources of Connacht was intensified by the thousands of refugees fleeing westwards from the Williamites. Many, especially from Ulster, brought their cattle, and the available fodder was quickly consumed. A Williamite officer recalled the pitiable state of the civilians, trapped in a starving condition between the armies:

> These wretches came flocking in great numbers about our camp devouring all the filth they could meet with. Our dead horses crawling with vermin, as the sun had parched them, were delicious food to them; while their infants sucked those carcasses, with as much eagerness, as if they were at their mothers' breasts.[28]

An additional problem was caused by ten thousand Ulster and Connacht Irish who rallied to form a private army in north Connacht under Brigadier Hugh Balldearg O'Donnell. This former officer in the Spanish army arrived in Ireland in 1690 to champion the Gaels. His contribution to the Jacobite war effort was, in the end, negligible and he changed sides in 1691. In an effort to enlarge the quarters, Sarsfield and Berwick led an attack on Birr in mid-September, which was repulsed. However, a substantial part of west Munster remained in Jacobite hands, and in the midlands the Irish were able to utilise much of no man's land immediately east of the Shannon. There were raids and skirmishes along the frontier, and Sarsfield fortified Bally-more as a counter to the Williamite stronghold of Mullingar. In the end, despite hardship and near starvation, the Jacobite army managed to emerge from the winter substantially intact.

The Williamite quarters were richer and better supplied, but their troops were widely dispersed and vulnerable to attacks by the Irish rapparees. These were pro-Jacobite guerrillas, whose name came from *rapaire*, the Irish word for a half-pike, the weapon that they frequently employed. The rapparees raided supplies, murdered stragglers, interfered with communications, stole horses, and generally harassed the Williamite army and the Protestant population. To a large extent they represented the reaction of the countrypeople to widespread abuse and plunder by the Williamite soldiers, the Ulstermen especially being reported 'very dextrous at that sport'. There was a long tradition of irregular warfare in Ireland and the rapparees had the support and encouragement of the Irish army, which valued their contribution as auxiliaries. Even after the establishment of a Protestant militia in 1691, the rapparees proved difficult to suppress. Operating in small parties, they were indistinguishable from the rest of the population and continued to be a factor of military significance up to the end of the war. A Williamite source describes how they operated:

> When the rapparees have no mind to show themselves upon the bogs they commonly sink down between two or three little hills, grown over with long grass, so that you may as soon find a hare as one of them: they conceal their arms thus, they take off the lock, and put it in their pocket or hide it in some dry place; they stop the muzzle close with a cork, and the touch-hole with a

small quill, and then throw the piece itself into a running water or a pond; you may search till you are weary before you find one gun: but yet when they have a mind to do mischief, they can all be ready in an hour's warning, for every one knows where to go and fetch his own arms, though you do not.[29]

In September 1690 the Dutch general Godard van Reede de Ginkel became commander of the Williamite forces in Ireland. He was a capable professional soldier – solid, cautious and adept at uniting the many disparate nationalities in the army. His overriding concern was to end the war as quickly as possible. He did not rule out a compromise and was soon in touch with the Jacobite peace party.[30] However, the negotiations ended abruptly when the militants intervened and the leading members of the peace party were dismissed or arrested. The peace initiative seems to have been linked to a brief mid-winter Williamite offensive, but the defence of the Shannon crossings was vigorously and successfully organised by Sarsfield from headquarters at Athlone.[31] A subsequent declaration by Ginkel, offering 'reasonable terms' to all who submitted, met with no response. Irish Protestant opinion was strongly opposed to concessions to Catholics; a fresh peace offer published the following July was less generous than Ginkel wished, although it eventually provided the basis of the settlement that ended the war.

Sarsfield was created earl of Lucan by James and promoted, apparently, to lieutenant-general, but command of the Jacobite army for the campaign of 1691 went to the marquis de St Ruth, who arrived at Limerick in May. He was an experienced French general with a reputation for courage, who had been favourably impressed by the Irish soldiers of Mountcashel's brigade, which he had commanded in Savoy in 1690. He soon won the respect of the Irish army and displayed great vigour in preparing it for the coming campaign. French engineers were put to work on the fortification of the major strongholds. About ten thousand troops were left in the garrisons, and soon after mid-June, a force of twenty-one thousand took the field, about a quarter of which was cavalry and dragoons. A French convoy with a limited quantity of arms, ammunition and supplies had accompanied St Ruth to Ireland. Although many shortages still remained, and there were no French troops, experience had improved the Irish army; St Ruth had more confidence in it than any of his predecessors.

The bulk of Ginkel's forces assembled at Mullingar. After capturing Ballymore, he was joined on 18 June by the troops that had been quartered in the south. At full strength the Williamite army comprised twenty cavalry regiments, five of dragoons and forty-two infantry battalions, a total of about twenty thousand men, which was much the same size as St Ruth's field army but significantly smaller than the force commanded by William in 1690. Ginkel's equipment included an impressive artillery train of over thirty siege cannon, six mortars and twelve field guns. A pontoon bridge, which had been shipped from England, was on its way from Dublin. An offensive was

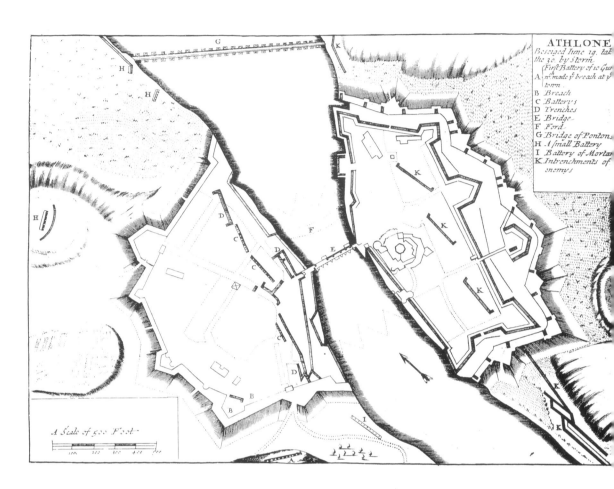

A Scale of 500 Foot

Plan illustrating the siege
and capture of Athlone
by Ginkel in June 1691,
from Story's *Continuation
of the Impartial
History . . .* (1693)

Siege of Athlone, 1691; a
wildly imaginary Dutch
print in which Athlone
looks like Heidelberg.

planned, with Athlone – the principal Jacobite stronghold on the middle Shannon – as the immediate objective.[32]

Athlone was a walled town divided by the river into two parts, which were linked by a narrow, sixteenth-century stone bridge. The Leinster town, east of the river, was easily stormed by the Williamites on 20 June. But the Jacobite resistance there was only a delaying tactic to give St Ruth time to bring the main army up to the support of the Connacht town, on which the Irish defence was concentrated. A French lieutenant-general, the marquis d'Usson, then took charge of the garrison, which was regularly relieved by fresh relays of troops from the main Irish camp a few miles to the west. The arches at the Jacobite end of the bridge had been broken down, and a line of defence works, including the medieval castle, protected the west bank. It seemed that an attack across the river would be a formidable task for the Williamites; St Ruth was reported to have said that Ginkel deserved hanging for attempting to take Athlone, as did he if it should be lost.

The Connacht town was heavily bombarded by Ginkel's artillery. In all, his guns fired off twelve thousand cannonballs, six hundred bombs and 'a great many tons of stones shot out of our mortars'. Despite severe damage to the defences, the Irish resistance remained strong. The hottest action was at the bridge. With great difficulty, the Williamites repaired the broken arches, only to have the new work demolished by an Irish detachment, which showed 'courage and strength beyond what men were thought capable of'. The pontoons, when they arrived, proved impossible to erect under fire. With his horse fodder almost exhausted, Ginkel was close to lifting the siege when success finally came on 30 June. Late in the afternoon, a picked force of two thousand men waded across a ford that had been discovered a few yards south of the bridge. D'Usson was absent in the Irish camp and the suddenness of the attack took the garrison unawares. Under a hail of hand grenades, the raw troops manning the defences panicked and fled. Within half an hour the Williamites were masters of the Connacht town. The castle was the last position to surrender. No counterattack was possible: Ginkel's men lined the western ramparts that the Jacobites had unwisely neglected to demolish, and St Ruth withdrew to the west.

It was a great success for the Williamites to have captured Athlone. Ginkel now had a secure bridgehead from which to advance across the Shannon into Connacht. On the Jacobite side there was consternation and the high command was sharply divided on future strategy. Sarsfield, Tyrconnell and d'Usson all favoured conserving the infantry in Limerick and Galway, sending the cavalry to harass Ginkel's rear in Leinster and Munster. St Ruth disagreed. Smarting from the loss of Athlone, he decided to take the gamble of giving battle while his army was still intact. The site he chose was beside the village of Aughrim, in County Galway.[33] The Jacobite army was drawn up facing east. Its lines extended about a mile and a half southwards from the village, along the eastern slope of Kilcommadan (or Aughrim) Hill to the Tristaun River on its right flank. To the east, a river and bog, running in front of the hill for most of its length, formed a major obstacle to assaulting troops, especially cavalry. The only 'passes' were at either extremity and guarded by the Jacobite cavalry. In the centre the Irish infantry was securely posted behind sod field boundaries, which had been adapted as breastworks. The position enjoyed undoubted defensive strength, but the topography did not favour an all-out counterattack of the kind St Ruth would have needed for a really decisive victory. His flag was at Kilcommadan church on the right wing. The comte de Tessé, his second in command, was in charge on the left.

The Williamite army moved forward from Athlone on 11 July. The next day there was skirmishing as it came into contact with the Jacobite outposts. After consulting his generals, Ginkel decided to attack without delay. Like St Ruth, he adopted the conventional deployment of infantry in the centre and cavalry on the wings. The sun and breeze were in the faces of his men when at about 5 p.m. his left advanced across Urraghry, the southernmost of the two passes leading to the Jacobite position. A sharp struggle soon developed as the Williamites engaged the Jacobite right. A declivity gained by the Huguenot brigade is still known as 'Bloody Hollow' from the ferocity of the fighting there. The Jacobites resisted with great determination. Their infantry made skilful use of their improvised breastworks for a system of 'defence in depth', and Ginkel's attack at Urraghry made slow progress. Before the battle, St Ruth and the Catholic chaplains had done what they could to raise Irish morale, and there must have been a widespread realisation that the army was making its last stand. Afterwards the Williamites said that 'the Irish behaved themselves like men of another nation', which was intended as a compliment.

To strengthen his embattled right wing, St Ruth switched troops across from his left. This encouraged Ginkel to make a major attack on the Irish centre-left. Ten battalions of infantry waded through the bog, with mud and water up to their waists, only to be routed by a determined Irish counterattack in which the Jacobite Footguards and Colonel Gordon O'Neill's Ulstermen plied pike and musket butt until 'the blood flowed into their shoes'. The Williamite troops were rallied by General Thomas Talmash, but it was clear the attack had failed.

St Ruth was jubilant. He declared the enemy forces were broken, and boasted that he would drive them back to the gates of Dublin. But soon afterwards, he was killed instantly when struck on the head by a chance cannon shot. Throughout the engagement he had been constantly on the move and at the time of his death was riding across to the northern sector, where a Williamite cavalry probe was seen to be making headway along the narrow causeway near Aughrim village that constituted the second of the two passes into the Jacobite position. Initially this force was commanded by the Scot Hugh Mackay, but after Mackay was thrown heavily from his horse, the Huguenot General Ruvigny took charge. It was the job of the cavalry on the Irish left wing to respond. However, the news of St Ruth's death brought their war-weariness and demoralisation to a head; they offered no resistance

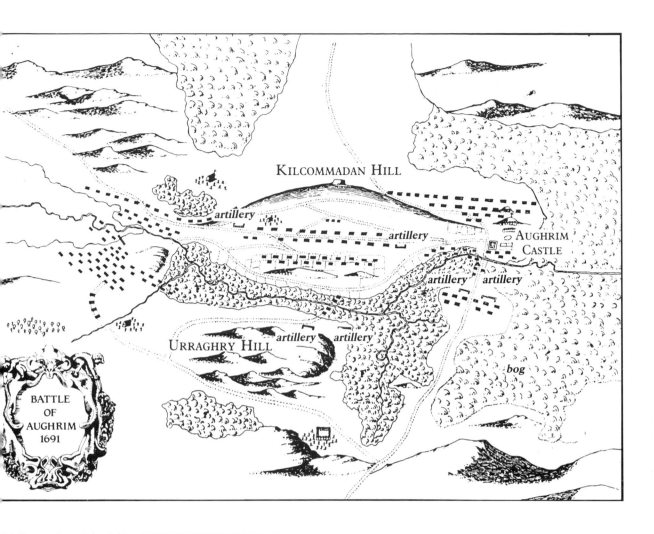

KILCOMMADAN HILL

artillery

artillery

AUGHRIM CASTLE

artillery   artillery

URRAGHRY HILL   artillery   artillery

bog

BATTLE OF AUGHRIM 1691

Bird's-eye view of the field of Aughrim, 12 July 1691, adapted from Story's *Continuation of the Impartial History . . .* (1693)

Dutch print illustrating the battle of Aughrim, 12 July 1691

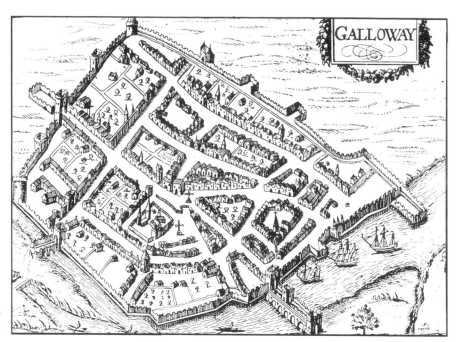

German plan of 'Galloway'
(Galway), 1691

to the Williamite advance and rode away from the battlefield to the west. Simultaneously, the infantry battalion defending the ruins of nearby Aughrim Castle ran short of ammunition.

The decisive point of the battle had now arrived. Caught on their unprotected left flank by Ruvigny's horsemen, the Irish centre crumbled. Talmash renewed the Williamite infantry attack across the bog. The Irish right, at last, also gave ground. As the Jacobite army fell back in dismay and disorder across Kilcommadan Hill there was no one to take control; de Tessé had been wounded in an abortive counterattack and left the field without making provision for a successor. Sarsfield's relations with St Ruth had been strained and he had not played an active role in events while the French general was in command. Now, with a force of cavalry, he did his best to cover the retreat, but he was unable to save the infantry from wholesale massacre. A Danish chaplain described the horrific scene:

> The Irish fled all over the fields . . . not knowing what to do or where to turn, since from all sides the inescapable violence meets them . . . throwing away their arms and finding no place to make a stand within a distance of seven miles. The women, children, waggoners, like madmen, filled every road with lamentation and weeping. Worse was the sight after the battle when many men and horses pierced by wounds could have neither flight nor rest, sometimes trying to rise they fell suddenly, weighed down by the mass of their bodies; others with mutilated limbs and weighed down by pain asked for the sword as a remedy, but the conqueror would not even fulfil with sword or musket the desire of him who implored him; others spewed forth their breath mixed with blood and threats, grasping their bloodstained arms in an icy embrace, as if in readiness for some future battle and that I may say it in brief, from the bodies of all, blood . . . flowed over the ground, and so inundated the fields that you could hardly take a step without slipping . . . O horrible sight![34]

Only dusk and the descent of a misty rain brought the slaughter to an end and allowed the survivors to escape towards Limerick and Galway.

Ginkel, after a shaky start, had won an overwhelming victory. With good reason, he publicly embraced Ruvigny on the battlefield. Irish losses were as many as 7,000 killed and 450 taken prisoner, to about 2,000 Williamites killed and wounded. All the Jacobite baggage and artillery were captured, together with eleven cavalry standards and thirty-two regimental colours. Although less famous than the Boyne, Aughrim was the greatest defeat in Irish history and, in military terms, the decisive battle of the war. The Jacobite army was shattered, its commander amongst the slain, and the numerous other casualties included members of many of the leading Catholic families.

It was clear that an ultimate Williamite victory was now inevitable. Galway capitulated a week later. Its leading citizens were supporters of the Jacobite peace party and had no appetite for further resistance.[35] The surprisingly favourable terms they secured were a signal of Ginkel's anxiety for an early end to hostilities. Sligo, which had put up a brave resistance in the north-west, surrendered in September. The Jacobite forces were concentrated on Limerick, their last major stronghold. Measures were taken to rebuild the army, but the French generals were pessimistic. The veterans who had died at Aughrim could not be quickly replaced, nor morale easily revived. D'Usson, the new commander, was an uninspiring successor to St Ruth, and the sudden death of Tyrconnell, who had become an advocate of continued resistance, was a further setback.

The Williamite army recrossed the Shannon at Banagher and invested Limerick on the south and east at the end of August. There was naval support from an English squadron off the west coast.[36] Compared to that of the previous year, however, the siege of August 1691 was conducted in a low key. There was an artillery bombardment but Ginkel made no attempt to storm the city by a full-scale assault. Instead, he concentrated on persuading the Irish to negotiate. At first they seemed determined to hold out, but the failure of a promised supply fleet from Brest to materialise gradually sapped

View of Galway from the sea, 1685, by Thomas Phillips

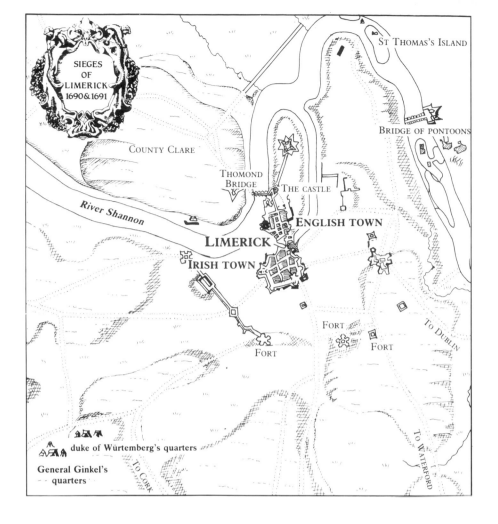

their resolve. Officers with estates to lose grew anxious to come to terms before it was too late. The cavalry were cut off from the Limerick garrison after the Williamites extended the city's investment to the west on 22 September. This was the occasion of sharp fighting in the vicinity of Thomond Bridge; next day the Jacobites asked for terms.

It surprised everyone that Sarsfield, who had previously headed the resistance party, now took the lead in the negotiations with Ginkel.[37] He was chiefly interested in taking the Irish army to France, an objective that the French generals also shared. Ginkel readily conceded the point and even agreed to furnish the necessary shipping. The arrangement had obvious advantages for the internal security of Williamite Ireland after the war. Additional transport was provided by the French fleet of Admiral Chateaurenault, which belatedly arrived in the Shannon estuary on 20 October. Fifteen thousand Jacobite soldiers eventually sailed for France, where for a number of years they formed a distinctive force, at Louis's expense, but under James's control. This arrangement terminated after the treaty of Ryswick ended the European war in 1697. Many of the Irish soldiers were disbanded, but a cavalry regiment and five battalions of infantry were incorporated into the French army, which already included the three regiments of the Mountcashel brigade. Sarsfield was mortally wounded at the battle of Landen in

1693; Mountcashel died in the south of France the next year. These units gave distinguished service.[38] There was active recruitment in Ireland up to the middle of the eighteenth century and a handful of distinctive Irish regiments, dressed to the end in their traditional red Jacobite uniforms, continued to be part of the army of the king of France up to the Revolution.

In Spain nine Irish regiments served in the army of the Bourbon kings. These units wore the red uniforms of the Jacobite army until 1806. The last three to survive – named Hibernia, Irlanda and Ultonia – were disbanded only in 1818. Another, Limerick, had transferred to southern Italy in 1735 to help form the nucleus of a new army in the Bourbon kingdom of the Two Sicilies. Large numbers of Irishmen also served in other European armies, mainly those of the Catholic states, especially Austria. Peter Lacy, who became a famous Russian field marshal and was the father of Field Marshal Francis Lacy of Austria, had commenced his military career as a thirteen-year-old Jacobite ensign at the second siege of Limerick. The 'Wild Geese', as these exiled soldiers came to be called, were only one section of an uprooted society: as a result of the Jacobite defeat Irish Catholics of all walks of life were dispersed throughout Europe in the eighteenth century.

There was hard bargaining at Limerick over the civil articles, which were concerned with the terms to be granted to the Jacobites who remained in Ireland. Eventually Catholics were promised such freedom of worship as was 'consistent with the laws of Ireland or as they did enjoy in the reign of King Charles II'. This formula was so vague that it was virtually worthless, as the subsequent enactment of the penal laws made clear. Those who were in Limerick, or otherwise under the protection of the Irish army, were promised their property, provided they took an oath of allegiance to William. This saved the estates of several hundred Catholic landowners from confiscation. The articles, which came to be called the treaty of Limerick, were signed on 3 October 1691 and brought the war in Ireland to a formal end.

Although in form a compromise, the treaty, in reality, marked a decisive victory for William and his supporters. A formidable Franco-Jacobite challenge to the Glorious Revolution was overcome and William's grip on his newly acquired kingdoms consolidated. Nevertheless, there was some consolation for Louis: for several years his relatively modest investment in Ireland had seriously hampered his opponents' war effort on the Continent, and the addition of the exiled Jacobite soldiers to his military capacity was an extra bonus. The Irish war also helped lay the foundations of an enduring Anglo-Irish military tradition. Three of the Enniskillen corps escaped the disbandments that followed the treaty of Ryswick to become the 5th and 6th Dragoons and the 27th Foot. The 18th Foot was another survivor at that time. It had originally been one of the units sent over to England by Tyrconnell to support James in 1688. Because it contained a significant number of Protestants, William preserved it after the Revolution. In this way it was unique in being the only regiment of James's Irish army to survive in British service until it was disbanded in 1922.

5
THE WAR AT SEA

A.W.H. PEARSALL

On the face of it, the Anglo-Dutch navies contributed in only a minor way to the outcome of the war in Ireland. By ensuring to William III the free use of the sea, however, they gave him an essential advantage in the struggle to defend and consolidate what he had gained by his invasion of England in 1688.

The perceptions of the three kings concerned in the conflict greatly influenced the course of events in Ireland. To William, preoccupied with his coalition against Louis XIV, Ireland was at first a nuisance. To the exiled James II, however, Ireland represented the most hopeful route for recovering his thrones. To Louis, who like William was principally preoccupied with European affairs, support for his fallen colleague provided a useful opportunity for a diversion, but only up to a point. James's efforts to recover England by way of Ireland with Louis's help, and William's attempts to prevent his succeeding, made Ireland for a time the crucial theatre of operations; and the fate of Ireland largely depended upon who controlled the seas around the British Isles and beyond. This point is perhaps so obvious, and the course of the naval war so much less spectacular than that of sieges and battles on land, that its importance tends to be overlooked or at best taken for granted. Nevertheless, although in the end the fate of Ireland was settled by the outcome of the military struggle, the conditions of that struggle were largely set by the ability of the Anglo-Dutch and French navies to supply and reinforce their respective armies there. The struggle for Ireland, furthermore, was to be the first chapter in the long Anglo-French rivalry for empire.

The navies of Europe in 1689 were in an evolutionary state, as the demands of the new war, in a new theatre, with new economic conditions were to affect the practice of sea war most markedly. All navies of the period had hitherto provided for operations in the traditional summer campaigning season, and in most cases not too far from their home ports. Pressure of events brought a new-style naval war – characterised by much cruising but few actions, the use of practical control of the sea, even if not confirmed by battle, the origins of

the two rival doctrines of 'ulterior motive' and of the 'fleet in being',[1] and finally, an increasing preoccupation with war on trade.

Hostilities opened with some hesitation and delay. As late as April 1689 the English admiral Arthur Herbert was seeking clarification and authority to attack French ships. After the uncertainties of the winter of 1688–9 in England, the navy was in some disarray, money and supplies were short, and only in April did any force begin to assemble. It had been agreed that the Dutch would contribute to the Allied fleet in a ratio of three to five, but they too were slow to appear. The French fleet, however, was better prepared: on 12 March James was landed at Kinsale with some supporters, while a further expedition was preparing with a considerable quantity of supplies and many advisers. This latter force, covered by the Brest fleet under Admiral Chateaurenault, sailed in April, and the supplies and advisers were landed in Bantry Bay. By most previous or subsequent standards this was early in the campaigning season and gave the French (and James) a good start.[2]

Although the English ministers had anticipated such a movement in giving Herbert instructions to cruise in the Chops (approaches) of the English Channel to prevent landings, Herbert did not get to sea until mid-April and then with only twelve ships of the line, not very well-fitted at that.[3] Arriving off the Irish coast, he discovered what had happened, and four more ships having joined his fleet, followed the French to Bantry. May 1 saw a battle in the bay. With an offshore wind, the French came out to cover their

93

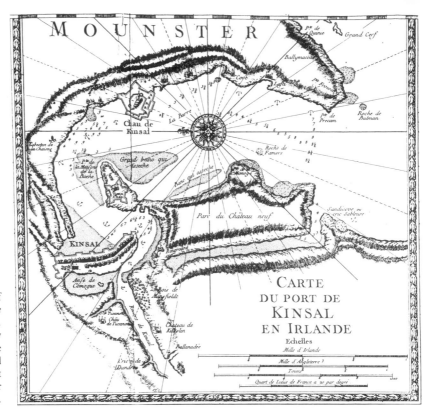

French chart of the port of Kinsale, Co. Cork, from *Le Neptune François* (1693). Before their capture by Marlborough in the autumn of 1690, Cork and Kinsale were the most convenient Irish ports for the French.

transports and engaged the English fleet on parallel courses heading out to sea. However, although the fighting was fierce and both sides suffered much damage, the engagement was like so many fought with simple 'line' tactics – inconclusive because not all the ships could get into action. Herbert was obliged to withdraw to repair damages, and Chateaurenault returned to his transports, completed the landing and soon sailed for Brest. Although no ships were sunk on either side, Bantry Bay was nevertheless the greatest naval battle ever fought in Irish waters.

Subsequently, Herbert, now earl of Torrington, resumed cruising at the western end of the English Channel with forty English and eleven Dutch ships of the line, in order to prevent any further French descents. Thus while the French were able to achieve their object, the English asserted control of the sea in practice.

With the arrival of James and the French, the Stuart cause in Ireland seemed likely to carry all before it. At first William underestimated the importance of the struggle there and his military response was slow. However, the danger of James or his supporters attempting to reach Scotland was appreciated: instructions were sent to Herbert to detach a force to prevent any communication between Ireland and Scotland. He selected for this command George Rooke, captain of the *Deptford*, one of the rising officers of the service. Making his way to the North Channel, Rooke sent the *Dartmouth* to bring to him, from Hoylake at the mouth of the River Dee, the few other ships previously allotted to the Irish Sea. Hoylake was to be the principal port used in these campaigns. In April one of these ships, the *Swallow*, had already escorted two regiments to Lough Foyle in the first abortive attempt to relieve Londonderry.[4]

Meanwhile, Rooke responded to an appeal for help from the commander of troops in Kintyre, who was anxious to quell Jacobite activity in Gigha. Afterwards he cruised between Rathlin Island and Kintyre, waiting for further relief forces. First he met Jacob Richards's reconnoitring mission to Lough Foyle, with the *Greyhound*, which on 8 June made an unsuccessful effort to relieve Londonderry by water, engaging Culmore Fort but going aground while doing so and suffering damage by gunfire. A few days later the Hoylake ships arrived, much delayed by adverse winds, with the transports of Major-General Percy Kirke's relief force. Rooke saw them into Lough Foyle, leaving some of his smaller ships to assist the military. He then returned to watch the North Channel, but failed to intercept three French frigates under the command of Duquesne-Monnier, which landed some troops in Lochaber and captured two Scottish warships before returning to Kinsale.[5]

The crucial importance of controlling these northern waters in the summer of 1689 arose, of course, from the continuing siege of Londonderry: had the city fallen, James would have controlled the whole of Ireland, and it

The battle of Bantry Bay, 1 May 1689, by A. van Diest. Both sides claimed to have won this indecisive encounter. Hearing the French claim outright victory, James II in France is said to have remarked, 'It is the first time, then!'

Jean-Bernard-Louis
Desjeans, sieur de Pointis
(1645–1705). A naval
officer, he was responsible
for the construction of the
boom at the siege of Derry,
1689, where he was badly
wounded.

could be relieved only from the sea. The long delay in making the relief attempt subsequently caused much controversy. The approach up the River Foyle was not easy. The loss in April of the fort at Culmore, at the entrance to the river proper, was certainly a handicap, but it was viewed with more respect than its meagre strength justified, possibly as a result of the *Greyhound* episode. The activity of the French naval officer the sieur de Pointis, with his strong boom across the river and its powerful covering batteries, taken in conjunction with the navigational hazards, also contributed to the apparent awe in which the obstacles were held by the council of war of 19 June. Obviously one answer was to employ local seamen and this was done. Another problem was that few of the warships were of shallow enough draught to work in the river; the *Dartmouth*, commanded by Captain John Leake, was one. Nevertheless, it is not entirely clear why the action of 28 July could not have been taken earlier. Rooke seems not to have concerned himself with Derry, merely allotting ships to take their orders from Kirke, though Rooke and his ships readily assisted in the movement of troops to Inch Island in Lough Swilly, and the *Bonaventure* was dispatched to Killybegs in County Donegal with some officers, arms and ammunition to assist the garrison of Enniskillen, a replenishment which proved timely and successful.[6]

Sir George Rooke (1650–1709), by M. Dahl. Rooke took part in the battle of Bantry Bay in 1689, commanded the squadron that relieved Derry in the same year, and played a decisive role at La Hogue in 1692.

The battle of La Hogue,
23 May 1692, by A. van
Diest. The destruction of a
large part of the French
fleet, which was to have
conveyed invasion forces
(including Patrick Sarsfield
and the Irish army) to
England, ended James II's
hopes of restoration.

Eventually, convinced of the desperate situation of the city, Kirke realised he must act. Leake and the masters of the two victuallers, *Mountjoy* of Derry and *Phoenix* of Coleraine, made plans to use the flood tide of the evening of 28 July. The *Dartmouth* engaged Culmore Fort from upstream while the victuallers passed behind her on the tide. The boom proved more of an obstacle, and the *Swallow*'s longboat, suitably built up, accompanied the victuallers to deal with it. The boom broke – as booms often did – weakened by the shock of impact, as well as by the efforts of the longboat's crew. And so, despite a crisis when, for a time, the *Mountjoy* grounded, the victuallers passed through and the city was relieved.[7]

The relief of Derry was the turn of the tide. William's foothold in Ireland was safe for the remainder of 1689, and the fear of an Irish army crossing to Scotland could be dispelled. But even before the relief, Rooke was off to Carrickfergus, where he had to meet the army under Schomberg. Captain Henry Wickham of the *Antelope* recorded the kind of difficulties always faced by these assemblages: on 8 August at Hoylake 'they began to embark soldiers on board the ships for Ireland, a company of Col. Herbert's Regiment was put aboard us & himself'. Winds were adverse until 12 August when

the wind blew fresh at EbN fine weather. Duke Scomberg put out to sea in the Cleavland yacht at 5 in the morning, there sailed along with him the Bonaventure and near 120 Sail of Merchantmen. In the afternoon we sailed having orders to bring up the rear of the fleet and to rendezvous at the Isle of Man in Ramsey Bay. In the evening we lost sight of the van of the fleet. About 12 in the night reckoning we were near the length of the Isle of Man, we layed by till morning.

97

Sir John Leake (1646–1720), by Kneller. Leake was captain of the *Dartmouth* in 1689 when he played a leading part in the relief of Derry, and captained the *Eagle* in the expedition to Cork in 1690.

On 13 August

> the wind blew fresh between ENE & ESE – indifferent good weather – in the morning we stood under the lee of the Isle of Man and was told by a small vessel the Duke passed to the southward of the Isle the last night steering towards Caracfergus we bore away and made what sail we could to follow him at 7 in the evening we anchored in the Bay of Caracfergus off Bangor where the Duke and most of the soldiers were already landed.[8]

On 16 August the *Princess Ann* took ninety ships back to Hoylake; on 18 August the *Antelope* met sixty more coming in, escorted by the *Portland*, *Charles* and *Supply*, and at Ramsey Bay she found forty ships on 20 August, and twenty more anchored that night; thirty more arrived in Belfast Lough on 24 August – all of which gives some idea of the scale of the transport operations.

At this time Carrickfergus was still in Jacobite hands. Other possible ports were, however, too close to Dublin, so Carrickfergus had to be used. Rooke had reported it in May to be 'very weak'. On 25 August the *Antelope*, in company with other ships and shore batteries, 'threw several Carcasses and Bombs into the town'. The place surrendered two days later.

The main fleet, meanwhile, was concerned in uneventful but nevertheless interesting operations. Now that he had more ships – his fleet of fifty-one increasing to over seventy with the arrival of more Dutch ships and the return of Admiral Killigrew's squadron from the Mediterranean – Torrington resumed a scheme, proposed by William earlier, of blockading Brest. With this large force he was able to remain cruising in the Soundings (the south-west approaches) until the end of August, a considerable feat by contemporary standards; but then, with much sickness and short of victuals, the fleet was obliged to anchor at Torbay. Even though the blockade had not been complete, the cruise had been quite effective while it lasted, and presaged many similar voyages.

The French had not been inactive. Louis realised that he must concentrate his entire fleet to counter the Anglo-Dutch force, so he ordered the Toulon squadron under the comte de Tourville to leave the Mediterranean. It reached Brest in July, at a time when Torrington had been blown offshore. Later, the combined French fleet left Brest and cruised in the Bay of Biscay, partly to exercise together, and partly, no doubt, as a threat, although it seems that no serious operations were ever intended. It was back in Brest by the end of August. Torrington was aware of these movements, and while the French were in the Bay of Biscay, he had covered the entrance to St George's Channel and the south coast of Ireland to foil any ventures in those directions.

William's ideas now clashed with those of his naval advisers. It was the beginning of September, when the 'great ships' customarily came in for the winter. William wanted the fleet to stay out longer to prevent any more French expeditions, and actually embarked troops to take Kinsale and so eliminate it as the French landing place. He wished too, for political reasons, to send squadrons to the Mediterranean and to convey the newly-married queen of Spain from Holland to her new country. In the end, the wind remained persistently adverse, equally so of course for the French, and so all that transpired was that a squadron under Lord Berkeley cruised in the Soundings from October until December. Little more could be done, for the long summer cruise had worn out the ships, there were no reliefs, and the victualling crisis was both serious in itself and the cause of much sickness and low morale.[9]

In 1690 the war at sea was still open. William was increasingly preoccupied with his Mediterranean ventures, which became inextricably connected with the transport of the queen of Spain: for reasons of prestige no less than protection, this voyage clearly required a respectable force. It was therefore combined with the squadron to convoy the Mediterranean trade, which had been held up in 1689. However, the whole affair dragged on so long, both in

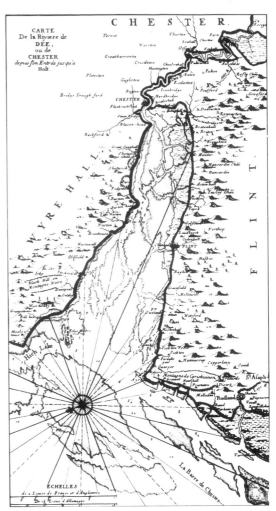

French chart of Hoylake
('Hich Lake') and the
estuary of the River Dee,
where the Irish expeditions
of Schomberg and
William III assembled and
embarked.

preparation and in execution, that nothing Louis could have done would have been a more effective diversion. Moreover, this large force accomplished nothing towards its true objective, either to create a diversion to occupy the Toulon fleet, or to check the movement of that fleet into the Atlantic. Leaving in February 1690 and escorting over four hundred sail, William's Mediterranean force under Killigrew met persistent winds. Russell left the fleet and took the queen to Corunna, returning to England in late April; but the main force was still away when the crisis broke.

William realised that matters in Ireland had reached such a pitch that he must tear himself away from continental campaigns and go there in person. First, a squadron similar in size to that of 1689, this time under the other rising star of the navy, Sir Cloudesley Shovell, was dispatched to the Irish Sea as early as February: and troops were directed towards Chester, where transports assembled. The brigade hired from Denmark crossed in March. Shovell's route was an obvious target for attack and he feared that his force was inadequate. Moreover, although a strong English Channel force was to be prepared from the remaining warships, they were so far behind in refitting that no cruising squadron was available for the Soundings in the first three months of 1690.

Sir Cloudesley Shovell (1650–1707), by M. Dahl. Shovell was knighted for his services at the battle of Bantry Bay, 1689, and played an important part in the operations in the Irish Sea in 1690. His breaking of the French line in the early stages of the battle of La Hogue in 1692 made his name.

Shovell's fears were well-founded, for once again dilatory preparations were forestalled by French action. This time the French admiral, the marquis d'Amfreville, sailed out with 6,500 troops for Ireland and landed them at Cork in April. Fortunately for Shovell, as in 1689, the French did no more than return at once to Brest, apparently without the English knowing. The Toulon squadron was also ready, and having on 10 May outsailed Killigrew in the Straits of Gibraltar, it reached Brest, to bring the main French fleet up to seventy sail.[10]

Free from hostile attentions, Shovell carried on with his task of protecting the transport of the army to Ireland. He cruised between Anglesey and Dublin with his larger ships, while the smaller vessels escorted groups of thirty to forty transports from Hoylake and Carrickfergus, until the king crossed in mid-June. These little-regarded transport operations were, however, an index of the growing maritime resources of England, for it is recorded that there were three hundred to four hundred ships in Belfast Lough when William landed; he then ordered Shovell to join the main fleet.[11]

Torrington in his turn was slowly assembling his reduced fleet – about fifty-six of the line. For this campaign Tourville received definite instructions to seek out and destroy the Allied fleet. In the circumstances, Torrington was not anxious for action, but his hints of withdrawing eastwards led to Mary and her council, fearful that such a move would leave the coast and ships to the west in peril, sending him positive instructions to engage. The result of these diverse movements was that the culmination of the 1690 campaign, both on land and sea, came on two successive days.

On 30 June was fought the battle of Beachy Head, or Beveziers, in which Torrington's fleet, especially the Dutch van, got the worst of a fierce action and had to withdraw up channel, through the Downs and into the Thames estuary. It there adopted the role that it might have taken from the outset, described so aptly by Torrington at his subsequent trial as a 'fleet in being'. Next day, 1 July 1690, the military decision in Ireland was largely achieved with William's victory at the battle of the Boyne.

In London, gratification at the victory in Ireland was submerged by the fear that the French might invade the undefended south coast of England. Unaware of William's order, the Admiralty recalled Shovell, though he was told to go into Plymouth if the French fleet was to the westward. Next came an alarming report of twenty-eight French frigates in the Irish Sea, so Shovell was soon diverted to look for them in St George's Channel, while the transports were hastily concentrated in Dublin. As Shovell left Plymouth he met the long-missing Killigrew with his twelve of the line, victim of numerous accidents and head winds but warned of the crisis.[12]

King William's landing at Carrickfergus, Co. Antrim, in June 1690; inset from a chart of 'Carreckfergus Lough' by Greenvile Collins, published in 1693. William made the crossing from Hoylake in the yacht *Mary* (A), of which Collins was captain.

However, the apparent loss of control of the sea was transient. For their part, the French seemed to have no idea what to do with their superiority; the risk of an attack upon the lines of communication in the Irish Sea did not appeal to them: there were few important ports open to attack; no troops were available for an invasion; and the Allied fleet was still 'in being'. So after some cruising, they delivered an onslaught upon the inoffensive port of Teignmouth in Devon, and then returned, with mounting sickness, to Brest.

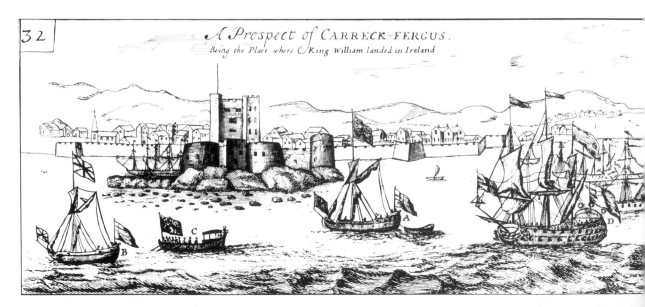

32

A Prospect of CARRECK-FERGUS.
Being the Place where King William *landed in Ireland.*

Certainly French ships did appear at Kinsale and later at Limerick, under Job Forant and d'Amfreville, but their purpose seems to have been only to succour the French on shore. Presumably these forces were the '28 ships we have so long been menaced with', as Sir Robert Southwell wrote to the earl of Nottingham.[13]

The Allies, on the other hand, quickly pulled themselves together. Even before the end of July Shovell had returned to the Irish coast, where the mere appearance of his ships induced the governor of Duncannon Fort, in County Wexford, to surrender. Dublin, Waterford and Wexford had already fallen to the Williamite army. Barely a month after the Boyne, Churchill, now earl of Marlborough, proposed to a council of war an effort to wind up the Irish affair by capturing the ports used by the French. Despite the alarm of the rest of the council, Russell and Nottingham supported him, and this resolute group obtained the approval of the king, who was engaged in the siege of Limerick. Indeed, he appointed Marlborough to command the force, and during August, the fleet, sailing from the Thames and from Plymouth, assembled at Spithead to cover the expedition. Adverse winds prevented its immediate departure; only in mid-September could it sail, in face of the French fleet. The Allied fleet landed heavy guns, while a bomb vessel shelled Cork, which was soon taken, followed quickly by Kinsale. Shovell proceeded along the west coast as far as Galway to intercept the French ships, but they had departed. Although fighting went on through 1691, and a few ships watched the Irish coast, the French for most of that year seemed unable, even if willing, to give support by further naval action.[14] After the Jacobites' disastrous defeat at Aughrim in July 1691, the French did finally get together another formidable expedition, which Chateaurenault once more guided without difficulty – this time to Limerick – but it arrived too late to prevent the capitulation of the city.

English naval efforts during these years had largely centred on Ireland. A large preponderance of the ships of the navy were involved either in operations in the Irish Sea or in the protective work of the main fleet. On 1 August 1690, for example, twenty-eight rated ships and many smaller vessels

View of Passage, Co. Waterford (right) and Waterford Harbour, looking seawards, by Thomas Phillips, 1685. Duncannon Fort, where James II boarded a Saint-Malo privateer for the first part of his flight to France in 1690, is in the far distance on the left.

are shown as engaged in Irish Sea tasks. When the strength of the main fleet (about sixty) is added, at least half of the total force is taken up. There was little to spare. Only a few ships were in the West Indies and one or two in North America, with twenty ships on convoys in the North Sea and the Mediterranean.

Although it is easy to see that in 1689 the English fleet operations were directed towards the prevention of a further French descent on Ireland, its operations in 1690 became more diffuse, a development largely accounted for by the battle of Beachy Head and the withdrawal of the Allied fleet to the east. In fact, the French executed an able combination to secure a superior fleet, but failed to take advantage of their success. Owing to the dependence of the Williamite army on supplies from England, an attack on the transports in the Irish Sea could have been most effective. Furthermore, the French should not have allowed the attack on Cork and Kinsale in autumn 1690 to pass unchecked. With the force available to Tourville, they could easily have been disorganised.

These criticisms are so obvious that they must lead us to the question of what the French were in fact seeking in Ireland. The English army had to be transported to Ireland and then, in that devastated country, kept supplied; the Irish effort depended on supplies and troops from France, yet no real effort was made to attack the English communications, or to give the Irish much maritime support. Late in 1689, the earl of Melfort, seeking aid for James, received from French ministers many excuses why little could be done, mostly based on caution induced by the existence of the Allied navies, although no difficulty seems to have been found in practice in supplying Ireland. When one looks at the overall picture, one realises that in reality these were the excuses of men who did not want to do too much for James.

In the departure of the French fleet and its subsequent inactivity at so favourable a moment, we may recognise a mixture of practical naval problems and policy. As to the former, fleets of that period, medical knowledge being what it was, were unable to remain long at sea in good health, and it was the universal custom to bring in the 'great ships' about the end of August. As to the latter, the tame return to Brest after the two spring voyages of 1689 and 1690 marks the appearance of the insidious doctrine of 'ulterior motive'. These two factors, combined with Louis's generally pessimistic view of the Irish and of James, a view shared by his advisers and reinforced by the unhappy experiences of the officers sent to Ireland, explain France's weak commitment to the Irish war.

The Allies used their fleets sensibly, apart from the aberration of Beachy Head. Unlike the French, they had positive commitments to support and protect, and necessity had led to operations running on into the autumn. William's preoccupation with grand strategy, however, induced him to ask too much of his resources and to ignore the chance circumstances of the sea, which so often delayed and bedevilled operations. In this respect the Irish commitment either drew in forces that he hoped to use elsewhere or left

CANAILIE
T. CANAEL UYT

Canailje t'Canael Uyt (sweeping the scum from the channel), a triumphant Dutch print celebrating the victory at La Hogue in 1692. Its democratic tone, with a French officer begging to surrender to a Dutch rating, is remarkable.

inadequate forces available. Most notably, little could be done to prevent the French supplying Ireland because the English army had to be protected. William's Mediterranean ambitions were also thwarted, and the protection of commerce, in particular, suffered. Shipping losses were consequently heavy, and there were great delays to trade waiting for convoy, which in some cases never came.

The campaigns at sea offered little excitement, and indeed present the paradox that those who came off worst in the two rather indecisive actions nevertheless achieved their objectives in the end. At the crucial moment the Allied resources were handled with resolution to dispatch Marlborough's expedition to consolidate the military supremacy gained in Ireland. The inaction of the French fleet reflected a loss of interest in Ireland and disillusionment with James, but also, perhaps, a failure to realise the opportunities of the new maritime situation. As the risk to William's crown in England and Scotland was thereby removed, so Louis's most formidable opponent was freed from a potentially exhausting Irish diversion. In this somewhat negative way, sea power decided the future of Ireland.

6
THE PROPAGANDA WAR

DAVID HAYTON

In the sense in which we commonly understand it, the term 'propaganda' is a nineteenth-century coinage, and indeed the concept does seem more appropriate to the modern age of instant mass communications and democratic political systems than to the relatively primitive technologies, deferential societies and oligarchic governments of the seventeenth century. And yet if we look closely, we find that there existed in the kingdoms of the later Stuarts both a ready audience for political propaganda and a variety of means through which that audience might be entertained. Historians may argue over the degree to which the outcome of the Glorious Revolution depended on political rather than military factors, but there can be little doubting the considerable emphasis placed by the Prince and Princess of Orange on winning the hearts and minds of their new subjects. The 'political nation' in England had to be dissuaded from giving resistance to the Dutch invasion, and subsequently persuaded of the legitimacy of the Williamite regime, or at least of the advisability of admitting William and Mary as king and queen in preference to the return of James II. No such conditions prevailed in Ireland, of course, where the violence of politico-religious antagonisms polarised opinion more completely. There to be Catholic was to be Jacobite; to be Protestant, Williamite. The 'middle ground' of moderation and neutralism was very sparsely populated, and the Irish conflict of 1689–91 was therefore much more clearly a military than a political one. Even here, in preaching to the converted, propaganda could still have its uses – to encourage morale, to stiffen the will to resist or the resolve to overcome. But it was in England that the prizes of the propaganda war were principally to be won, and to a lesser extent on the Continent, for the Revolution and the ensuing Irish campaigns were part of a wider European struggle; and it was in England and on the Continent that this war of words and pictures was principally waged.

A remarkable variety of events and artefacts could serve as vehicles for propaganda.[1] Naturally the printed word bulked largest, a sea of publications spreading from the dense polemic of tracts and sermons out to the shallows of the newspapers, squibs and broadside ballads. Pictorial representations could be even more effective, presenting a simpler and more striking message, whether through the medium of the engraved print, often satirical in tone, through the stylised images of coins and medals, or through the decoration of some household object, such as a plate or a pack of playing cards, both of which were used in this period to carry political statements. And finally there was the street theatre of public pageantry: formal state occasions and organised political demonstrations, complete with bonfires, fireworks, and assorted festivities.

To make an accurate assessment of either the size or the social profile of the audience reached through any of these seventeenth-century 'mass media' would be exceedingly difficult. There is, for instance, no detailed records of the print-runs of pamphlets, let alone broadsheets or engravings. An estimate can be hazarded on the basis of the number of editions a publication may have gone through, but even this would only give a rough idea of how many copies had been sold, not how many readers had seen it.[2] It might be tempting to assume that written propaganda catered for a better-educated audience than pictorial propaganda; that is to say, at the very least, a literate

Firework display on the frozen Vyver lake at The Hague, by Romeyn de Hooghe, from *Komste van Koning Willem in Holland*. The display was part of the lavish ceremonies to welcome William on his return to Holland in 1691.

Left: Dutch plate with portraits of William and Mary, *c.*1688; *right:* Lambeth delft charger with an equestrian figure of King William

audience. However, those who could not read might still listen. Newspapers and newsletters were read aloud in taverns and coffee-houses, and ballads and doggerel verse were composed to be learnt by heart and recited. Furthermore, items like medals and even engravings were luxury goods, with a relatively narrow and select circulation. Far from being crude woodcuts, the satirical prints of the period were cleverly and expensively manufactured works of art, sometimes adorned with colour and usually imported from the Continent. In any case, they had frequently to be accompanied by a lengthy commentary, necessary to decipher the full satirical message. In all probability, therefore, the safest way to evaluate the audience for propaganda is to infer it from the content of a particular piece, whether it be a complex satire requiring a high degree of political awareness, or a simple slogan appealing to the most obvious of contemporary prejudices. Using this rule of thumb, we may conclude that while some propaganda was intended to mould the opinions of the enfranchised 'political nation', there was also a powerful element of rabble-rousing populism.

Much of this output was not the direct responsibility of the royal courts or governments whose interests it served. Many of the pamphleteers, poets, playwrights and preachers who enlisted their talents under the Williamite or Jacobite banner did so on their own initiative, some out of a principled attachment to the cause, others for the less respectable but probably more common motive of personal advancement. Once the issue of the conflict was effectively decided – in England and Scotland in 1688–9, in Ireland in 1690 – it was the Williamites who were the greater beneficiaries of careerist penmanship: few would consider it worthwhile to pay court to a losing side, and those Jacobite authors like the Irish nonjuror Charles Leslie, who had not accompanied their sovereign into exile and who continued to write under difficult and dangerous conditions at home, can only have been motivated by principle or sentiment. Oddly enough, the Jacobite cause was probably

Allegorical print by G. de Lairesse, 1691, showing Fame revealing a portrait of William crowned with victor's laurels.

better served in these adverse circumstances than it had been before. Besides the advancement of fortune and worldly reputation to be gained by hack writing for a successful party, there were considerable financial attractions for the commercial entrepreneur in this field. Money was to be made from the marketing of tracts, broadsides and prints, and from the distribution of newsletters. These last are an even better example of 'free enterprise' propaganda, operating beyond the sphere of government, since unlike printed publications, the handwritten newsletters were not subject to the attention of the censor. Still more flagrantly commercial were the cards, delftware and other suchlike 'souvenirs' with which manufacturers hoped to exploit a popular mood of Orangeist triumphalism.

While the volume of propaganda in circulation in 1688–91 was thus inflated by careerist or commercially-minded opportunism, there remained a significant element at the core, which was directed, inspired or controlled by James and William themselves or by their ministers and officials. Both kings made public appearances that were contrived for special effect. Both made

French print of 1690, produced in the mistaken belief that William III had been killed at the Boyne. Halifax, dressed as a French curé, leads the procession which carries William's body to its grave. On the right William is shown descending into hell to join Schomberg.

public pronouncements of policy, and issued proclamations and declarations: William's Declaration prior to his invasion in 1688, setting out the grounds for his action and defining only limited objectives, was later credited with hoodwinking a number of loyalist waverers into lending him their support, while James in exile produced not one but two such political manifestos, with less success, designed to prepare the way for a counter-revolution.[3] Both kings minted coins and struck medals that carried overtly political symbols. Both published official newspapers in England: William did so in Ireland too, with the *Dublin Intelligence* (beginning in 1690), and James may have done – at any rate, he appointed loyal Catholics as 'King's Printers' in Dublin in January 1690.[4] Both monarchs exercised a general supervision over the press through the system of licensing. William is thought to have encouraged and facilitated, perhaps even paid for, the publication of a host of tracts, broadsides and prints in England in 1688–9 to follow up his Declaration. Sometimes these actually bore his imprimatur: a pamphlet *Character* of the Prince of Orange, presenting a highly flattering picture of his ample virtues, which appeared during the sessions of the convention parliament at Westminster in 1689, proclaimed that it was published 'with allowance'.

A similar combination of direct and indirect influence marked the Crown's relationship with the London theatres. Intervention by the lord chamberlain forestalled the staging of plays like John Dryden's *Cleomenes* (1692), regarded as 'reflecting' excessively upon the Government, while the endorsement of royal patronage was given to other works with a more acceptable message, such as Nathaniel Lee's dramatisation of the St Bartholomew's Day atrocities in France a hundred years before, *The Massacre of Paris*, put on in 1689 in order to fuel fear and hatred of popery. On one remarkable occasion this tactic backfired. Queen Mary commanded a performance of Dryden's earlier anti-Catholic satire, *The Spanish Fryar* (1681), only to find herself

embarrassed by hard stares from some sections of the audience at references in the play to a daughter forcibly usurping the throne of her father.[5]

Mention of the influence that governments could exert over press and playhouse highlights an obvious point about the relative effectiveness of Williamite and Jacobite propaganda, that once William had gained control of London in December 1688 and his father-in-law had fled to France, he enjoyed an overwhelming advantage. He had the power to promote and disseminate his own views throughout England, Scotland and Wales, and to suppress or deter opposition. James was forced to rely on the assistance of his French hosts, who had other fish to fry; on the voluntary efforts of clandestine loyalists in England, who to begin with were intimidated by the risk of arrest; and for a time, on the activites of his Irish administration, which was ill-equipped to mount a sustained propaganda initiative. But William possessed other advantages too, which furthered his cause even before his invasion and were to enhance his position afterwards: the superior talents of his Dutch subjects and Protestant European allies in the realm of pictorial satire. The Dutch were at this time the acknowledged masters of the art of engraving, with their most renowned designer, Romeyn de Hooghe, the busiest and most effective exponent of the genre. The best medallists, as well, belonged to the Dutch school, men like Smeltzing, Borkam, and William's particular favourite, Arondeaux. Of the hundred or so propagandist medals struck for William and his supporters in the years 1688–91, the vast majority were manufactured in Holland or Protestant Germany.[6]

The superiority of the Dutch in visual satire was not simply, or even necessarily, a matter of technique (though at its best, Dutch engraving was

III

French print satirising William's reception by the people of London in 1688.

technically unsurpassed), but of imagination. French engravers and medallists could also produce fine work, but it generally lacked political bite. Their prints made little use of the emblematic style so characteristic of the Dutch, which served as an ideal vehicle for barbed political commentary. On the rare occasion that a French artist did venture some satirical allusion the Dutch were able rapidly to turn his weapons back upon him. When Parisians were regaled with a false rumour that William had met his death at the Boyne, a print was issued portraying what the designer imagined to be the gleeful reactions of hypocritical courtiers and oppressed subjects in England (and Ireland). This composition was subsequently adapted by the Dutch and transformed into a picture of the deathbed of Louis XIV, to emphasise the expiry of French ambitions.[7] The French king's medallists, for their part, were more accustomed to apply their art to propaganda purposes, but it was a different and less penetrating form of propaganda than that of their Dutch and German counterparts, deploying the symbolism of absolute monarchy simply in order to glorify Louis as the 'Sun King', while Dutch medals not only praised William as a hero but effectively denigrated his enemies: an example from 1688 shows Louis and James joining hands with the Sultan of Turkey and the ruler of Algiers to form an 'Antichristian Confederacy'.[8]

This important divergence in approach is perhaps symptomatic of deeper differences between the respective governments of France and the United Provinces, and by extension, the French-supported King James and the Dutch King William. The French monarchy may be seen as content to bask in its own *gloire*, whereas the more open political system of the Dutch, in

VIII. *S.K.H. werd ontfangen in London,*
Den 1⁸⁄₂₈ D.cemb. 1688.

VII
His R. H. reception at London,
Desmb. 18. 1688.

B

C

D

E

't Amsterdam by CAROLUS ALLARD, *op den Dam;*
Met Privilegie van de Edele Groot Mogende Heere Staten van Holland en Westfriesland.
Amsterdam by CHARLES ALLARD *an the Dam;*
With Privilege from the Great & Mighty States of Holland & Westfriesland.

William's reception in London, 1688, by Romeyn de Hooghe (detail). In contrast to the derision of the French print, this was a Williamite propaganda version of the event.

Lambeth delft charger.
The mounted figure copies
that of an earlier king,
simply changing the label
to indicate King William.

which representative institutions played a major part, encouraged appreci-
ation of the value of manipulating 'public opinion' in a more active way. It is
equally plausible to depict the two principal protagonists in the Glorious
Revolution as embodying these opposing attitudes. Not that one would wish
to represent William, whose desire to safeguard and extend his powers as
king of England was much the same as his father-in-law's, as notably liberal.
Rather, his sensitivity to the value of propaganda showed a shrewd grasp of
the ways in which the English political system could be managed.

William's exploitation of the power of the press to undermine James's
position antedated the Revolution. He had, for example, directed the
publication of Pensionary Fagel's *Letter* to criticise James's proposals to
repeal the penal laws in England against Catholics. We have seen how he took
care to preface his expedition in November 1688 with a cleverly crafted
declaration of intent, distributed throughout England and Scotland and
consolidated with other tracts and broadsheets. William's gratitude to those
who had helped him in this endeavour, such as the lone English printer of the
Declaration, later accorded a trading monopoly in his home city of York,
speaks volumes for the new king's personal involvement, as does his
rewarding of Romeyn de Hooghe for services rendered, and the subsequent
appointment not only of a royal engraver but a royal medallist to carry on the
good work.[9]

William also took a close interest in the styling of his public image. The
interpretation of his role in the events of 1688–91 in terms of a providential
instrument of deliverance, a theme that was to become the great cliché of
Williamite writing and preaching on the anniversaries of 1688 and the
Boyne, was articulated at the time by the king himself. Replying to Bishop
Dopping's speech of welcome outside Dublin in July 1690, he announced: 'I
have come hither to deliver you from the tyranny of popery and slavery, to
protect the Protestant religion and to restore your liberties and properties.'[10]
There is even the tantalising possibility that the image of the king as a hero on
a white horse, that most enduring and evocative of Ulster's political icons,
may be traced back to the 1690s. Contemporary accounts do not give the
colouring of his mount at the Boyne itself, nor at the triumphal entry into
Dublin, but descriptions of William's ceremonial welcome to Exeter in 1688,
the first important English city to fall to his army, note that he appeared
riding 'a milk-white palfrey'.[11]

By contrast, James seems to have paid nowhere near the same attention to
cultivating a public image of heroic kingship, nor even to the business of
putting his political views across in the most favourable manner. Instead he
seemed often content to rely on his authority as the divinely anointed king.
Attempts by his administrations in London and Dublin to make some use of
the press were half-hearted. His Irish printers, for example, appear to have
produced a news service of sorts in 1689–90 in the same way that Williamite
printers, official and unofficial, were doing in England, issuing a series of
broadsheets with an update of political and military information. But while

the news emanating from the London presses was generally slanted in favour of William and his armies – accounts of 'signal victories', 'great defeats' for the enemy and so forth – and might be spiced with tales of the brutality of the Irish and French forces under James or even of the faithlessness of James himself, the surviving Jacobite news-sheets display an admirable, if politically unrewarding, objectivity in their reporting.[12]

The exiled king can scarcely be blamed for his party's failure to match the Williamites in areas like the publication of satirical prints, where the Dutch were particularly strong, but James may be fairly charged with failing to make the most of those opportunities that did arise. The birth of his son, the Prince of Wales, in the summer of 1688, provides a good example. If we look at the commemorative medals struck on this very significant occasion, we find that James, despite having access to able artists in England and France, suffered another propaganda defeat instead of recording a success. A royal medal did illustrate the new prince as an infant Hercules, but this message was drowned by the Dutch counterblast, which drew on the malicious rumour of the child's suppositious origin – the 'warming pan' theory – to depict him as an unlawful heir, the tool of the Jesuits and the papacy in their unholy conspiracies against the English.[13] These contrasting responses cannot simply be explained by reference to the greater resources enjoyed by William and his party. James's flaccid approach may reflect the fact that, as the man in possession of the Crown in 1688, he did not feel so strongly impelled to court public opinion. He may have relied too much on the doctrines of nonresistance and passive obedience, preached to Englishmen by high-flying clerics on his behalf; or it may just have been a matter of temperament. Whatever the reason, it seems clear that the most effective pro-Jacobite propaganda was produced not from above at the behest of James or his ministers, English or Irish, but on the initiative of the pamphleteers and versifiers who, in the years after 1688, fired off an increasingly intensive barrage of tracts, squibs and ballads attacking the Williamite regime from below.

William had one further important advantage over his rival, namely that in the years 1688–91 he could be reasonably confident of the strength of his case. In propaganda terms at least, his were the arguments likely to weigh most with Protestant Englishmen. In brief, as the inscription to one medal put it, William had come to England as 'the restorer of religion and liberty', and these two themes – defence of the Protestant religion and the restitution of the ancient liberties of Englishmen – formed the basis of the Williamite message.[14] Frequently they would be conflated by a reference to 'papal tyranny', the idea that Catholicism was in itself an oppressive political system that throughout Europe served as the handmaiden of arbitrary rulers.

Anti-popery was of course one of the most profound emotional forces in seventeenth-century English politics, helping to bring down Charles I and threatening to topple Charles II at the time of the Exclusion Crisis.[15] Some of the traditional elements of Reformation bigotry still featured strongly: a

he ſcientiſik three horned Doctor, Father PETERS, a great Labourer; in Works of Darckneſs

belief in some quarters that the pope was Antichrist, and the rather more widespread view that the Catholic clergy were corrupt and mercenary, duping their flocks with mumbo jumbo in order to feather their own nests, characteristics personified in the popular imagination by the sinister figure of James's confessor, Father Petre, who was portrayed on one occasion in the guise of a satanic magician.[16] But by the later seventeenth century, denunciations of 'popery' were tending to concentrate more on the political dimension to the Catholic bogy. The emphasis in sermons, pamphlets and parliamentary speeches was on the connection between Catholicism and persecution, Catholicism and absolutism. Oppression of the Huguenot minority in France, and James's attempts to interfere with the liberties of borough corporations, universities and finally (in the persons of the Seven Bishops) the Church of England itself, took their places at the end of a long history of oppressions and atrocities, beginning with the Spanish Inquisition and Mary Tudor's burning of Protestants at Smithfield.

James's main arguments touched emotions that ran just as deeply in seventeenth-century Englishmen, but in the years 1688–91 they did not have the force of the 'no popery' cry. The Jacobite case rested upon the principle of divine hereditary right and the illegality of breaking the line of succession and transferring the Crown to William and Mary. The new king and queen were branded as 'usurpers', and their English followers as 'Commonwealthmen' and 'Republicans'. In a society that was as yet far from being secular or

Catastrophe Gallia, & Hiberniae Restitutio.

A N

Impartial Judgement,

Reduction of Ireland.

Denoting the

This Revolution, &c (reding Men in the 9 that is a)

ALSO, THE

Conquering of *Lewis* XIV. prefent K. of *France.*

By His sacred Majesty

King William III.

In a few Years,

Prophetically Deduced

From the

Characters of Heaven.

Likewise,

The Planets Attributes, according to the Doctrine of *Hermes.* With a Philosophical Discourse of the Four Elements, and the Nature and Powerful Influence of the Heavenly Bodies. Also, A second District of Prophesy, demonstrated from the Ten Seals, and of the seven deirful Prophecies on our Blessed Saviour, long before his Birth. To which is added, *Scotia Calhedera, or a Whig's that deserves victory.*

By Richard Darby, Phil: & Astro. & Medica.

LICENSED, And Entered according to Order.

London, Printed for the Author...

Title page of *Catastrophe Galliae & Hiberniae Restitutio* (1690), by Richard Kirby, an astrologer who predicted William's victory in Ireland from the stars. Though no longer credited in intellectual circles by the end of the seventeenth century, astrological prediction was still a respectable profession.

rationalist, and in which religion and religious divisions were of the first importance in men's lives, the appeal of divine-right theory should not be underestimated.[17] Some Englishmen found the events of 1688–9 profoundly shocking and the setting aside of the lawful king wholly unacceptable; many others were only brought to acquiesce in the Revolution after a crisis of conscience; and even those who were the architects of the political settlement, the Whigs, did their best to disguise the reality that one king had been deposed and another chosen by parliament with a series of constitutional expedients and desperate fictions, such as the 'warming pan' theory, to deny that the Jacobite Prince of Wales was the lawful heir.[18]

Loyalty to the monarchy, in its traditional form, had been a source of great political strength to Charles II in the aftermath of the exclusion crisis, and to James II at the very outset of his reign. The difference between these years of loyalist ascendancy and the situation in 1688, however, was that in the earlier period devout royalism was enhanced by devout Anglicanism. The identification of the monarchy with the interests of the Church of England had created a loyalist (Tory) majority among the nobility and gentry and even a powerful strain of popular loyalism in London and other cities.[19] What had hurt Charles II's opponents then was not so much the accusation of republicanism as their association with Nonconformity. By his religious policy, James had deprived himself of this valuable propaganda ploy. In seeking an alliance between Catholics and Protestant dissenters to overturn the Anglican monopoly, he had cut himself off from the mainstream of loyalist political argument. Significantly, in 1688–91 the Jacobites seem to have made little of this attempt to secure religious toleration. The Williamites mentioned it only to discount it as a deception, a Trojan Horse to hide the reintroduction of popery.[20] Potentially the issue was a problem for William, since he was a Calvinist who himself favoured toleration. In later years this was to cost him dear, but in 1688 his stand as the saviour of Protestantism outweighed other considerations. Anglican objections to his Calvinism, and loyalist qualms about his position outside the direct line of kingship, had to be set against darker fears. Faced with the alternative of a Catholic on the throne, most Englishmen put Protestantism first.

On a less exalted level than the Jacobites' legitimist arguments were their *ad hominem* attacks on William and Mary in ballads and satirical verse.[21] These should perhaps be viewed primarily as an appeal to the lower orders, and as a response to some of the cruder aspects of anti-Catholic propaganda, though they were also matched on the Williamite side by innuendoes concerning Mary of Modena, pictured either as a partner in Father Petre's lusts or as the secret mistress of Louis XIV.[22] In return, the Jacobites portrayed William as a hook-nosed, dwarfish hunchback, impotent with his wife but guilty of 'unnatural practices' with his favourite Portland; William looked like a beast – 'he has gotten in part the shape of a man, but more of a monkey, deny it who can' – and behaved like one.[23] The impact of such scurrilous abuse on William's popular reputation cannot be gauged, and has in any case to be balanced against the many representations of the king as a conquering hero, like Hercules, or as the 'Belgic lion', which was a particularly common device in medallic illustration. But in the long run, when the unwelcome consequences of the Revolution were being felt – most notably England's involvement in a costly European war – William's less attractive physical attributes were given a more critical public scrutiny. So too was the most damning of his faults, in the eyes of his new subjects, his nationality. Seventeenth-century Englishmen were notoriously xenophobic, and William's Dutch ancestry was to be his most vulnerable point, though despite the efforts of some Jacobite sympathisers, it does not seem to have been sufficiently abhorrent to Englishmen in 1688 to counterbalance his main virtue: his Protestantism.

The conclusion that the religious issue was probably the most important one in the propaganda war is borne out if we look at the way in which the Williamites handled the major themes of their campaigns: the restitution of the Protestant religion and the liberties of the subject. In the rhetoric of speeches, whether they be the king's own pronouncements or the orations of his supporters, Protestantism and liberty were set side by side. 'Are we Christians, Protestants, Englishmen,' George Walker asked the defenders of Derry, 'and shall we doubt to defend our religion, our country, and our liberties?'[24] The medals issued on William's behalf, perhaps the clearest statement of an 'official' line, combined both themes, with William being shown, for example, carrying the cap of liberty and a Christian banner, or as being aided by Providence in his recovery both of the true reformed religion and of Magna Carta, which before his arrival had lain broken and neglected. Not surprisingly, perhaps, those medals that relate directly to his reconquest of Ireland tend to place religion above liberty on the scale of priorities, but still include political symbols alongside the Bible and the Ark of the Covenant.[25] For more popular consumption the emphasis is sharper: a periodical like the *Roman Post Boy*, which appeared in London in 1689, is an example of a publication pandering to vulgar anti-Catholicism, with its broad humour at the expense of the Jesuits and the Irish. Satirical prints concentrate heavily on this aspect. No representation of the courts of James or Louis is complete without some monk or priest holding aloft a papal flag or counting his beads. Here some allowance has to be made for the national obsession of Dutch artists with the danger posed to their own country by the forces of the Counter-Reformation. One print portrayed James's embarkation for Ireland as the start of an avowedly Catholic crusade.[26] Naturally, given the situation of the Dutch, their primary fear was of the French. It was Louis rather than the pope whom they depicted at the head of the international Catholic conspiracy. This was not quite the English view. While English Protestants hated and feared Louis as a tyrant, and indeed might regard James after 1688 as no more than the French king's tool, they did not easily relinquish their old papaphobia. In contrast to the Dutch vision of Louis as the arch-enemy, an English print of 1690 shows William and Mary holding the pope's nose to the 'Protestant grindstone' in retribution for past persecutions.[27]

The involvement of Irish Catholics in James's crusade was of particular value to the Williamite propagandists, since they were able to exploit traditional prejudices to blacken still further their picture of the wickedness of their Jacobite enemies.[28] All Catholics were assumed to be naturally cruel and deceitful. Heinous crimes were blamed on French troops in Ireland, and James himself was frequently accused of breaking his word. But in the case of the Irish there was something worse to be feared: a streak of barbarity, even of bestiality, which the English had long assumed to be innate in the Gael. This view of the native Irish as a people from whom every excess of savagery was to be expected, including cannibalism, had been nourished by a decade or more of English Whig propaganda, beginning in 1679 with the republication of Temple's history of the 'horrid villanies' perpetrated in the 1641 rebellion. The result was the panic of November 1688, when wild rumours swept England that James's Irish troops were committing mayhem as they roamed the countryside.

The news from Ireland in 1689 and 1690 provided another crop of atrocity stories, such as the report that some forty thousand to fifty thousand

An English anti-papal print, showing William and Mary holding the pope's nose to a grindstone, which is being turned by two Anglican bishops while Catholic clergy lament.

The Protestant Grind-Stone.

Queen   King   Schomberg

Old Holy Father, there was once a time
When Clemency was thought a mortall Crime
Er Hereticks no pitty you could find:
But most severely did their Faces Grind.

The time's now turn'd, harsh Stripes upon you fall
Too well deserv'd, and this is done that all
Who see the Whore of Babylon may Say
Shee's pox't because her nose is worn away.

In this English print, Louis XIV's 'habit' (dress) is composed of towns and fortresses he had seized. His hat, representing Limerick, lies on the table and an onlooker remarks, 'He begins to unrigg', a reference to the surrender of Limerick in 1691.

Protestant prisoners had been paraded naked through the streets of Dublin.[29] The sufferings of Irish Protestants, subjected to the summary justice of Jacobite officers and the violence and depredations of their men, were related in Williamite news-sheets, illustrated in engravings, one of which pictured a mass hanging, and gathered together in publications whose titles are self-explanatory: *The Discovery of the Lord Tyrconnel's Design to Surprise and Massacre All the Protestants of Ireland; The Narrative of the Murders, Cruelties and Oppressions Perpetrated on the Protestants of Ireland . . .* and so on. The moral that the English reader was expected to draw was spelt out by one writer: 'It will appear beyond contradiction,' he wrote, 'how the Protestants [in England] are to be treated if King James should carry his point.'[30]

English attitudes to the Irish were not simply characterised by fear, however. On stage or in popular literature there had always been a strong element of ridicule in the portrayal of the Irishman, and this trend had grown more pronounced in the Restoration period. The comic Irishman was becoming a stereotype, and the publication in *c.*1680 of a volume of Irish

A

Full and Impartial Account

Of all the

SECRET CONSULTS,

Negotiations, Stratagems & Intriegues

OF THE

Romiſh Party

IN

IRELAND,

From 1660, to this preſent Year 1689.

For the Settlement of Popery in that Kingdom.

LONDON,

Printed for *Richard Baldwin* at the *Black Bull* in the *Old-Baley,* M DC XC.

jokes, *Bogg-Witticisms*, fixed this standard interpretation of Irishmen and their country as absurd and contemptible. The *Roman Post Boy* made full use of this stereotype, as did some of the plays staged in London during the Irish war, notably Thomas Shadwell's *The Amorous Bigot* (1690), which re-created his earlier comic character, the villainous Irish priest, Father Teague O'Divelly.[31] Even the news-sheets peddling their horror stories qualified their picture of the wild Irishman with touches of humour and disdain. An account of the reception afforded James at his landing at Kinsale described the 'barbarous' manners of the Irish who greeted him, 'making a garland of a cabbage stump'.[32] At other times it was the supposed ignorance of the natives that drew laughter. The Williamite general Schomberg reputedly frightened the Irish to such a degree that they believed him to be a giant, sixteen feet tall and with moustaches 'like two barbers' poles'.[33] The assumption of Irish cowardice implicit in this anecdote is highly significant. James's army was frequently presented as a rabble, easily driven into retreat by inferior numbers of Williamite troops. (Interestingly, James himself was also denounced as a coward.[34]) Much of the commentary in the news-sheets was designed to be ultimately reassuring to English readers. In the same way, the constantly disparaging tone of 'Lilliburlero' and other English broadside ballads in their references to all things Irish, and the triumphal note struck by plays such as *The Royal Flight* (1690), *The Royal Voyage* (1690), and *The Siege of Derry* (1692), which re-enacted William's campaigns on the London stage, demonstrated that final victory in the Irish war should not be in any doubt. The only surviving print to make any reference to Irish barbarity did so in a confident, almost jocular, fashion, featuring an Irish 'monster', ludicrous in appearance (at least to modern eyes), which had formerly been devouring men but had since been captured and was now safely under control.[35]

In reporting the events in Ireland, English writers often used the terminology of a national conflict: the Protestant community in Ireland constituted the 'English interest'; the Catholic enemy were 'the Irish' *tout court*, ignoring any distinctions between 'Old English' and 'Old Irish'. But in Ireland William was sometimes obliged to dress himself in different attire, for the Anglo-Irish Protestants were developing an alternative concept of nationality, in which they considered themselves in some degree Irish.[36] They still called themselves 'English', in order to distinguish themselves from their Catholic adversaries, but simultaneously they could visualise Protestant Ireland as a sister kingdom to England. Thus the Church of Ireland clergyman Edmund Arwaker, in an elegy for a Williamite hero, wrote first of William having quelled the rebellion of (Catholic) Ireland, and then of the restoration of (Protestant) Ireland to its liberties. The coexistence of these contradictory interpretations of nationality was reflected in some Williamite propaganda, especially in the medals issued to mark the victory at the Boyne and the conclusion of the war. One has a legend, 'the Irish defeated'; another has William 'restoring . . . Ireland'.[37] Both kinds of rhetoric in their

1690

'The Irish Monster', an anti-Irish print published in Hamburg in 1690. The German text refers to the taming of such a monster by King William, a reference to his victory at the Boyne.

different ways appealed to the Anglo-Irish. However, the most attractive message as far as they were concerned recalled their special identity as Protestants. Soon after William had landed in 1690 he had been addressed by some Ulster supporters, who had begged him to 'revenge the affronts of poor distressed Sion'. When this had at last been done, he struck a medal which said simply: 'He has preserved our hearths and altars.'[38]

These items of propaganda, produced in Ireland, were only partly intended for the Anglo-Irish. They would have resonated in England too, which after all was William's prime political concern. He did not have to worry about the loyalty of Irish Protestants to his cause. In terms of propaganda, Ireland was of interest to him almost solely as a means of highlighting the weaknesses of his enemy, and his own self-proclaimed virtues as the restorer of Protestantism and liberty to a benighted people. For James, on the other hand, Ireland represented, in propaganda terms, one of his greatest liabilities. He too could be confident of the loyalty of his Irish followers, which scarcely required to be cosseted or encouraged, but his identification with their cause cost him dearly in England – the real seat of his ambitions. Perhaps this was not the least of the reasons why, having left Ireland for good in the aftermath of his defeat at the Boyne, he was hardly ever to bother his head about the country again.

121

BRASS MONEY

ROBERT HESLIP

In the popular memory of Irish Protestants the two afflictions associated with popery from which William of Orange saved them were 'brass money and wooden shoes'. The undesirable footwear, particularly repugnant in a well-brogued land, was the sabot, symbol of French domination, a threat ironically removed by the forces of another clog-wearing nation. William arrived too late, however, to prevent brass money. What was this instrument of economic terror? Why did an interesting economic experiment come to be seen as the greatest of many impositions?

An adequate supply of money, what an Irish Jacobite bewailing its scarcity called 'the sinews of war', is one of the most important elements in winning any armed conflict. The seventeenth century is no exception to this rule. One of the crucial factors in the struggle between James II's father, Charles I, and parliament during the English Civil War was the latter's control of London and the mint, which was much more than just a factory for making coins. The scale of that conflict was reflected by the size of the coinages produced by both sides. In 1688 the situation was rather different: having fled England, James removed himself from the centres of financial power in a more complete manner than his father had, and was thus heavily dependent on subsidy from France and whatever funds could be raised voluntarily from his supporters, or wrung from the general population. To make his problems worse, Ireland, although geographically a convenient base for his attempt to recover the throne of England, was hardly swimming with wealth, and the state of its coinage probably failed to reflect even what limited prosperity there was. The fact that a large part of the available money was in the hands of economically active but politically hostile Protestants compounded the problem. The way in which he attempted to cope with this situation reveals not only the workings of an economy under stress conditions, but also explains quite a lot about seventeenth-century perceptions about money and how it functioned.

Ideally one would like a complete audit of the Irish economy, paying

Sir William Petty, 1683; frontispiece to his atlas of Ireland *Hiberniae Delineatio* (1685)

particular attention to the money supply, in 1688 and again in 1691, but the information does not exist and we must make what we can of contemporary evidence. If the situation in Ireland before James landed was known, we would be better able to estimate the strains war put on the economy and the effect (and effectiveness) of gunmoney. Sir William Petty, in his *Political Anatomy of Ireland* (1672) and his 'Treatise of Ireland' (1687), does at least provide well-informed estimates of the situation, though the polemical nature of both works must be remembered. (Petty himself was aware that he was writing in a period of change and his intention was to influence government policy.) He estimated 'the whole Cash of Ireland' to be no more than £400,000 or, put another way, 'The Coyned and Currant Money, now running in Trade, is between 300 and 350,000 l. or the 50th part of the value of the whole Kingdom', and elsewhere he repeats this estimate and suggests that £590,000 is required to 'drive the Trade of the Nation'.[1] The point of his argument was that Ireland was under-capitalised and that an injection of cash would bring a quantum leap in prosperity. His figures need to be adjusted

GUILELMO III

HISTOIRE
METALLIQUE
DE
GUILLAUME
III ROY
DELAGRANDE
BRETAIGNE

R de Hooghe inv

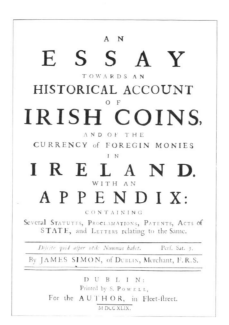

AN

ESSAY

TOWARDS AN

HISTORICAL ACCOUNT

O F

IRISH COINS,

AND OF THE

CURRENCY of FOREGIN MONIES

I N

IRELAND.

WITH AN

APPENDIX:

CONTAINING

Several STATUTES, PROCLAMATIONS, PATENTS, ACTS of
STATE, and LETTERS relating to the Same.

Ditate quid alper utile Nummus habet.   Perf. Sat. 3.

By JAMES SIMON, of DUBLIN, Merchant, F.R.S.

DUBLIN:
Printed by S. POWELL,
For the AUTHOR, in Fleet-ftreet.
M DCC XLIX.

Title page of James Simon's Essay *(1749), still the best source of information on James II's emergency coinage*

up, to allow for the rise in prosperity, reflected by an increase in rentals, between 1684 and 1687, and then down for the subsequent decline. The sum potentially available to James in terms of ready cash is unlikely to have exceeded £450,000.

If Petty provides some suggestions as to the resources available to James when he landed, there are fewer accurate indications as to the state of Ireland when he left. The subject was a favourite one with propagandists, but the state of the coinage, when not associated with wooden shoes, was one in which they showed little informed interest. Opinion is not in short supply (the issue was still a live one to Simon writing nearly sixty years later), facts are. Further confusion is produced by the quite violent variations in the state and value of the English coinage.[2] What one can suggest, however, is that the effects of '1690 and all that' were less marked than those experienced in the aftermath of the earlier civil war, probably by a factor greater than can be explained by the relative shortness of the later struggle. The overall situation which resulted in the economic devastation affecting much of Ireland in 1690–1 will have determined the operation of the coinage.

The notional £450,000, which may have represented the actual cash in Ireland, will have been radically altered by both a rapid outflow of money from those who had the means to export capital (and this outflow will have been exaggerated in terms of ready money by the transportability of coin against goods), and by the disappearance of cash into hiding as a security measure, even on the part of those who may have supported the Jacobite cause. Bishop King writes: 'Merchants have generally their Stock in Moveables, so that it is easie for them to transport themselves and their Effects into another Country . . .'[3] In 1672 Petty estimates that the 'Owners of about ¼, both of all the real and personal Estate of Ireland, do live in England', and in 1687 estimates the total wealth of Ireland, other than real property: 'the Value of the Cattle, Corn, Merchandize, Shipping, and Money of Ireland will be about 7 millions, and that 4 millions and a half thereof doth belong to

Title page of Chevalier's Histoire metalique de Guillaume III. *The figure at bottom right is using a fly press to strike medals, the same process used to produce James II's gunmoney coins.*

125

Brass large half crown, 1689

British Protestants'. The flight of capital started even before James left England: Petty remarks that the 'late changes' (the effects of Tyrconnell replacing Clarendon) 'have made [the "Value of Ireland"] fall from 3 to 2' in comparison with 1684. It is entirely possible that this is an exaggeration, made for political reasons, but the situation at this early stage cannot have been as frightening as it was to become for the Protestants later.[4] Everyone would have been apprehensive about the presence of large numbers of soldiers, whatever their allegiance. A modern authority notes that the proceeds from import duties were remarkably large in 1691 and 1692, the highest since the tax began, and sees the figures as reflecting in some part the return of goods by Protestants, as well as simple restocking after a period of shortage.[5] Again it must be emphasised that the outflow in cash must have been many times greater than in goods.

Shortages of coin are consistently complained about throughout Irish history. On landing, James found the problem aggravated and probably worsening. His first steps to meet it were far from dramatic. He issued a proclamation on 24 March 1689 revaluing a whole range of foreign and English coins: for example, the eight reales (most in the form of 'cob' silver dollars from the mines of Spanish South America) was increased from 4s. 9d. to 5s. 0d., an effective devaluation of 5 per cent, which is fairly consistent across the silver pieces; for gold the amount was more variable but averaged about 10 per cent, all against a base given by the proclamation of 6 June 1683.[6] This suggests an immediate change of just under 5 per cent.[7] The apparent premium put on gold may either reflect a change in the international ratio between it and silver (a constant problem in a bimetallic coinage system within which the proportions were fixed), or the actual situation in Ireland, where there was probably a greater shortage of gold, compared with England, which also suffered in this way. High-value coins will have been the first to be hoarded or exported. The change in values may also have been intended to keep money within the country, a seventeenth-century equivalent of raising the interest rate. King claims 'that most of the current Coyn in the Kingdom came into the Treasury once in a year'.[8] Even if this is an exaggeration, the public sector may have been able to exercise considerable control over values and exchange in the short term.

Brass small half-crown, 1690

Brass sixpence, 1689

Limerick 'Hibernia', 1691

Brass crown, 1690

Brass small shilling, 1690

There was a limit to the degree to which it was desirable to raise the value of coin, as this was in fact depreciating the currency against bullion and generating inflation, contrary to the modern situation in which token currencies reverse the effect. Such measures might in themselves be counterproductive by inducing panic. D'Avaux suggested that Louis XIV should make half a million livres available, but these were obviously needed for paying foreign troops and the international purchase of supplies. Very few seem to have got into or stayed in the hands of the Irish. The solution to the shortage of money, both physical and fiscal, was the issue of promissory notes in metallic form. A proclamation was issued on 18 June 1689 revealing to the public that 'we have ordered a certain quantity of copper and brass money to be coyned to pass current . . . for remedy of the present scarcity of money' and that these coins were to pass for sixpence. Taken with a proclamation of 4 May 1689, making the French coin of three sols six deniers legal tender,[9] it is obvious that it is not an out-and-out shortage of money that was being addressed, but rather the provision of small change.

The presence of troops and James's court must have stimulated the local economy into some form of boom, at least in the short term, and may have more than compensated for the other disruptions. Petty probably expressed the general view when he wrote: 'nor are such Tokens base as are coyned for Exchange in retailing by Particular men (if such men be responsible and able to take them back, and give Silver for them)'.[10] There had been extensive issues of low-value tokens by merchants in both England and Ireland in the 1650s, 1660s and 1670s, and the main official objection seems not to have been an economic one, but rather that they infringed the royal prerogative. The proclamation of 18 June clearly stated the temporary and token nature of the coinage:

we have caused the said copper and brass money to be made current money for present necessity, and therefore do not intend that the same shall continue for any long time. We do . . . promise and engage to all our subjects here, that as soon as the said money shall be decried and made null, that we shall thereupon receive . . . such proportion of the said money as shall be, and remain in their respective hands at the time the same shall be so decried and made null [and] either allow for the same the value thereof . . . out of what rent, duties or debts

Pewter coins, 1690

Brass large shilling, 1689

Pewter coins, 1689

127

they respectively shall owe us, or to make them full satisfaction for the same according to the rates aforesaid, in gold or silver of the current coyne of this kingdom.[11]

The new coins were to be legal tender except explicitly for the payment of goods on first importation, import duties, money left in trust, mortgages and debts due by record, et cetera. These provisions point up at least two of the problems the new coinage had to face – that it was not internationally acceptable, and thus of little value to any merchant importing goods; and that public opinion was not prepared to accept it as an alternative to precious metal, if such metal was available. The exceptions listed indicate that there was a feeling that money laid out in gold or silver should not be returned as brass money.

It appears that the situation was perhaps more immediately serious than had been realised, because a further proclamation dated 27 June 1689 was issued, making shillings and half-crowns current. This differs from the first in that payment for imports (or import duties) is no longer excepted, and punishment is threatened for those who refuse to take the new coins. An order dated 4 July 1689 was sent to the commissioners of the mint[12] telling them to give 20s. 6d. in the copper money to those who brought 20s. of gold or silver for exchange. This was a normal device to get base metal coinages into circulation and should not be taken as indicating any particular problem.

The 'Commissioners of His Majesty's Mint', who were also 'Commissioners for His Majesty's Revenue', were asked to meet on 2 July 1689 to 'consult what is to be done to advance the coynage'. They replied that

considering we stamp all night as by day we may be allowed a double set of men to each mil [press], each set to attend and work 12 hours. For the mil at present working we humbly propose [there follows a list of four named comptrollers, two feeders] Four laborers for the Fly. Two Porters.[13]

It seems that although work on the project may have been going on for some time, the additional denominations were proving a strain. This is also an indication that demand had so far made the new coinage a success.

As for the coins themselves, although now they are almost always called 'gunmoney', that term does not appear to have had contemporary usage, 'copper' or 'brass' money being used instead. Cannons were undoubtedly melted down, and even imported from France for the purpose, but in fact any 'hamered or forged copper and brass'[14] was sought, as well as bells and ordnance. The major source of metal may well have been the three-legged bronze cooking pot. Proclamations specifically refer to copper *and* brass. It was obviously a matter of little concern whether pure copper or an alloy was used, though the latter was more readily available. The variety of colours exhibited by the coins indicates the number of alloys used. The standard design was a profile bust of James, in at least as grand a style as on any of his previous coinages, with a crown and crossed sceptres on the reverse and a 'J'

Mint workers making coins in the eighteenth century, from Diderot's *Encyclopédie*.

and 'R' either side. The denomination is given above and the month of issue below. It is this last feature that is both unusual and significant. Although it is not stated, the purpose was probably either to allow the redemption of the coins in order – though whether this would have worked in practice once a mix of dates had occurred is doubtful – or to emphasise the promissory nature of the coins. There is a close historical parallel, both in function and outcome, in the large amounts in bank notes issued by the Confederate states during the American Civil War.

Luckily for James there already was a mint available in Dublin. A patent was held for the production of halfpennies by Colonel Roger Moore, who had two presses, which, after royal seizure, were christened the James and the Duchess.[15] The building used was in Capel Street. It does not appear from Royal Mint practice that sufficient men were provided to allow round-the-clock working, at least over a long period. Craig gives some figures from the period of the Great Recoinage 1696–7, when shillings were struck at a rate of thirty per minute, albeit in annealed silver, which was softer than the miscellaneous brasses and bronzes available to James's men.[16] In London a crew of seven was allocated to a press, with three resting while four worked a twenty-minute spell, so that a man actually worked making coins for only five hours out of a ten-hour day, the remainder being taken up with other duties. These workers, however, were protected by centuries of acquired privilege and were working in good conditions, if under considerable pressure at the time. The amount of effort required to strike coins depended not only on the hardness of the metal but also on the size of the coin: the large brass were the same size as the silver shillings, about 25 mm. in diameter, but the large half-crowns, later over-struck to make crowns, were 32 mm. (Sixpences and small shillings were 20 mm.) It may be that the staffing levels at Capel Street were increased later, but the sense of grievance implied by Simon on behalf of these workers may have had some justification. Rough calculations based on the highest week's output we have record of before the coins were reduced in size, 1–8 March 1690, show that at the Royal Mint rate it would have taken seventy-two hours to make the shillings, sixty-four hours for the half-crowns (assuming that they will have struck at three-quarters of the shilling rate), and twenty-eight hours for the sixpences (assuming production at one and a half times the shilling rate).[17] Even allowing for the fact that the silver coins had to be struck to an exact weight, it can be seen that there was little leisure at the Capel Street premises.

Absolutely central to any assessment of the brass money must be an estimate of the quantity produced. Such estimates have been made, both at the time of issue and since; most tend to be of the order of £1.5 million. It is generally unclear whether they include the output of the Limerick press, but it seems likely that this was the Duchess moved from Dublin, rather than being simply additional.[18] The Madden MS, for example, gives figures for each denomination, but omits crowns from the list. Story 'enquired of some people concerned with the Treasury in James's time and they told [him] that there had not been much above 1,100,000 l. Brass money coyned during all the time it passed'.[19] Calculations are complicated by the introduction of the crown at the end of April 1689 and the reduction in size of the other denominations (with the sixpence almost becoming redundant) in April.[20] Again this measure does not seem to reflect any attempt to devalue the coins, but is instead a reflection of the shortage of metal; it also speeded production. By far the best indication is a statement that gives the output of the James press in Capel Street from 3 August 1689 to 17 May 1690 in terms of coins produced, and the amount of money paid to the treasury. This in itself is of interest because the former amount does not match the latter exactly, giving some indication of the actual demand for money. The ratio between the denominations may also be significant: if the need was for large sums rather than change, then half-crowns would have been favoured over shillings and sixpences. The total amount produced, including pewter pennies and halfpennies, comes to £777,762 13s. 11d., of which £757,369 13s. 6d. was paid to the treasury, leaving £20,393 0s. 5d. at the mint on 17 May 1690.[21] On the basis of this evidence, one authority estimates a total production of c. £950,000 for the life of the Dublin mint, taking into account only the James press, and then goes on to suggest that up to £2 million might be the overall total.[22] This does not appear to allow for the crowns, the smaller size of the coins after April 1690, and cessation of the sixpences. If the weekly production of half-crowns for the five weeks before the reduction in size and for the six weeks after is averaged, then it can be seen to have doubled, to over

£20,000 a week. That of shillings increased by a factor of about 1.6, to £7,250. The total production in the last week for which we have figures was over £38,000. The proclamation announcing the issue of crowns was not made until 15 June 1690, but the new crowns would have been stockpiled and are by no means scarce now, suggesting that a considerable number were made in the limited time available. It looks, therefore, as if existing estimates are likely to be under rather than over the actual figure.[23] This was an impressive feat of organisation: by way of comparison the total amount of silver struck in the Royal Mint between 1666 and 1689 was £3,330,641.[24]

How well did the experiment work before the ultimate disaster? This question seems to have received little attention, the final ignominy of crowns being devalued to a penny (or worse – according to Story, 'our soldiers got . . . about 4000 pounds in Brass money, a good deal of which the soldiers threw about the Streets as not thinking it worth the Carriage'), overshadowing all other considerations.[25] James was unfortunate in that Louis, with his own financial troubles, was not able to devote as much money to the struggle as it warranted, and what fiscal intervention he did make further undermined James's position. Brass money depended for its success on two things: confidence in final victory and, just as important, the lack of a substitute. Confidence was easily measured by the rate of exchange between the brass and gold and silver. Even in normal times, scarcity and movements of the bullion market frequently led to large premiums being paid for guineas. The English Jacobite officer Stevens writes with feeling of the problem and puts the blame firmly on the French, who were paid in gold and silver while the rest of the Jacobite army had to make do with the brass. Under 4 and 5 October 1689 he writes: 'The army was punctually paid, and the brass money passed as current and was of equal value with silver', and he goes on to list prices paid for commodities by the army, which he regards as extremely cheap, sensibly attributing this to a lack of buyers at the normal markets.

The introduction of the French silver 'was no small damage and discouragement to the rest of the army who received none but the brass money'.[26] A proclamation was issued on 15 June 1690 threatening death to the 'several covetous persons, who have a greater regard for their own private interest, than for the publick good, have given of late intolerable rates for gold and silver . . . to the great disparagement of the brass and copper money', and limits the amount to be paid to 30s. 0d. for a pistole, 38s. 0d. for a guinea, and 7s. 6d. for a crown. This compares with 19s. 0d., 24s. 0d., and 5s. 5d. respectively, under the proclamation of 24 March 1689.[27] Such threats were bound to be ineffective, and the rates probably indicate the very minimum that was being paid. Conversely, French silver has left little mark on the physical record. Only one firmly provenanced find of a low-value coin has come to my attention, namely, a twelfth écu (worth five sols six deniers, rather than the coin of three sols six deniers usually mentioned), which was discovered in a hoard of gunmoney found near Clonmel, County Tipperary, and believed to have been concealed in August 1690. The implication is that such a vast injection of cash – one source suggests the military cost of the war to the French as being in excess of 889,200 livres[28] – had little lasting effect because foreigners were able to keep control of specie in ways that were not open to natives. James was also unfortunate in that, as well as having the structural difficulties inherent in the operation of the brass money, there were international complications: the price of bullion soared and both Louis in France and William in England had difficulty in coping.

It would be fascinating to be able to discover what the rates were immediately before the Williamite forces landed in Ireland, and thus estimate how much of the rise in the value of the gold and silver coins was due to normal economic factors, and how much to panic. A shortage of goods is one such factor: sellers could afford to be more selective in how they took payment, as well as raising prices. The Irish market – always particularly subject to the vagaries of supply and demand, regional and seasonable, because of limited size – had contracted to a level where the relation between

View of the walled city of Limerick in 1685, by Thomas Phillips

price and a willingness and ability to sell was extremely exaggerated. This is confirmed by the statement that soldiers paid thirty sols in France need only be given five or six sols in Ireland, because of the shortage of silver.[29] In other words, prices may actually have deflated in real (international) terms, and it was gunmoney that had depreciated. Stevens gives the rates set by Tyrconnell on 16 September 1690, which are the same as those in the royal proclamation of 15 June, but goes on to say that pistoles were being sold for £5 in brass and that the French gave a gunmoney crown for a three-sou piece. Tyrconnell's measure can only have been an attempt to bolster confidence at a time of desperation, undermined once again by French access to specie. Departing troops can only have valued the brass money as souvenirs: their very leaving ensured that its promises would never be redeemed. In January the brass crown was devalued to 5d., and pro rata for the smaller denominations.[30] The end had surely begun.

During the second siege of Limerick, in August 1691, large and small

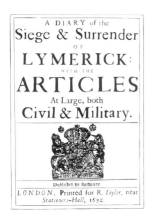

shilling-size coins were overstruck to act as halfpennies and farthings, the undertypes frequently showing through. These coins are crude, as befits their status as siege money, but have been unfairly neglected by scholars, as they at least deserve notice for providing the first representation of Hibernia on a coin. This type, a seated female leaning on a harp and holding up a shamrock,[31] is very close to the Britannia introduced on Charles II's English halfpennies, with the exception of the spear with which Britannia is armed. The precise date in 1691 when the Hibernias (as the Limerick money was known) were issued is unknown,[32] but it may have been the occasion described by the anonymous author of 'A Light to the Blind' when he writes under March 1691 that 'the duke Tyrconnell, finding that the brass money hitherto used had become of no value' ordered the commissioners of the mint to keep a count of the coins brought in by individuals, 'to the end that the subject might not be the loser thereby, when it should please God to return the King'.[33] Whatever the date, one can argue that the issue of the Hibernias marks the true end of the ill-fated Jacobite monetary experiment. We know very little about conditions inside the town during the latter period of the siege of Limerick, but at first sight they would seem to have been ideal for gunmoney to flourish, especially as communication with the surrounding area diminished and the internal economy became more and more isolated.

Did the inflation that had plagued gunmoney since the introduction of the French specie become irrelevant in the endgame of the desperate struggle? There cannot have been much in the way of gold and silver left within Limerick, as the regular purchase of supplies in the earlier stages of the siege would have bled away what little may have been available. In such a situation, gunmoney may have been the equivalent of matchsticks in a prisoner-of-war card game, as good a mechanism as any other for the conduct of whatever commerce survived. There is no mention of actual shortages of petty coinage in the sources for the earlier parts of the war, the halfpennies minted for Ireland during the years 1685–8 by Charles II and James perhaps proving sufficient. Indeed, as prices, denominated in gunmoney, rose and rose there would seem to have been little scope for purchases as small as a halfpenny. Prices rise within besieged areas, shortage and hazard demanding monetary reward. The Hibernias, which were struck in some quantity, may indicate that within the pressure of the beleaguered walls, with no alternative available, the feasibility of the promissory coinage was at last proved.

There is one further element that deserves mention, for the sake of completeness rather than because of any visible economic effect. In the midst of difficult fiscal manipulation, at a time when by any reckoning the presses must have been busy, a further and, if the arguments about small change given above are correct, unnecessary coinage was embarked upon. On 1 March 1689 the commissioners of the mint were ordered to strike two sorts of coin, 'one about the bigness of a shilling to be made of white mix'd metall . . . to pass as a penny': the other, the size of a sixpence to pass as a halfpenny. A proclamation offering these coins 'for remedy of the present scarcity of pence and halfpence in this our kingdom' was dated 28 March 1690. A further proclamation dated 21 April 1690 made white metal crowns legal tender.[34] All these pieces, in what appears to be pewter, including a small half-groat also dated 1689, are extremely scarce.[35] The fragmentary mint record shows a total of £492 12s. 0d. being made in pennies, and £212 6s. 5d. in halfpennies.[36] Far commoner survivals are 'proofs' of all denominations struck in silver, the commonest of these being halfpennies struck on silver French twelfth écus. In the absence of concrete evidence one might postulate that, given the previous (and subsequent) shortages of halfpennies that afflicted Ireland and England, a shortage either arose or was feared late in 1689, but only a little later increased inflation made the pewter pieces irrelevant.

The story of the brass money is both frustrating and instructive. It has aroused interest from its inception, but little comment has been either informed or to the point. Essential to any understanding is some sort of accurate estimate of the size of the coinage. This must probably await an exhaustive examination of numismatic evidence. In particular, an estimate of the ratio of Limerick-struck coins to Dublin-struck coins in the month for which we have figures might clear up several puzzles.[37] The coinage, like so many other aspects of the struggle, is submerged beneath a tide of partisan comment, which has diverted attention from a consideration of its working as a practical expedient. Assessment of the brass money must still be provisional, but it seems, like many of James's affairs, a good idea gone wrong.

PART THREE

THE CONSEQUENCES

THE LAND SETTLEMENT

W.A. MAGUIRE

The war in Ireland was part of a much wider European struggle between Louis XIV and William of Orange; and William's victory at the Boyne was rightly seen as an important European event. So far as people in Ireland were concerned, however, what was at stake was not so much the balance of power in Europe as religious freedom (it might be truer to say religious supremacy) and the ownership of Irish land. It is worth pointing out that while the outcome of the struggle in Ireland was of vital importance to fervent adherents of every religious group in the country, at every level of society, those directly concerned with the ownership of the land were a comparatively small group of people. In 1688 the Catholic landowners numbered about thirteen hundred; and all land in Ireland was owned by no more than four or five thousand people.

It is true of course that the interests of a good many more than that were also at stake; notably members of landowning families who might not possess an acre themselves but whose social status depended upon their kinship with those who did. In a world where one's place in society and one's ability to exercise power were both based upon ownership of land, it was certainly a serious matter to lose one's connection with it; conversely, to be able to acquire landed property, if one had made a fortune in trade or war, was the route to social advancement and political power. Nevertheless, it remains true that the number of people directly concerned was comparatively small. At that time, and for long after, most Irishmen did not and could not hope to own land, and were subservient to those who did, whether the gentry above them were Catholic or Protestant. But precisely because landowners wielded so much social and political power, the freedom of the rest of the population to worship as it pleased might depend upon the outcome of the struggle for the land.

To look back no more than three decades, the reason for that struggle lay in the settlement that followed the restoration of Charles II in 1660. Under Oliver Cromwell in the 1650s most of the Catholic proprietors in Leinster

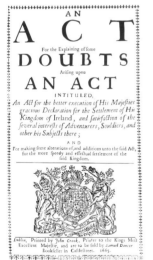

THE

STATE

OF THE

Papiſt and Proteſtant

PROPRIETIES

IN THE

Kingdom of Ireland,

IN THE

Year 1641. when the then *Rebellion* began, and how
diſpoſed in 1653. when the *War* and Rebellion was
declared at an End, and how diſpoſed in 1662. upon the
Acts of Setlement, and now the Proprieties ſtand this preſent Year
1689: with the Survey, Loſs, Coſt and Charge of both Parties by the
aforeſaid War, or Rebellion

WITH

Inferences and *Expoſtulations* from thewhole, faithfully Cal-
culated in ſo conciſe a Method and Order as was never done before.
Humbly tendred to the Conſideration of the KINGS moſt
Excellent MAJESTY, and the PARLIAMENT of
LORDS and COMMONS now Sitting at *Weſtminſter.*

To which is added,

A Liſt of the preſent Nobility of *IRELAND* *Proteſtant*
and *Papiſt.*

LONDON,
Printed for *Richard Baldwin* in the *Old-Baily.* 1689.

Williamite pamphlet tracing the changes in Irish landownership between 1641 and 1689. For both sides in Ireland, land was one of the chief issues at stake.

AN ACT

For the Explaining of ſome

DOUBTS

Ariſing upon

AN ACT

INTITULED,

*An Act for the better execution of His Majeſties
gracious Declaration for the Settlement of His
Kingdom of Ireland, and ſatiſfaction of the
ſeveral intereſts of Adventurers, Souldiers, and
other his Subjects there;*

AND

*For making ſome alterations of, and additions unto the ſaid Act,
for the more ſpeedy and effectual ſettlement of the
ſaid Kingdom.*

Dublin, Printed by *John Crook,* Printer to the Kings Moſt
Excellent Majeſtie, and are to be ſold by *Samuel Dancer*
Bookſeller in Caſtleſtreet. 1665.

Title page of the Act of Explanation (1665), the final statutory basis of the Restoration land settlement.

and Munster, whatever their racial origin (Gaelic Irish, Old English or Elizabethan settler), had forfeited their lands; few Protestant royalists who had fought for Charles I against parliament lost their estates, with the notable exception of the duke of Ormond, who recovered his when he returned to Ireland as lord lieutenant after the Restoration. The land confiscated at that time had been given to English 'adventurers', who had financed the Cromwellian conquest, and to Cromwellian soldiers in lieu of arrears of pay.

By the time Charles returned in 1660, then, a large part of Ireland was owned by a new class of proprietors. These new men, for the most part, were willing to support the return of the monarchy, provided they could keep their property and their power. For his part, anxious to be restored to all three kingdoms with as little trouble as possible, Charles was willing to come to an arrangement with them, provided the interests of some of those who had suffered for supporting his father and himself were looked after and some obvious injustices removed. In effect, the Acts of Settlement (1662) and Explanation (1665) confirmed the Cromwellian proprietors (with the exception of the regicides) in most of the lands they had held in 1659, but modified the Cromwellian settlement in order to restore some 'innocent papists' and others with claims to royal favour. A court of claims sat in Dublin to hear cases.[1] By August 1663, when the process was to have ended, the commissioners had dealt with eight hundred cases and had given seven hundred decrees of innocency. Thousands more were waiting to be heard; if most of them were declared innocent as well, there would be little left for the Cromwellians. In the end, by the terms of the Act of Explanation, most of the Cromwellians agreed to give up one-third of what they had received under the Act of Settlement in order to secure the rest, while the remaining claimants were left unsatisfied. A quarter of a century later, the maintenance or reversal of this settlement was to be one of the main points at issue between the Jacobites and the Williamites.

The Restoration settlement pleased hardly anyone. On the one hand, the more extreme Protestants objected to surrendering any land at all to the old proprietors, whom they regarded as conquered rebels. The author of a 1689 pamphlet went so far as to say that the victors were not

> permitted to enjoy what they had justly won by the sword, while the Irish were restored to what they had as truly forfeited by their cruel disloyalty, by which partial piece of justice the victors were indeed subdued and the conquered were in the conclusion victors.[2]

On the other hand, many Catholic families, especially those of Gaelic stock, failed to recover any of their ancestral property; others, including a number of English origin, got back very little. A later Protestant comment summarised the course of events quite succinctly:

> King Charles II upon the Restoration shewed [the Catholic Irish] some Favour, set up a Court of Claims, and the Estates of some of those that had been Loyal were restored to them; but in the main, very many of them by the Act of Settlement were debarred in a great Measure of their Antient Patrimony, and the Cromwellian Soldiery and others confirm'd in their Possessions.[3]

These expropriated persons, described in 1684 as the 'old proprietors who evermore haunt and live about those lands whereof they were dispossessed', were to exercise an important influence on the attitude of Irish Jacobites to the dismantling of the Restoration settlement by James II's parliament in 1689.

The forfeited lands taken from the regicides, an area totalling some 120,000 'profitable' Irish acres scattered throughout sixteen counties, were not returned to the (mainly Gaelic) families that had once owned them. Instead, Charles granted them to his brother James, duke of York, as his 'private estate'. The great estate of the head of the Dempsey family in Leix and Offaly was granted to Charles's English favourite, the first earl of Arlington.

In the later years of Charles II's reign, and under the reign of James, the Restoration settlement was somewhat modified by Catholic purchases of land. The outstanding estate thus acquired was that of Sir Patrick Trant, who bought it from Arlington. Richard Talbot, who helped many Catholic families through his influence at court and who in the process helped himself, acquired most of his own estate in this way. As a result, by 1688 Catholic proprietors had improved their position somewhat and held between a quarter and a fifth of all the land in the country. The proportion of Catholic land varied greatly from one area to another. It was at its greatest – nearly a half – in the counties beyond the Shannon, at its smallest in Ulster (where it consisted mainly of Lord Antrim's large estate, along with the substantial but much smaller properties of the fourth earl of Abercorn and Sir Neil O'Neill). Elsewhere, though not very numerous, Catholic landowners included magnates with great local influence, such as Lord Clancarty (MacCarthy) in Cork and Sir Valentine Browne in Kerry, and peers representing notable Old English families, such as the Butlers (Lords Cahir, Galmoy and Mountgarret) and the Plunketts (Lords Louth and Fingall). There were also numerous gentry such as Bagenals, Fitzgeralds, Nugents, Dillons and Sarsfields in Leinster.

The accession of a Catholic king in 1685 naturally raised the hopes of the dispossessed and the discontented, more especially when his old comrade-in-arms Talbot – soon created earl of Tyrconnell – became James's chief man in Ireland. Protestant fears rose with Catholic hopes. Sir William Petty, the distinguished political economist who had surveyed Ireland under the Commonwealth in the 1650s and had acquired large estates in Kerry (which he was allowed to keep intact at the Restoration), became very concerned that the settlement would be reversed. In interviews with Petty, Tyrconnell made soothing noises, and James himself promised that he would not break the settlement. Nevertheless, Petty's 'Treatise of Ireland', presented to James in September 1687, expressed apprehension and referred to a sharp fall in Irish land values and the start of a migration of Protestants to England.[4] The migration became a flood in 1688, and when James was replaced on the throne of England by William and Mary, most of the remaining Protestants who could safely do so declared for the new regime.

When James arrived in Ireland in March 1689 and summoned a parliament – overwhelmingly Catholic in its composition, following Tyrconnell's remodelling of the boroughs – the pressure on him to repeal the Acts of Settlement and Explanation and to pass an Act of Attainder against the Williamites proved irresistible.[5] Knowing what the effect in England would be, he did his best to resist, but in the end he had to agree to what (if it had come about) would have been little short of a complete Catholic resettlement, in which the heirs of the proprietors in 1641 (when Catholics owned two-thirds of the profitable land and all the unprofitable) would have recovered their ancestral estates in full, and the forfeited property of 2,400 listed Williamites would have become available to compensate other claimants. James's 'private estate' was to be thrown into the settlement and he was to be 'reprised' with the estates held in 1641 by a Protestant. Although James could not prevent the acts repealing the Restoration settlement and attainting the Protestant landowners since he was bluntly told by some of his Irish supporters that if he did not satisfy them, they would not fight for him against William, he could and did ensure that nothing much was done officially to put the acts into effect during the short period when most of the country remained under Jacobite control. Then and later, of course, a good deal of Williamite property – especially the property of those who had fled – was seized informally by the Jacobites.

William's victory at the Boyne and the subsequent retreat of James's forces

Anno undecimo & duodecimo

Gulielmi III. Regis, &c.

An A C T for Granting an Aid to His Majesty, by Sale of the Forfeited and other Estates and Interests in Ireland, &c.

Most Gracious Sovereign,

Hereas soon after Your Majesty Your late Royal Consort of ever Blessed Memory were Graciously Pleased to Accept the Crown and Royal Dignity of this Kingdom, and the Dominions thereunto belonging, many of Your Majesties Subjects, contrary to their Duty and Allegiance, Traiterously adhering to Your Majesties Enemies, Levied and Maintained, within Your Realm of *Ireland,* a Desperate and Bloody War and Rebellion against Your Majesties, who by the Blessing of God upon Your Majesties Royal Conduct and Courage, and the Assistance and very great Expence of Your Majesties *English* Subjects, were reduced to their due Obedience to the Crown of *England*: And whereas 'tis highly Reasonable, That the Estates of such Rebels and Traytors should be Applied in Ease of Your Majesties faithful Subjects of this Kingdom, to the Use of the Publick : We Your Majesties most Dutiful and Loyal Subjects, the Commons in Parliament Assembled, most Humbly beseech Your Majesty, that it may be Enacted : And be it Enacted by the King's most Excellent Majesty, by and with the Advice and Consent of the Lords Spiritual and Temporal, and Commons in Parliament Assembled, and by the Authority of the same, That all and every the Honours, Manors, Baronies, Castles,

For Applying the Estates of the Rebels and the Rebels and Ireland to the ease of His Majesties English Subjects, who were at a very great Expence in Reducing that Kingdom, ence of the Crown of England.

Preamble to the Act of Resumption, which revoked most of William III's grants and applied the proceeds from the sale of forfeited estates towards paying the cost of the war in Ireland.

Lady O'Neill, widow of Sir Neil O'Neill, by Garret Morphey. Though she failed to recover outright ownership of her husband's confiscated estate, Lady O'Neill was granted a forty-one-year lease of it by the trustees.

143

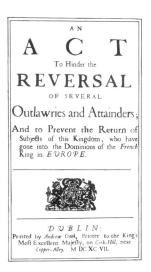

AN

A C T
To Hinder the
REVERSAL
OF SEVERAL
Outlawries and Attainders;
And to Prevent the Return of
Subjects of this Kingdom, who have
gone into the Dominions of the *French*
King in *EUROPE*.

DUBLIN:
Printed by *Andrew Crook*, Printer to the King's
Most Excellent Majesty, on *Cork-Hill*, near
Copper-Alley. M DC XC VII.

This act of 1697 by the Irish parliament was in reaction to William's use of royal pardons for individuals, which had restored the estates of a number of prominent Catholic families.

to the line of the Shannon brought similar informal seizures of Jacobite lands, till the restoration of civil administration and the courts put everything on a more regular footing. William's courts were established in Dublin in November 1690, almost a year before the war came to an end. Already, however, a number of leading Irish Jacobites had been indicted in England for treason; the list included peers such as Clancarty, Galmoy, Gormanston, Limerick and Bellew (and of course Tyrconnell), as well as other notables.[6] Despite no fewer than seven attempts by William's English parliament, however, no general act of attainder (like the Cromwellian act of 1657) was passed against the Irish Jacobites. William had good reasons to frustrate such a measure. Apart from his own more tolerant and detached view of such things, he wanted to end the war in Ireland quickly, and to be free, if necessary, to offer generous terms in order to do so; and he did not want his parliament to dictate the disposal of such Irish land as might become available by forfeiture. At any event, the prevention of a general attainder act during the period 1689–91 was to have an important effect in limiting the scope of the confiscations.

Instead, individual Jacobites were indicted for high treason in Ireland, and if convicted, were outlawed and forfeited their property (no one was executed). The indictments began in the autumn of 1690 and went on until the end of the war; there were very few thereafter. This in effect confined the proceedings to the twenty counties under Williamite control. The total number of those whose names appeared on the county lists was 2,603, but there was a good deal of duplication (Tyrconnell, for example, was indicted in several counties where he had no property). Most of the sentences of outlawry were also passed before the end of the war; most of those who had been indicted but not convicted by that time escaped altogether. Attempts made later to prosecute Jacobites in Connacht who had not been indicted earlier and who could not claim the protection of the articles of Galway and Limerick failed miserably because the Connacht juries – composed largely of Catholic freeholders who had been Jacobites themselves but had retained their estates under those articles – refused to convict. By that time even Protestant gentry in Leinster and Munster were apparently reluctant to disturb Catholic neighbours who had survived without being prosecuted until then.

In addition to the numbers indicted and outlawed for high treason in Ireland, more than 1,200 were listed for treason abroad. In all there were nearly 4,000 outlawries. At first sight there is an apparent contradiction between this large number of forfeiting persons and the much smaller total number of Catholic landowners in 1688 – a mere 1,300. The fact is that many of those listed were not the owners of freehold property but younger sons, tenants, merchants and traders, even artisans. Their property was still forfeit but it was not freehold land. Only 457 landed estates were actually affected. Some of these were very large, however; the total amount of profitable land declared confiscated was over a million Irish (1,700,000 statute) acres.

Elizabeth Villiers, countess
of Orkney (1657–1733), by
Sir Peter Lely. Even the
king's friends found it hard
to defend William's grant
to his former mistress of
the 'private estate' of
King James.

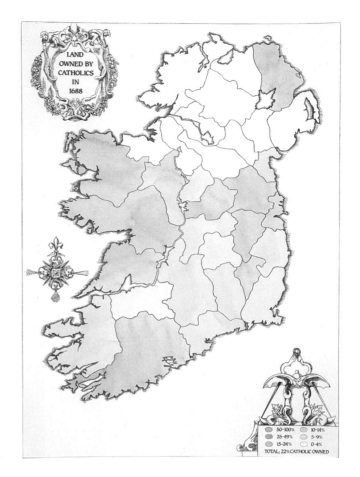

LAND
OWNED BY
CATHOLICS
IN
1688

50-100%   10-14%
25-49%   5-9%
15-24%   0-4%

TOTAL; 22% CATHOLIC OWNED

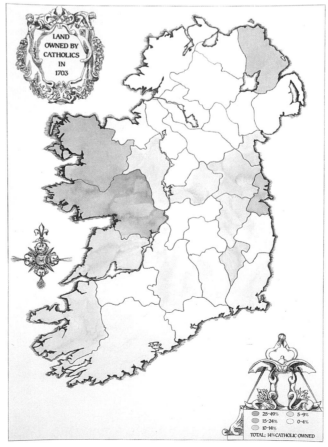

LAND
OWNED BY
CATHOLICS
IN
1703

25-49%   5-9%
15-24%   0-4%
10-14%

TOTAL; 14% CATHOLIC OWNED

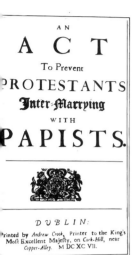

AN

ACT

To Prevent

PROTESTANTS

Inter-Marrying

WITH

PAPISTS.

DUBLIN:

Printed by *Andrew Crook,* Printer to the King's
Most Excellent Majesty, on *Cork-Hill,* near
Copper-Alley. M DC XC VII.

The purpose of this 1697
act was to prevent
Protestant property passing
to Catholic control by
marriage.

Anxious to bring the war in Ireland to an end before another campaigning season became necessary, William empowered his commander Ginkel to offer generous terms to the Jacobite garrisons of Galway and Limerick. Ginkel pledged that William and Mary would try to reduce the number of attainders. Jacobite officers, if they rejected the alternative of leaving the country to join a foreign army, could keep their estates, provided they swore allegience to William and Mary. So too could 'all such as are under their protection in these counties' (Limerick, Galway, Clare, Kerry, Cork, Mayo) and the inhabitants of Galway, Limerick and other garrisons. 'All such as are under their protection in these counties' was the famous 'omitted clause', left out in the copy of the original articles sent to London by the lords justices, but reinserted by William when he signed the treaty in February 1692. When the articles were eventually ratified by the Irish parliament in 1697, the clause was again omitted. However, its omission in the legislation does not appear to have made much difference so far as the judgment of claims was concerned.[7]

One way of reducing the number of attainders was by giving royal pardons to forfeiting persons who could not claim the benefit of the articles. Of the forty-four pardoned in this way, twenty-four owned estates amounting to 88,000 Irish (142,560 statute) acres. Some of those pardoned had submitted after the Boyne, such as Richard Talbot of Malahide, County Dublin (who had been James's auditor-general); others who surrendered early were not so lucky. Some had been outlawed by mistake. A royal pardon in 1697 enabled the third Lord Bellew to recover his estate, which had been granted to Lord Sydney six years earlier. Bellew's kinsman, John Bellew of Barmeath, County Louth, outlawed by his own consent in order to conceal his employment by the Williamites in the negotiations leading to the peace, was also pardoned. The attainder of the seventh Viscount Dillon, killed at Aughrim, was reversed in order to benefit his son, who was within the articles.[8] The granting of pardons was criticised by both the English and Irish parliaments. The Irish Commons in 1695 deplored the 'countenance and favour' thus shown to Catholics; and two years later the Irish parliament passed an act 'to hinder the reversal of several outlawries and attainders', forbidding further pardons except in accordance with the articles of Galway and Limerick. Named exceptions included Nicholas Taafe, second earl of Carlingford, killed at the Boyne, to benefit his brother Francis, the next earl, who was one of Emperor Leopold's generals; and Sarsfield's father Patrick, to benefit his grandchild Charlotte.

Much more important than royal pardons in limiting the extent of the confiscations were the claims made under the articles. These numbered 1,283, all but 16 of which were admitted. Each claimant had to produce three witnesses, one of whom must be a Protestant. The claims were adjudged in two periods, separated by an interval of nearly three years. Between April 1692 and the end of 1694 a comparatively small number were dealt with by the privy council in Dublin. Hearings resumed at the end of October 1697

Alexander Macdonnell, third earl of Antrim (1615–99), by an unknown artist. During his long life he saw his family's estates twice confiscated and twice restored.

and continued until September 1699 before a court of claims which consisted of nine judges. No fewer than six hundred claims were settled during the last three months of that period. The total amount of land returned to claimants under the articles was 525,000 Irish (848,500 statute) profitable acres. This turned out to be nearly half of all the land remaining in Catholic hands in 1703.[9]

One of the greatest Catholic estates to escape confiscation in this way was that of Alexander Macdonnell, third earl of Antrim. The hopes of his many enemies in the north, who had gained temporary possession of his vast property, were disappointed when he claimed the protection of the articles. The frustration felt by the predators at the likely escape of so rich a prize was frankly expressed by William Conolly (later Speaker of the Irish House of Commons, who made a fortune by dealing in forfeited land) in a letter to the corporation of Derry, for whom he acted as agent. Hearing news that Galway had surrendered on good terms, he wrote: 'Its feared the Lord of Antrim is there, if not hee is in Limerick, to which place the General [Ginkel] wrote to Tyrconnell offering the same terms, which is thought hee and many others

Sir Richard Cox (1650–1733), by an unknown artist. Though an ardent Protestant, Cox dealt sympathetically with Catholic claims under the treaty of Limerick.

will accept of.' Conolly wrote later, 'I feare hee will be restoured, for wee have no evidence against him.'[10] Eleven Catholic peers successfully claimed the benefit of the articles; twenty-eight Fitzgeralds and twenty-two Nugents, among many other well-known gentry, also succeeded, as well as a number of the Os and the Macs (O'Briens, MacNamaras, McGillicuddys, Reillys, Kellys). One Protestant, who had sat in the Dublin parliament of 1689, also benefited.

The leniency with which the articles were interpreted, and which resulted in the success of all but a handful of the claimants and a consequent large reduction in the amount of land permanently forfeited, led to fierce criticism from two quarters. In Ireland the more extreme Protestants, wanting to crush their opponents beyond hope of revival, were alarmed that so many Catholic Jacobites had managed to hold on to their property, especially in Connacht. James still had an army in France, and he might make another attempt to recover his kingdoms. In England the Commons – anti-Catholic, anti-Irish and determined to use forfeited Irish land to defray the cost of the conquest and the burden of William's war in Europe – also viewed the shrinkage of forfeited land with alarm. The ideal situation so far as the

Protestant extremists in Ireland were concerned was expressed by James Bonnell, the Irish accountant-general: 'Had the Irish been totally reduced by the loss of all their estates, this country would have been looked on by the English as a secure place and many would have flocked here.'[11]

The Whig Lord Capel, who was appointed lord lieutenant in 1695, was violently anti-Irish. His appointment, and the parliamentary debates leading to the ratification of the Limerick treaty in mutilated form in 1697, effectively put an end to adjudications between 1694 and 1697. During that period, those who had agreed its terms and, following William's wishes, had interpreted them liberally, were abused and attacked in the Irish parliament. A particular target was the lord chancellor, Sir Charles Porter, one of the signatories of the treaty and prominent in its early implementation. Porter was forced to attend the House of Commons to defend himself in person, and he routed his opponents. Sir Richard Cox, one of the judges concerned in adjudicating claims during the later period, answered his critics in ringing terms:

> What is but common justice they may call favouring the Irish and a lessening of the forfeitures, and we cannot help that. We got nothing but trouble and censure by that court of claims, and if the justice we administered there will distinguish us and preserve us from the destroying angel when he comes to punish the oppressions and perjuries, notorious and public, committed against the claimants it is all the reward we desire or expect.[12]

It was not only the interpretation of the articles of Limerick, however, that roused the wrath of a large party in the English House of Commons. The fact was that the disposal of the Irish forfeitures became an issue between the new king and his parliament. This struggle over Irish land, only one aspect of a larger struggle for political control which continued for the whole of William's reign, went through three phases. During the war in Ireland and for three or four years after, the abortive attainder bills were accompanied by a variety of schemes to ensure that the forfeitures would be used primarily to pay the arrears due to the army, and that only soldiers who had actually served in Ireland would get royal grants of land; foreign favourites and courtiers should not be beneficiaries. William dodged all these attempts to limit his prerogative by proroguing or dissolving parliament, though he was forced to give what many took to be a promise not to proceed without its approval. During this difficult period, he made few substantial grants, apart from one to Lord Sydney.

During the middle years of his reign, when he relied on the Whig Junto to control parliament for him, William acted with less restraint and made large grants to forty-four individuals. The two largest were Lord Clancarty's estate of 135,820 Irish acres, granted to Lord Woodstock, son and heir of William's Dutch adviser Hans Willem Bentinck, whom he had created earl of Portland; and 108,633 Irish acres, forfeited by Lord Clare and others, to his younger Dutch favourite Joost van Keppel, earl of Albemarle. Other

Hans Willem Bentinck, earl of Portland (1649–1709), by an unknown artist after Rigaud. The earl of Clancarty's enormous estate, which William intended for his unpopular Dutch adviser, was granted instead to Bentinck's son Viscount Woodstock.

large rewards were given to foreigners such as the Huguenot Ruvigny, Viscount (later earl of) Galway, and Ginkel, earl of Athlone, the victor of Aughrim. In fact seven foreigners got the greater part of the area granted. Among the rest, Charles Hamilton, earl of Abercorn, who had turned Protestant, was given the forfeited estate of his Catholic brother Claud. Another Hamilton, Gustavus (not to be confused with the Gustavus Hamilton who was governor of Enniskillen), who had led the storming of Athlone, got 3,482 Irish acres; he fought under Marlborough and later became the first Viscount Boyne. James Corry of Castle Coole got the estate of his late neighbour Cuchonnacht Maguire, the last remaining Irish landowner in Fermanagh, who had been killed at Aughrim. Thomas Prendergast, a Catholic Jacobite who had revealed the plot to assassinate William in 1696, got the forfeited O'Shaughnessy estate at Gort in County Galway.

The most controversial grant was made to William's mistress (or ex-mistress) Elizabeth Villiers, or Countess of Orkney as she became after her marriage in 1695 to George Hamilton, earl of Orkney. No great beauty – according to her friend Dean Swift, she 'squinted like a dragon' – but very

149

Claud Hamilton, fourth earl of Abercorn (d.1691), by an unknown artist. His forfeited estates were granted by William to his Protestant brother Charles, but the grant was annulled by the Act of Resumption (1700) and the property was vested in the trustees.

intelligent and sensible, this former lady-in-waiting to Queen Mary was given James's 'private estate', later valued at £26,000 a year (less annuities payable to two of James's mistresses, Arabella Churchill and Susannah Bellasis; the former was Marlborough's sister and the mother of James's illegitimate son James FitzJames, duke of Berwick). At first transferred to trustees in order to conceal its ownership, the grant was never confirmed by an act of parliament, despite Lady Orkney's efforts. The status of the 'private estate' – had James rightly forfeited it, since he was never attainted? – made the grant uncertain, and there was bitter controversy about it in the parliamentary debates. Even William's friends found it hard to defend.[13]

The third phase of the struggle between William and his English Commons over the forfeitures came in the later years of his reign, after the conclusion of the peace of Ryswick had left parliament free to concentrate on domestic matters. The court could count on a majority in the House of Lords, but by 1699 the majority in the Commons was so opposed to the king and so determined to get its way that it forced through a bill to take account of the Irish forfeitures by 'tacking' it on to a finance bill that the Lords would

Sir Richard Levinge (d.1724), by Ralph Holland. An Englishman from Derbyshire, Levinge made his career as a lawyer in Ireland, where he was solicitor-general and Speaker of the Irish parliament in the early 1690s. He was one of the three forfeiture commissioners who refused to sign the report in 1699.

hesitate to throw out. Seven commissioners were appointed – Lord Drogheda, John Trenchard, Francis Annesley, Sir Francis Brewster, James Hamilton of Tollymore, Henry Langford, and Sir Richard Levinge – of whom the last five were members of the Irish House of Commons.

During 1699 the commissioners carried out their investigations in Ireland and quarrelled furiously about their report, which in the end was signed by four of them (Annesley, Langford, Hamilton and Trenchard) and opposed by the other three. The chief issue that divided them was whether or not the 'private estate' should be included in their calculations. Hamilton, despite being kin and friend of Lord Orkney, gave his casting vote in favour of including it. Annesley presented the commissioners' report to the English Commons on 15 December 1699.[14] The Commons at once decided to bring in a bill to resume (that is, take back) all the grants made since 13 February 1689, and to use for public purposes all the estates and other property

James Hamilton of Tollymore (d.1701), by an unknown artist. Hamilton was both a commissioner and a trustee, but died shortly after his appointment to the trust.

forfeited in Ireland. Despite all the efforts of his supporters in the Lords, the mortified William was eventually obliged to accept the resumption bill early in 1700, after it was again 'tacked' to a bill to raise taxation. Elizabeth Villiers's brother Lord Jersey is said to have persuaded the king that it would be dangerous to continue his opposition any further.

The decision to resume the grants was based upon an optimistic calculation by the commissioners of how much money was likely to be raised by the sale of the forfeited estates – £1,500,000, they reckoned, including the 'private estate'. Accordingly, under the Act of Resumption[15] thirteen trustees were appointed, with wide powers, to administer the estates, to hear claims, and eventually to sell whatever property remained. The money raised was to go only towards paying the arrears of the soldiers and debts to contractors and others, apart from payments to the inquiry commissioners and the trustees themselves (each trustee was paid the large sum of £1,500 a year and expenses). The majority commissioners (Annesley, Hamilton, Langford and Trenchard) were included among the trustees, though Hamilton died in 1701 shortly after his appointment. The most distinguished

Title page of the report of the forfeiture commissioners (1700), which was printed along with reminders of William's promises not to dispose of the spoils of war without consulting parliament.

member (and chairman) was Sir Cyril Wyche, a former president of the Royal Society who had been an Irish lord justice in 1694–5, and ambassador at Constantinople. Francis Annesley kept detailed records of the work of the trustees, very fortunately for historians, since the official records were largely destroyed in 1922; his eleven volumes of minutes, with reports and accounts and lists of sales, now in the Public Record Office of Northern Ireland, are a major source of information.[16]

The trustees took over the estates of all those convicted or attainted of high treason between 13 February 1689 and the last day of Trinity term, 1701. In theory, the property of some Jacobites indicted but not yet convicted might thus have been added to the rest (this was one of the many optimistic aspects of the commissioners' report), but in practice this expectation was disappointed. In addition to the estates of those actually convicted the trustees were to deal with estates of those declared to have died or been killed in rebellion since the start of the reign. Outlawing of people after their death had already been introduced by the Irish parliament, in an act of 1697, and a number of estates actually forfeited belonged to people who had died 'in rebellion'. The question of the 'private estate' was finally settled by including everything James had possessed in Ireland. No one who had been judged entitled to the articles of Limerick or Galway, however, was to be disturbed; in fact all such adjudications were confirmed. All the grants made by William, with some minor exceptions (amounting to 31,000 Irish acres) to people who had distinguished themselves in the war or to dependants of individuals – including some Jacobites – were declared void and the land handed over to the trustees.

The whole affair of the forfeited estates had gone on so long that a new group of proprietors had appeared by that time. These were the so-called 'Protestant purchasers', who had bought or leased land from William's grantees. Albemarle, Ginkel, and others, aware of the uncertainty of their position, had very wisely sold their Irish estates for moderate sums. The one hundred or so purchasers, who included many of the leading Irish Protestants (and two Catholics), had paid out nearly £60,000. The Act of Resumption allowed them only £21,000 in compensation, which caused uproar in Ireland. After agitation by William Conolly and others, the purchasers were permitted to buy the estates from the trustees at thirteen times the annual rent, but were allowed two-thirds instead of one-third of what they had paid to the grantees. This did much to quiet the opposition in Ireland to the trustees and their activities, an opposition roused not only by resentment at the English parliament's acting over the head of the Irish Protestants but also by the fact that the trustees took over Chichester House in Dublin, the meeting place of the Irish parliament (which did not meet between 1699 and 1703).

Any person who claimed to have had an interest in a forfeited estate before 1689 had to enter the claim by 10 August 1700 (the trustees sat till midnight 'to give the claimants fair play'). Over three thousand claims of various kinds

A LIST of the CLAIMS, as they are Entred with the TRUSTEES.

No.	Claimants.	The Estate or Interest Claim'd.	By what Deed or Writing.	On what Lands.	County and Barony	Late Proprietor.	
1	Nathaniel Desbrowe, Administrator of John Desbrowe.	Estate for Years, commencing the 1st of May 1671.	By Lease dated the 28th of March 1671. Witn. *M. Wren, A. Turner, Tho. Heywood.*	Crumlin, Gortnefickan, Burresnow als Ballynebrogue	C.Tipperary B. Ikerrin.	Private Estate.	*Dismissed for want of prosecution,,*
2	Peter Duffresnoy, and Susanna his Wife. the Relict of Daniel Day.	105 *l.* Rent Arrear for 3 Years, ending May 1689.	By Lease dated the 27th of June 1686. from Dr. Day. Witnesses, *H. Beily, M. Hicky, Bar. Russel.*	Lands Purchased from Nicholas Monckton, Esq;	C.Longford	Roger Farrell, Lessee.	*Do:*
3	William Francis.	The Sum of 30 *l.* 19 *s.* 8*d.*	Book Debt due from Coll. Pat. Sersfield.				*Do.*
4	Peter Duffresnoy.	334 *l.* 10 *s.* 0 18 *l.* 19*s.* 7*d.* 353*l.* 9*s.* 7*d.*	By Bond dated the 29th of October 1688. Witnesses, *J. Kelly, J. Eddrige.* Book Debt. Due from Coll. Sarsfield.				*Do.*
5	John Usher, Esq; Executor of Sir Tho. Newcomen.	Estate for Years, commencing the 1st of May. 1669.	By Lease dated the 28th of March 1671. Witnesses, *M. Wren, A. Turner, T. Heywood.*	Naule, Little Rath, Lackingstown, Flackstown.	C. Dublin. C.Balrothery.	Private Estate.	*Allowed*
6	The same.	Estate for Years, commencing the 1st of May 1669.	By Lease dated the 12th of May 1669. made to Tho. Cusack and Assigned to Sir Tho. Newcomen, by Deed dated the 23d of December 1669. Wit. *N Cusack, J.Connell, E. Maclaghlin, H.Brady.*	Lands formerly belonging to Tho. Cusack.	C. Meath, and Kildare	The same.	*Disallowed*
7	John Clayton, Parson of St. Michans.	Estate in Fee, to the Incumbent and his Successors.	By Letters Pattents under the Great Seal of Ireland.	A Slated Stone House in Church-street	Dublin City	Sir Will. Ellis.	*Allowed, with a Saving to the other Two Parsons of St. Michan's*
8	Fra. Flood.	Estate for Years, commencing the 1st of May 1689.	By Lease from Sir Edw. Tyrrell, dated the 10th of June 1689. Witnesses, *C. Tyrrell, Th. Duckinfeild, N. Dalton, C. Birmingham, Edward Tyrrell.*	Simondstown, Stonestown, Bagstown.	C. Westmeath.	Sir Edw. Tyrrell.	*Dismissed*

The first page of *A List of the Claims* (1701). Nos 1, 5 and 6 concern parts of the 'private estate' of James II.

were submitted, many of them from Protestants who had financial interests such as mortgages. Leaseholders sought to safeguard their leases, widows and daughters to secure jointures and dowries. Some of the claims were very long shots indeed, notably that of Sir Edward Smith, by a grant of 1570, 'to such rights which he hath or may have, in the manors etc. in the little Ards and several other lands' in Ulster.[17] This and similar claims were dismissed. A small number of estates, amounting in all to about 70,000 Irish acres, were restored to families of forfeiting persons; Lords Gormanston and Trimleston, and Thomas Fitzgerald Knight of Glin, County Limerick, recovered theirs, for example. In some other cases, only the life interest of the forfeiting

James Hamilton, sixth earl of Abercorn (1656–1734), by an unknown artist. In 1703 he purchased from the trustees the forfeited estates of his Catholic cousin Claud, fourth earl.

person was disposed of by the trustees, and the families eventually recovered possession.

The hearing of the claims by the trustees went on for two years. Although Protestant pamphleteers claimed that the trustees favoured Catholics and discriminated against Protestants, the record shows that most of the claims of the latter for mortgages and leases were allowed but that fewer than half of those who tried to recover estates under deeds of settlement succeeded in doing so. One who did was Brian Maguire of Tempo, whose father Cuchonnacht had raised a regiment for James and had died at Aughrim. The estate, surrounded as it was by the properties of Fermanagh planters, was seized at an early stage and granted to the Reverend Andrew Hamilton (one of the leaders of the Enniskilleners). After Hamilton's death, it was declared forfeit by a local jury in 1692 and subsequently granted to James Corry. The Act of Resumption deprived Corry in 1700. Thereafter, Brian Maguire successfully claimed it from the trustees on the grounds that his father, by his marriage articles, had possessed only a life interest.[18] Altogether, Catholic claimants recovered 137,000 Irish acres by this means. A different case was that of Agmondisham Vesey, son of the Protestant archbishop of Tuam, who had married Patrick Sarsfield's niece Charlotte after she had got possession of the forfeited manor of Lucan in 1696. Under the Act of Resumption the trustees seized the estate and rejected the claim made on behalf of Vesey and his daughters (Charlotte having died). Vesey had sufficient influence in England, however, to get a private act passed there, by which he got possession after paying three times the yearly rent the trustees had fixed for the property.[19]

When all the claims had been dealt with, the trustees were left with 481,000 Irish acres to sell; the articles of Limerick and Galway, royal pardons, and their own judgments had accounted for 750,000 Irish acres. By the time they came to sell, between October 1702 and June 1703, the bottom had dropped out of the market in Irish land and they had great difficulty in getting rid of estates to Protestants, who were the only permitted purchasers. When much remained unsold, they were forced to knock down the rest at bargain prices to a consortium of London merchants calling themselves the 'governor and company for making hollow sword-blades in England'. The Hollow Blades company bought over a quarter of a million Irish acres; only six years later it decided to sell out. The rest of the forfeited land, formerly belonging to 179 proprietors, was bought by 360 purchasers, most of whom were Irish Protestants. A substantial number of the purchasers were members of the Irish House of Commons in the late 1690s or early 1700s.[20] These legislators thus acquired (or enlarged) the strongest of interests in maintaining the Williamite settlement.

When all was over, the net effect of the events of the 1690s and the Williamite confiscations was to reduce the proportion of land owned by Catholics from 22 per cent in 1688 to 14 per cent in 1703.[21] The Restoration settlement, which had established a Protestant ascendancy, was thus confirmed and strengthened. Whether it would this time survive unchallenged remained to be seen. Considering the scale of the upheaval and the passions involved, the actual confiscations turned out at the time to be remarkably moderate. Yet when the writer Arthur Young visited Ireland in the 1770s, he guessed that the proportion of land then remaining in Catholic hands was no more than 5 per cent. This decline was the effect of the working of the penal laws on Catholic property, most landowners preferring to conform to the Established Church rather than risk losing their estates and their standing in society. Conversion thus completed the process that confiscation had left unfinished. This was the result foreseen in 1710 by the author of *The Present State of Great Britain and Ireland*:

> Since this time [1691] all proper Methods have been used to put the Remains of that Nation from being ever in a capacity to make another Revolt; and a very effectual Course has been an Act . . . to divide the Estates of the Roman Catholicks amongst all their Children, except any become Protestants, who in such Cases are to inherit the whole; so that if this Law were put in due Execution, there would be scarce a Man in the Compass of 50 Years that could have a Fortune above that of a Peasant.[22]

9
THE PENAL LAWS

S.J. CONNOLLY

The ending of the war in October 1691 left James II's Irish supporters defeated but not broken. Of the Jacobites still under arms, those who wished were permitted to leave the country to continue their struggle for the restoration of a Catholic monarch. The rest stayed in Ireland, under the apparently liberal guarantees incorporated in the treaty of Limerick. Adhering to the terms of this agreement, the Government forbade reprisals against Catholics or Jacobites. Hearings began of the cases of those claiming to be protected against forfeiture of their estates under the provisions of the treaty, with the great majority of such claims being allowed. In addition, sentences of outlawry and forfeiture earlier passed against a number of persons not protected by the treaty were reversed by royal pardons.

All this was deeply resented by Irish Protestants. Six weeks after the treaty of Limerick was signed, Anthony Dopping, bishop of Meath, was invited to preach a sermon of thanksgiving for the reduction of Ireland. He delivered an impassioned diatribe, arguing that Irish Catholics had over the years displayed such consistent and unrelenting malice towards Protestants, and had been guilty of such treachery and deceit, that no trust could be placed in any treaty concluded with them. Dopping was punished for his outspokenness by being dismissed from the privy council, but his views were shared by many. Inevitably there was resentment that men accused of having plundered or murdered Protestants during the war should, as James Bonnell put it, 'under the subterfuge of the articles of Limerick, Galway etc. have sheltered themselves from common justice, and live splendidly and securely upon the spoils of ruined Protestants'.[1] There was anger that the Catholics as a body could not be forced to pay the cost of the war they were felt to have caused. Most of all there was the recognition that the Catholic interest had not after all been crushed for ever, but could await an opportunity to resume the attack. As one observer noted in November 1691: "Tis plain the Irish are in much better condition than we hoped they would be in the end of this war, and by consequence the condition of the Protestants so much worse.'[2]

Behind such complaints lay a fundamental divergence in interests and outlook between Irish Protestants and their new monarch. William III had accepted a generous settlement with the defeated Irish Jacobites because he saw this as a reasonable price to pay for the return to the main European theatre of the resources he had been forced to divert to Ireland. He was willing, to some extent at least, to see the fulfilment of the terms of the treaty signed in his name as an obligation binding in honour.[3] In addition, both William and his successors were to be influenced by diplomatic considerations: harsh treatment of Catholics in Britain and Ireland could only damage relations with the different Catholic powers with which England was from time to time allied, as well as undermining attempts to persuade Catholic

James Bonnell (1653–99), accountant-general of Ireland under both James II and William III

Irish House of Lords, c.1708

rulers to show greater tolerance towards minority Protestant populations within their dominions. Irish Protestants, by contrast, were more narrowly concerned with the affairs of their own small island. There they were outnumbered three to one by Catholics. A well-developed tradition of polemical history had taught them to see their country's past as a series of determined assaults by this implacable enemy. Most of all, the experience of James's reign seemed to confirm that no compromise was possible between Catholic and Protestant interests. What had begun as an attempt to give Catholics some share in power and privilege had ended in the packing of corporations and the judiciary with Catholic majorities, the creation of a Catholic army, and ultimately the sequestration of Protestant land by a Catholic parliament. For all these reasons, the terms of the treaty, which to William had been a simple matter of strategic priorities, seemed to Irish Protestants to threaten their very survival.

Only a short time before, the discontent of men like Dopping and Bonnell would have counted for relatively little. Right up to the last decade of the seventeenth century, the Irish parliament was an institution of strictly limited importance. Between the civil wars and the Glorious Revolution there had in fact been only one Irish parliament, in 1661–6. The absence of effective representation had allowed Charles II largely to ignore Irish Protestant opinion. In 1670, for example, he had ordered a new lord lieutenant to adopt what amounted to a policy of open toleration towards the Catholic

Irish House of Commons,
*c.*1708

clergy. Despite the alarm it caused among Irish Protestants, this continued until 1673, when it was abandoned as a result of English, not Irish, pressure. After 1688, however, all had changed. The dramatic assertion of the central role of parliament implied by the rhetoric of the Glorious Revolution could hardly have failed to affect Irish Protestants. Even more important, the soaring financial demands of the war with France that began with the overthrow of James and continued with interruptions until 1713 provided a new opportunity to use the power to grant or withhold taxes in order to make the Irish parliament an integral part of the government of the kingdom. That parliament, it is true, remained a subordinate legislature, whose enactments had to be approved by the English privy council and could be superseded by English legislation. At the same time neither William nor his successors were able to ignore Irish Protestant opinion in the way that Charles II had done.

It was against this background that the apparently favourable conditions secured for Irish Catholics by the treaty of Limerick were eroded by a series of penal laws enacted in the 1690s and early 1700s. The first step in the process came when the Irish parliament met in October 1692.[4] It had been called in order to vote taxes and pass a series of measures drawn up by the Government. Instead the Commons revolted. Bills prepared by the privy council were rejected as unsatisfactory. Votes of censure were threatened against office-holders suspected of corruption. Most important of all, a finance bill was thrown out on the grounds that it had not been initiated by

Lieutenant-General Owen
Wynne (c.1665–1737), by
James Latham. As a young
man Wynne fought for
William at the Boyne; he
ended his military career as
commander-in-chief of the
army in Ireland.

Lieutenant-General Michael
Rothe (1661–1741),
attributed to Nicolas de
Largillière. Rothe fought
for James II throughout the
Irish war and thereafter
made his military career in
France, where he became
colonel of one of the
regiments (formerly
Dorrington's) of the Irish
Brigade and reached the
rank of lieutenant-general.

Title page of the Popery
Act of 1709

Title page of the
Disarmament Act of 1695

MPs themselves. The main motive behind all this was constitutional self-assertion. In wrecking a legislative programme on which they had not been consulted, and in asserting the sole right of the Commons to devise financial legislation, MPs were seeking to demonstrate that they were no longer content to be a mere rubber stamp for government measures. But their truculence also reflected resentment of the undue leniency that they believed had been shown, in the negotiation of the treaty and since, to the defeated enemies of the Protestant interest. A particular target for their hostility was the Irish lord chancellor, Sir Charles Porter. Porter was vulnerable because he had also served as lord chancellor under James. His real offence, however, was that he had been one of the signatories of the treaty of Limerick, and that he remained firmly opposed to punitive measures against the defeated Catholics. After the Irish parliament was prorogued, Porter's opponents mounted a vigorous propaganda campaign against him in England. In February 1693 they managed to procure an address from the English House of Commons to the king, complaining of the favour allegedly shown to Catholics by the Irish administration.

Faced with this new-found militancy among Irish Protestants, William and his English managers sought a compromise. Porter was kept in office, but a number of the leaders of the Opposition in the 1692 session were also given places in the Dublin administration. When parliament met again in 1695, the issue of financial control was resolved by having the privy council draw up a token money bill, thus preserving the claim of the Crown to initiate such legislation if it chose, while leaving most of the necessary taxes to be raised by measures devised by parliament itself. On the Catholic issue, too, concessions were made. The new lord lieutenant was Henry, Lord Capel, whose brother had died for his uncompromising Protestantism in Charles II's counterattack after the Popish Plot. Moreover, among the acts passed by the parliament in that year were two designed to ease fears of the Catholic menace. One sought to sever links between Irish Catholics and their co-religionists on the Continent, by forbidding them to go overseas for purposes of education. The second sought to reduce their military capacity by making it illegal for any Catholic to possess weapons, or to keep a horse worth more than £5. At the same time there were limits to what William, at this point at least, was willing to concede. Later in 1695, when the Irish Commons went on to introduce a draft of a bill to banish all members of religious orders from Ireland, it was suppressed by the English privy council, after the London agent of Emperor Leopold had made representations against it.

Divisions within the Irish administration on the policy to be adopted towards the Catholics continued for the next two years. In the autumn of 1695 Porter's opponents went so far as to try to have him impeached for, among other things, his supposed indulgence to the king's papist enemies, but failed to gain a majority. Thereafter, however, the balance of influence moved in favour of the anti-Catholic party. Porter's death in December 1696

161

removed the most powerful opponent of tough anti-Catholic measures, and there was also a deterioration in relations between William and Leopold. In 1697, when the Irish parliament next met, the bill to banish Catholic clergymen was once again introduced, and this time it was not blocked by the English privy council, even though the original measure had now been extended to apply not only to regular clergy (members of religious orders) but also to bishops and others exercising any ecclesiastical jurisdiction. Immediately after the act became law, the Government transported more than four hundred members of religious orders from Ireland to the Continent, while as many as three hundred more left of their own accord. In the years that followed, regular clergy continued to be hunted down and imprisoned or expelled, while the few Catholic bishops remaining in the country were also forced to go into hiding.[5]

The other main concern of the parliament of 1697 was with the still unresolved issue of the treaty of Limerick. The twelfth article of the treaty had bound William and Mary to use 'their utmost endeavours' to have the treaty confirmed by the Irish parliament. In the event, however, successive administrations had preferred not to raise the issue. The disarming act of 1695 had observed the spirit of the treaty by exempting from its provisions all those who had been inhabitants of any Jacobite garrison at the end of the war, but it had studiously avoided mentioning the hated articles by name. When a bill to ratify the treaty was finally introduced in 1697, it differed in important respects from the document agreed in 1691. One crucial omission was the clause extending the terms of the treaty not only to those Jacobites in arms at the time it was signed but also to all other persons in the territories they controlled. This was left out on the grounds that it had not been included in the actual copy of the treaty signed at Limerick, although William had subsequently issued letters patent, accepting that the omission had been a clerical error and ordering that the missing words were to be regarded as part of the treaty. Two other omissions lacked even this pretence. The second article of the treaty, stating that Catholics were to enjoy the same religious liberties they had had under Charles II, was not included in the ratifying act. Neither was article nine, under which no oath was to be required of Irish Catholics other than the oath of allegiance. These omissions had less immediate practical effect than might have been anticipated: in particular, there was no attempt to initiate the widespread forfeitures of property held by Catholics who had not actually been in arms in October 1691 that the omission of the 'missing clause' would theoretically have permitted. Yet by successfully opposing the ratification of the full treaty, the advocates of a tough anti-Catholic policy had both confirmed their influence and removed an obstacle to further penal measures.[6]

In the years immediately following these events the Catholic issue was temporarily pushed into the background by other concerns. There were bitter disputes over the disposal of forfeited lands, especially in 1700, when the English parliament invalidated the grants made over the previous ten

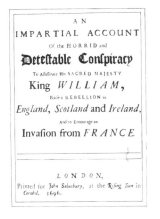

AN
IMPARTIAL ACCOUNT
Of the HORRID and
Detestable Conspiracy
To Assassinate His SACRED MAJESTY
King WILLIAM,
Raise a REBELLION in
England, Scotland and Ireland,
And to Encourage an
Invasion from FRANCE.

LONDON,
Printed for John Salusbury, at the Rising Sun in
Cornhil. 1696.

The assassination plot of 1696, which was revealed to William himself by one of the conspirators, an Irish Catholic named Prendergast, underlined the reality of the Jacobite threat in the 1690s.

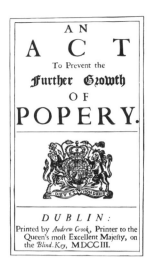

years by William, leaving Irish Protestants who had bought from the grantees badly out of pocket. In 1699 there was also the resentment created by another English act, banning the export of wool from Ireland. Faced with these discontents, the Government avoided for as long as possible summoning another Irish parliament. Parliament met briefly at the beginning of 1699, passing among other measures 'An act to prevent papists being solicitors', and was then dissolved. By William's death in 1702, however, it was clear that new taxation measures would soon have to be authorised. At this point the process of trading anti-Catholic legislation for parliamentary co-operation on other matters began again. When the lords justices met leading Irish politicans for preliminary discussions in November of that year, they heard predictable demands for the removal of restrictions on Irish trade, for a reduction in the share of military expenditure borne by Ireland, and for compensation for Protestant purchasers of forfeited lands. But there were also other suggestions for 'laws against the Irish inheriting while they continue papists, and for admitting no priests into the kingdom'.[7]

Facing what they knew would be a difficult session, the Irish executive took the hint. The bill that they drafted, however, was milder than their Irish advisers had called for. It confined itself to forbidding Catholics to acquire land owned by Protestants, or to sell off lands in order to prevent them descending to a Protestant heir. Even so, the bill was not approved by the English privy council. When the Irish parliament met in September 1703, it drafted its own bill. The suggestion that no Catholic should be permitted to inherit land was modified, the bill, instead, providing that the estate of a Catholic proprietor could not descend intact to a single son, but must be divided equally among his male heirs. There were also clauses making it illegal for Catholics to purchase or take long leases on land owned by Protestants. The bill was transmitted to London, accompanied by dire warnings of the difficulties that would follow in the Irish parliament if it were suppressed or watered down. In fact it returned strengthened, the ban on purchasing or leasing land from Protestants being extended to the acquisition of any land whatever.

Representatives of the Irish Catholics had lobbied against the bill in

London, arguing that it was a breach of the treaty of Limerick, and they were also allowed to state their case before the Irish Commons.[8] In each case, however, their protests were rejected. Meanwhile, the call for fresh legislation against Catholic clergymen was met by two acts, the first extending the penalties of the Banishment Act of 1697 to both secular (parish priests) and regular clergy who entered the kingdom after 1 January 1704, the second requiring all priests in the kingdom to register with local magistrates and provide security for their good behaviour.

For twelve years, starting with the parliament of 1692, the nature of the policy to be adopted towards Catholics was thus a central element in the bargaining that went on between English governments and the Irish parliament. After 1704 this was no longer to be the case. The politics of both England and Ireland now came to be dominated by the conflict between two parties, Whig and Tory. Religious policy was, it is true, one element in this conflict. Whigs in both countries generally advocated strong anti-Catholic measures, and accused Tories of a dangerous ambivalence towards popery. Tories were somewhat less concerned by the Catholic threat, and considerably more hostile to Protestants who refused to accept the authority of the Established Church.

Thus it was under the Whig administration of the earl of Wharton that the last of the major penal laws was introduced in 1709. This was intended to make the 1704 act more effective, by allowing any Protestant who discovered a Catholic purchasing land or taking a long lease to file a bill of discovery and so become entitled to the Catholic's share in the transaction. In addition, registered priests were to be required to take the oath of abjuration, denying the right of James's son, now defined as the Pretender, to the thrones of Great Britain and Ireland. By contrast, the Irish Tory administration that held power between 1710 and 1714 enforced the existing laws but did not enact any new ones. Yet these differences in attitude to Catholics and dissenters were subordinate to the central political issue of the preservation or reversal of the revolution of 1688. What obsessed the Whigs in these years was their fear that the Tories could not be trusted to maintain the Protestant succession on the death of Queen Anne but would seek to bring back the Pretender. Beside this awful possibility, questions of short-term policy towards Catholics or their Church were of secondary importance.[9]

Whig fears were proved groundless in 1714, when a Protestant prince, George, elector of Hanover, was installed unopposed in succession to Queen Anne. Yet the question of policy towards Catholics never regained its former central role. Nevertheless hostility to Catholicism remained intense. In 1719 a surge of concern over the number of Catholic clergymen reported to be entering the kingdom illegally led MPs to propose a ferocious bill providing that unregistered priests should be branded on the face, as well as further tightening the restrictions on Catholic property dealings. This was approved in both Dublin and London, but was eventually rejected by the Irish House of Lords. The objection was not to the branding proposal (for which the Irish

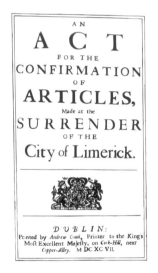

AN
ACT
FOR THE
CONFIRMATION
OF
ARTICLES,
Made at the
SURRENDER
OF THE
City of Limerick.

DUBLIN:
Printed by *Andrew Crook,* Printer to the King's
Moſt Excellent Majeſty, on *Cork-Hill,* near
Copper-Alley. M DC XC VII.

Title page of the act of 1697 confirming the treaty of Limerick. When the agreement of 1691 was at last ratified by the Irish parliament, the article relating to religious freedom for Catholics was deliberately omitted.

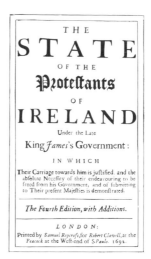

privy council had suggested substituting castration), but that the provisions invalidating certain types of land transaction were to apply to leases already made. The legal principle that legislation could not be retrospective was too important to sacrifice even in the cause of more effective anti-Catholic measures.

In 1723–4 renewed anger at the number and boldness of the Catholic clergy, combined with an upsurge of recruitment in the name of the Pretender, for the Spanish army, inspired a bill providing for the execution both of unregistered priests and of anyone convicted of harbouring a Catholic bishop. This was passed by the Irish parliament but suppressed in London. In the early 1730s there was a surge of complaints about the activities, particularly in the legal profession, of purely nominal converts. In this case an act was in fact passed in 1734 to ban converts whose wives were Catholic from acting as justices of the peace or from educating their children as Catholics. Apart from these specific incidents, however, most Protestants appear to have been reasonably satisfied with the existing state of the law. Certainly the promise of new anti-Catholic statutes was no longer a major card to be played in the management of the Irish parliament.

The one major addition to Catholic legal disabilities after 1714 was the act of 1728 forbidding them to vote in parliamentary elections.[10] (An English act of 1691 had excluded Catholics from sitting in the parliament of either kingdom.) At first sight it is surprising that such an obvious measure was not enacted much earlier. But in fact the ban was less important than it seemed. Of the 300 members of the Irish parliament, 234 sat for 117 boroughs, in most of which voting was confined to members of the corporation or to the freemen. Except for a brief period under James, Catholics had been excluded from membership of corporations since the 1650s. Even before the revolution, therefore, Catholics would have been able to vote in only a minority of constituencies. The popery act of 1704 reduced the number of Catholic electors still further, by requiring all voters to take the oath of abjuration. It is also important to remember that the Irish parliament, like the English, was a parliament of landowners, their dominance being due partly to their wealth and partly to the influence that they could exert over the votes of tenants and

Henri de Massue de Ruvigny, earl of Galway (1648–1720), by an unknown artist. In charge of the government of Ireland in 1697 at the time of the Banishment Act, Galway was long reputed to be the architect of the early penal laws. It has recently been shown, however, that he was the victim of a campaign of black propaganda directed by Louis XIV, who wished to discredit him because he had evidence that Louis was implicated in the plot to assassinate William III.

dependants. The drastic reduction after 1641 in the Catholic share of landed property had thus brought with it a corresponding fall in political influence. The combined effect of loss of acres and exclusion from corporations was already apparent in Charles II's parliament, elected in 1661, when only one Catholic was returned, his election being subsequently disallowed.

This, then, was the background to what have come to be known as the penal laws. These were not, as is often assumed, a systematic code designed by a united Protestant establishment to serve its agreed purposes. Instead they were a series of measures emerging piecemeal, over a period of almost twenty years, out of complex negotiations that involved successive Irish executives, their masters in London, and the parliaments with which they had to deal in Dublin. In these negotiations, members of the Irish Protestant élite traded compliance in other matters, such as financial legislation, for satisfactory measures to deal with the threat they perceived from Irish Catholicism. Yet this does not mean that the penal laws reflected the wishes of all Irish Protestants; if the treaty of Limerick was probably resented by most, not all were equally vehement. The militant anti-treaty party was able to insist on the disarming and education acts of 1695, and the banishment act of 1697, as well as the ratification of an incomplete version of the treaty. On the other hand, they failed to gain a majority for their attempt to impeach Lord Chancellor Porter. There was, moreover, a minority who regarded the treaty as a binding agreement and opposed the penal laws as a breach of its terms. Fourteen members of the House of Lords, seven of them bishops of the Church of Ireland, entered a formal protest against the mutilated form in which the treaty was ratified in 1697. Subsequent penal laws were similarly opposed by a minority, with bishops again prominent among the critics. The 1709 act, for example, was opposed by two archbishops, six bishops and six lay peers. In the mid-1720s, Henry Downes, bishop of Elphin, and Edward Synge, bishop of Tuam, proposed that the existing penal laws should be replaced by measures providing for a tolerated but strictly limited and closely supervised Catholic Church establishment.

If the Irish Protestant establishment was not wholly agreed on the policy to be adopted towards Catholics, it was to a much greater extent divided on the other main issue of religious policy, the treatment of Protestant dissenters. By the late seventeenth century more than half the Protestants of Ulster, and probably close to half of those in Ireland as a whole, were Presbyterians, mainly of Scottish descent. Under Charles II these had been alternately tolerated and harassed. After 1691 their status remained ambiguous. Presbyterian clergy received a salary, the *regium donum*, from the Crown. At the same time local magistrates often interfered with their activities, particularly if they attempted to establish new congregations, while the ecclesiastical courts of the Established Church sought to treat Presbyterian marriages as invalid. As in England, the issue was one of party politics: Tories sought to uphold the full privileges of the Established Church, while Whigs called for Protestant unity in the face of the common enemy, the exiled Stuarts and their Catholic supporters. When the popery bill of 1704 was being considered in London, a clause was added requiring all office-holders to qualify themselves by taking the sacrament in the Church of Ireland. The Whig opposition in the Irish parliament bitterly attacked this addition, but the move had been a shrewd one. Once a bill had been approved and returned by the English privy council, the Irish parliament could only accept or reject it as it stood. As the Tory ministry in London had foreseen, the prospect of a comprehensive bill against Catholic landownership was too attractive for the Whigs to sacrifice, and the bill was passed. The condition of the Presbyterians improved with the arrival of a Whig lord lieutenant, the earl of Wharton, in 1709. Under Ormond's Tory administration of 1710–14, on the other hand, interference by local authorities and Church courts reached new levels. Shortly before Queen Anne's death, in 1714, the *regium donum* was suspended.[11]

Although these divisions over the treatment of Protestant dissenters were real enough, they should not be seen as a simple opposition between tolerance and persecution. Whigs regarded harsh measures against dissenters as dangerous because they threatened to divide the Protestant interest; in

James Kirkpatrick (d.1744), by an unknown artist. Minister of the second Belfast congregation, Kirkpatrick was typical of most Ulster Presbyterian clergy of the time in being of Scottish parentage, a graduate of Glasgow University and a supporter of William III. His *Loyalty of Presbyterians* (1713) was written in reply to charges made against Presbyterianism by the Church of Ireland vicar of Belfast.

some cases they suspected a Jacobite plot to achieve precisely that end. But this did not imply any great sympathy for those who obstinately set themselves outside the state Church. On the contrary, landed gentlemen, whether Whig or Tory, could not but see in such dissidents a challenge to the orderly, hierarchical society they wished to maintain. This was particularly the case with the Presbyterians of Ulster. Their numbers, already large, were reinforced by a further wave of immigration in the 1690s and early 1700s, and their tight ecclesiastical discipline made them a particularly formidable group. William King, now archbishop of Dublin, writing in 1719, saw clearly that the central issue was not one of religious belief or practice, but of social and political authority: 'The true point . . . is, whether the presbyterian ministers, with their synods, presbyteries and lay elders in every parish, shall have the greater influence over the people, to lead them as they please, or the landlords over their tenants.'[12]

Under the succession of Whig administrations that held power after 1714, the Church of Ireland was discouraged from harassing Presbyterian congregations, or from enforcing the letter of the law against Presbyterian marriages. In 1719 the Irish parliament passed a limited toleration act, as well as an indemnity act protecting existing office-holders who had failed to take the sacramental test. This, however, did little to weaken the main practical effect of the test, which was to exclude dissenters from the share in local government which their numbers and commercial wealth would otherwise have given them. Yet attempts to have the Irish parliament repeal the relevant clause of the 1704 popery act failed decisively. After 1714 the Presbyterians were no longer so badly treated as either to disable them from defending the Protestant interest if it came under attack, or to risk alienating them from the state. At the same time they were in no position to challenge the privileges of the Established Church or of the landed élite. To the Anglican landowners who dominated the Irish parliament, this was clearly a very acceptable solution.

The legal restrictions thus imposed on Catholics and Presbyterians lasted for most of the eighteenth century. Relief acts in 1778 and 1782 removed the main limitations on Catholic landownership and on Catholic clergymen. The sacramental test was abolished in 1780. In 1793 the British government, alarmed by the threat of an alliance between Protestant radicals, inspired by the French Revolution, and Catholics disgruntled at their legal disadvantages, forced through the Irish parliament a bill permitting Catholics to vote in parliamentary elections. It was widely expected that the remaining disabilities – exclusion from the upper levels of the legal profession, from the higher offices of state and, most importantly, from parliament – would be removed at the time of the Act of Union in 1800. In fact it was not until 1829 that these last restrictions were removed, after a spectacular popular agitation, organised by the Catholic Association under the leadership of Daniel O'Connell, had brought Ireland to the apparent brink of civil war.

Where the Irish Catholic Church was concerned, the penal laws had less effect than might have been imagined. There was, after all, no actual prohibition of Catholic religious services. Priests who had registered under the act of 1704 were free to carry out their normal pastoral functions, though only in the parish for which they were registered. It is true that if the laws of 1697 and 1704 had been rigorously enforced, then – with no new priests permitted to enter the kingdom and no bishops remaining there to ordain them – the Catholic clergy would have died out in a generation. Whether such an outcome was ever seriously intended remains a matter of debate.[13] What is clear is that the laws were never effectively put into practice. Even where magistrates and others were disposed to enforce the laws, they did not have the resources to do so. The turning point in many ways came with the act of 1709 requiring priests to take the oath of abjuration, on pain of forfeiting the legal status they had acquired by registering. Only thirty-three out of over one thousand priests took the oath. Many of the remainder went temporarily into hiding, but within a few weeks it had become clear that the authorities had baulked at the task of coercing so many dissidents and had simply let the matter drop. Sporadic attempts to track down regular clergy and unregistered priests continued into the early years of George I's reign. But by the early 1720s, if not sooner, serious attempts at enforcement had been largely abandoned. Thereafter, the laws against Catholic ecclesiastics were for the most part a dead letter, although they continued to be threatened, and occasionally invoked, in cases of real or anticipated disorder.

In the absence of either effective repression or any sustained missionary effort by the Church of Ireland, progress towards the ostensible aim of extending Protestantism at the expense of popery was minimal. Between 1703 and 1789, a total of about 5,500 individuals registered themselves as converts from Catholicism to the Church of Ireland, most of them members of the landed or professional classes. The restrictions imposed by the semi-legal status of bishops and clergy probably contributed something to the weakness of internal discipline that was evident in the Irish Catholic Church of the mid- and late-eighteenth century. But even here it is difficult to separate the effects of sporadic official harassment from those of the ebbing of Counter-Reformation enthusiasm that was evident by this time everywhere in western Europe.

If the penal laws did little to inhibit Catholic religious practice, they had even less impact on the social and political condition of the great majority of the Catholic population. For the farmer, artisan or labourer, exclusion from sitting in parliament, from central or local government office, or from buying, inheriting or marrying land, was a wholly theoretical disability. Even the right to vote, under a system of open ballot, was for most men the right to vote as a social superior dictated. The restriction to leases of no more than thirty-one years certainly placed Catholic tenants at a disadvantage compared to Protestants. Once again, however, leaseholders were a minority within the rural population. Moreover, at a time of rapidly rising prices, as in the mid-eighteenth century, a thirty-one-year lease was enough to permit substantial profits, and it was, in fact, the very period that these laws were in operation that saw the emergence of a Catholic rural middle class of middlemen and strong farmers. It is of course true that Ireland remained throughout the eighteenth century an unequal and in many ways exploitative society, in which a small minority monopolised political power and the greater part of the nation's wealth. But this was not a result of the penal laws. A similar political and social structure existed throughout western Europe, whatever the religious composition of rulers and ruled.

To the commercial middle class the loss of political rights was undoubtedly more significant. Exclusion from voting and, more importantly, from a role in local government, was both a grievance in itself and an obstacle to the defence and furtherance of business interests. At the same time it is important to remember that even the Protestant middle classes were poorly represented in the landlord-dominated parliaments of the eighteenth century. Where economic opportunity is concerned, exclusion from the legal profession and from public service meant an undoubted narrowing of career opportunities. On the other hand, there was no serious attempt to limit Catholic participation in trade or to hinder the increase or transmission of non-landed wealth. At various times, in fact, contemporaries complained that Catholics had gained, or were on the point of gaining, a monopoly of the kingdom's trade, to the disadvantage of the Protestant interest. On the other hand, recent research has indicated that the Catholic share of merchant wealth was in fact less than half: a significant accumulation of wealth, but well below the Catholic share of total population.[14] The reason for this under-representation of Catholics in trade, however, was not any legal restriction but rather the collapse of Catholic landownership, at a time when land remained the main source of capital for trade and business.

Once again, therefore, we are brought back to the fact that it was the Catholic landowning class who were the main victims, as they were the main targets, of the penal laws. Indeed this was implicit in the content of the laws themselves: the so-called 'act to prevent the further growth of popery' of 1704, for example, was in reality an act against Catholic landed property. As a result of this and other penal statutes, Catholic landowners found themselves excluded from central and local politics, prevented from developing their estates by purchase, long leases, or strategic marriage, and faced with the prospect of seeing existing properties dwindle into eventual insignificance through repeated subdivision. The great majority, rather than suffer this fate, chose to conform to the Church of Ireland. By 1779, Arthur Young suggested, Catholics owned no more than 5 per cent of the land in Ireland. As a tribute to the effects of the penal laws, however, this statistic is less impressive than it seems. In 1688, on the eve of the fall of James, the Catholic share of profitable land was only 22 per cent. By 1703, confiscation of the estates of persons not protected by the treaty of Limerick had reduced this

Christopher Butler (1673–1757), Catholic archbishop of Cashel, by James Latham. Educated in France and consecrated in 1712, he seems to have administered his diocese throughout the early eighteenth century without much interference, despite the penal laws, perhaps because he had powerful Protestant kinsmen.

proportion to 14 per cent.[15] The collapse of Catholic landownership, in other words, had already taken place before the first penal law was passed. If Arthur Young was correct in his estimate, then the popery act of 1704, so rigorous and all-embracing in its provisions, served to change the religion of the owners of around one-tenth of the profitable land of Ireland.

What then was the significance of the penal laws? They did not create what was much later to come to be known as Protestant ascendancy in Ireland.[16] The transfer of wealth and power from Catholic to Protestant had been going on since the sixteenth century, and had been massively accelerated by the events of the 1640s and 1650s. The reign of James II saw a last desperate attempt to reverse this process. However much James himself might have wished to avoid the issue, his Irish followers were clear from the start that nothing less than the return to Catholic ownership of a substantial proportion of the land in Ireland could rescue them from a future of subordination. This was what the Irish Catholics who gathered at the Boyne, Aughrim and Limerick were fighting for. Even if they had won, of course, it is open to question how much difference that victory would have made to the daily lives of the rank and file who followed their traditional leaders into battle. As it was, the attempt at counter-revolution was defeated. What happened next was that the Protestant élite – or rather a vocal, well-organised section within it – used its new bargaining power to extort from successive British governments a series of further restrictions on Catholic landownership, religious organisation and political activity. The purpose of these restrictions was not to create a new social or political order, but rather to ensure that the existing one would never again be threatened as it had been under James.

Much later, of course, the penal laws were to assume a very different significance. In the 1820s, Catholic middle-class politicians were able to build up a mass following behind their campaign for the removal of remaining legal disabilities. By this time legalised discrimination had indeed become the mechanism by which these Catholic merchants and professional men were excluded from a share in political power that would otherwise have been theirs. 'Catholic Emancipation' – Ireland's first authentic popular political movement – equally became the symbol of a demand for political and, to some extent, social equality.[17] All this, however, took place in a world where land was no longer the sole key to power, and which was witnessing the beginnings of a genuine popular political awareness: a world, in other words, which neither the Protestant gentlemen who had pushed through the original penal legislation, nor the Catholic gentlemen who had been its main victims, could ever have imagined.

ARMY AND SOCIETY IN EIGHTEENTH-CENTURY IRELAND

THOMAS BARTLETT

Acutely aware of their numerical inferiority in relation to the Catholics of Ireland, and keenly conscious of their 'next to miraculous' deliverance from the hands of their enemies by the victories at the Boyne and especially at Aughrim, Irish Protestants in the eighteenth century, historians are generally agreed, had a fondness for a large military establishment, which was completely contrary to the attitude of their English cousins for whom (with painful memories of both Cromwell and James II still fresh) a standing army remained 'Slavery, Popery, Mahometism, Paganism, Atheism [and] Freethinking'.[1] Thus one historian in a recent account of the deployment and training of the British Army in this period comments that

> in Ireland the standing army was neither subjected to the abuse nor did it stir the same fears that it aroused in England . . . The supremacy of the Anglican ruling classes in that country rested ultimately (as in 1690 so in 1798) upon the army – and the ruling classes knew this only too well.

Another historian in his study of the army in Ireland in the eighteenth century remarks that

> the army was a popular cause in Ireland where there was no echo of the jealous apprehensions felt in England about the effect of a standing army on civil liberties.[2]

Moreover, so impressed have some historians been with the evidence for a disproportionately large military establishment in Ireland in the eighteenth century (apart from wartime, Ireland was home to half the British Army in this period, the remaining half being equally divided between Britain and garrison duty abroad) that they have concluded from it that Ireland was pre-eminently a violent country in which a large and embittered population was held in subjection only by a massive military presence and the operation of draconian laws. Thus the large number of barracks in Ireland is explained by the fact that the country 'was virtually a colonial territory occupied by an English army and the barracks took on the role of control posts, police stations and blockhouses': and we are told that 'martial law was routinely imposed [for] in Ireland the army was the force of government, freely and often applied'.[3]

In the face of such unanimity one hesitates to voice dissent; however, not only is there evidence to suggest that the attitude of Irish Protestants towards a large standing army was in fact rather ambiguous but also that the picture of eighteenth-century Ireland as a police state, if not actually as a military dictatorship, is one far removed from reality. In short, the subject of the army's role in eighteenth-century Ireland is a complex one that requires more investigation if it is to be properly understood.

The military facts are clear enough and at first glance would seem to lend support to Edmund Burke's withering dismissal of the Protestant ascendancy as having 'grown up under . . . military servitude'.[4] By the English Act of 10 William c. 1 (1699) the army in Ireland was limited in size to 12,000 men, but after 1769 it was permitted to augment its numbers to 15,325. By contrast, for most of this period Britain had, despite a much larger population, fewer than nineteen thousand soldiers. Since at least half and sometimes more of these were serving abroad at any one time (only four Irish regiments served outside Ireland), undoubtedly men in uniform were a much more common sight in Ireland than in England. Moreover, until 1769, when regiments on the British and Irish establishment were made equal in strength, regiments in Ireland had been considerably smaller than those in England (280 men in Ireland as compared to 500 in England), but this had not meant any reduction in an Irish regiment's complement of officers, with the result that the Irish establishment was top-heavy with underemployed officers. Furthermore, it was notorious that this military force was widely distributed throughout Ireland: with no fewer than 263 barracks in use in Ireland in 1704, and with 34 regiments of foot, dragoons, and horse quartered in 1752 in some 69 towns and villages (mostly south of a line from Dublin to Galway), allegations of a military occupation would seem to have some basis.

Again it is a point of some importance that, strictly speaking, there was no 'Irish army' in this period, but rather an army on the Irish establishment, limited in size by an English act and legalised by the annual British Mutiny

Loading and firing a flintlock musket, from a military manual of 1730. With basic bayonet drill, the whole procedure comprised thirty-eight operations for a soldier to master.

Act; not until 1782 was the Irish parliament permitted to pass its own mutiny act. The Irish army establishment was, furthermore, quite separate from that in Britain – the lord lieutenant having considerable power with respect to appointments and promotions – and there was also a separate Irish staff. So far as the composition of this force was concerned, it was expressly forbidden to enlist Irish recruits, and while this rule was occasionally relaxed where Anglicans were concerned (as in 1745), Irish Presbyterians were technically barred until 1780 and Irish Catholics until as late as 1793 from wearing the king's uniform. As F.G. James says, 'the rank and file of the army was an alien group: they came from England'.[5] On the other hand, Irish Protestants of an appropriate rank in society or from strong 'military' families were well-represented among the officer corps (in the cavalry). Finally, the role of this army was to act as a sort of strategic reserve to Britain's needs, to defend Ireland from invasion, to act in support of the civil magistrates, to assist in the collection of the revenue, and to keep an eye 'on the popish interest'.[6] Given that the force was as outlined above, it would seem that claims that eighteenth-century Ireland resembled a military colony were rather well founded; but in fact, on examination, it will be seen that this 'ideal' state of the army and of the army's role in Ireland was far from corresponding to reality.

In the first place, the army in Ireland in the eighteenth century was a byword for inefficiency, incompetence and shady practices. The widespread dispersal of troops throughout the villages and hamlets proved ruinous to discipline, for officers were frequently absent from such boring stations and, left to themselves, the men's efficiency suffered. But even in the big garrison towns, such as Galway, Dublin, Limerick, Cork, and Waterford, discipline and training were neglected. When General Parker inspected some four thousand men exercising near Kilkenny in 1750, he was so unimpressed by what he had seen that he 'ordered his coach home saying such a managed exercise would make a dog spew'. And when Winegarde's regiment (no Roman legion this!) marched into Limerick in the same year, an observer commented that 'they were proceeded [sic] by soldiers leading grayhounds, pointers, setters, spaniels, car dogs, [and carrying] fish rodds, and fowling pieces', having deposited their own arms on the baggage carts. Some months

later, in July 1750, Bragg's regiment left Limerick amidst scenes of considerable disorder. Great quantities of alcohol were consumed on the eve of the soldiers' departure, and 'after it grew dark there was such serenading, whooping and hallowing and riot thro' the streets that people did believe hell was broke'. With great difficulty – 'the very drummers [were] so far gone they were not able to beat a march' – the regiment, now reduced to between eighty and one hundred men, staggered out of Limerick the following morning, bearing their officer on a cart of straw and 'there he lay like a hog'. Such unseemly, if not unsoldierly, incidents could be multiplied, for as one contemporary remarked wryly, laxity of discipline was *quelque chose de règle en Irlande*.[7]

Much of the blame for the disorderly state of the Irish army must be laid at the door of the officer corps, which, it was claimed, 'conform to that glorious plan of freedom and ease which all polite society have established and which we are so constantly attached to in this our dear country', with the result that they spurned anything that looked like 'formal foppery or military pedantry'. Officers were notoriously reluctant to abandon the social whirl of Dublin for the tedium of provincial duty, where their quarters were sometimes built over the barrack stables, which occasioned 'a great source of noise and noxious steam'. Understandably, 'the busy, the idle, the gay or fops', who figured prominently among the officer corps, frequently cut more of a dash in the drawing rooms than on the parade grounds. As one ditty had it about 'spruce Captain Benson' and Miss Lydia Brown:

> The Captain is more to be loved than to be feared.
> He charms all hearts with his graces and airs
> When he simpers and smiles and leaps over chairs.

But somehow the soldierly language would out:

> Says Benson to Lydia, Pray dearest Miss Brown
> How can you exist in this hole of a town?[8]

In addition, officers were well aware that the path to advancement lay more through the operation of patronage than through diligent duty, and this was a further disincentive to accompanying their regiment. Admittedly, the reign of George II (1727–60) saw a determined effort to promote only deserving candidates, and recent researches among the 293 colonelcies bestowed in the British Army during the period 1714–63 reveal an admirable regard being paid to experience and service.[9] But in Ireland the picture is rather different, and there is a good deal of evidence to show that promotions there were regularly determined by a person's political weight rather than normal military criteria. Thus when Lord Chesterfield recommended a promotion to Lord Harrington at the war office in 1745, he commented that the candidate 'is an utter stranger to me and . . . my true reason for recommending his request is that he is brother to lord Lanesborough [and] is himself and has many relatives in the Irish Parliament'. And in 1763 the

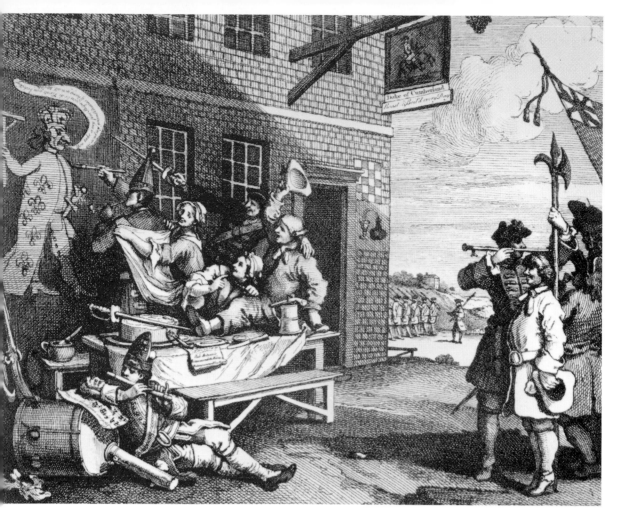

under-secretary in Dublin Castle, Thomas Waite, rather shamefacedly sent over to London a request from Lieutenant Coote Purdon that he be permitted to give up his rank and retire as a half-pay *captain*. Waite commented that while there were precedents for such an exchange in Ireland, it was unheard of in England and ought to be put a stop to. However, he did add, 'I must inform you that this Coote Purdon is connected with my Lord Shannon who I believe will be well enough pleased to get the thing done for him, tho' he does not write to ask for it.'[10]

The fact was that the army in Ireland and its supplies, its accoutrements, and its barracks were all integral parts of the political patronage at the disposal of the lord lieutenant, and were treated as such. Cadetships, ensigncies, and colonelcies were eagerly sought for the sons of the Anglo-Irish – realistically, apart from praying, what other career could they pursue? – and no lord lieutenant who valued peace was prepared to deny them. In England, by contrast, the army was much more under direct royal control, and when the duke of Cumberland was captain-general (1745–57), he 'paid scant regard to interest and looked out for the deserving' where promotions were concerned.[11] Lords lieutenant of Ireland could not afford to be so virtuous (or so sanctimonious).

Irregularity among the officer corps was, then, quite common on the Irish army establishment – so common in fact that one report sarcastically claimed that Irish officers were entirely 'regular' in their behaviour, 'here and there a few excepted who are but lately come amongst us and who as yet have not had time to learn that noble freedom and ease so customary with us'.[12] This laxity in discipline was, not surprisingly, reproduced lower down in the ranks. Military correspondence of the eighteenth century is filled with reports of brawls with civilians (admittedly, soldier-baiting was a favourite blood sport in both England and Ireland but Viscount Sydney was probably right when he commented that 'I have always understood that pelting the soldiers by the mob and firing upon them in return were events much more frequent in Dublin than in London').[13] There are also reports of riots (in 1765 soldiers of the Dublin garrison rioted, threw open the doors of Newgate gaol and released many prisoners[14]); and above all, of desertion on an epic scale (in 1783 the lord lieutenant referred to the Irish troops 'cherishing that spirit of desertion which is here truly a trade'[15]).

There were, moreover, frequent allegations of fraud and corruption in the funding of the army and also in the construction of barracks. In this latter respect, after a programme of barrack-building had been allegedly completed under the supervision of Arthur Jones Nevill in the late 1740s, a government report concluded that apart from massive irregularities in the building contracts, the barracks themselves that had been constructed were 'unfit for the reception and dangerous to the health of His Majesty's troops'.[16] Jones Nevill was censured and eventually expelled from the Irish House of Commons; but his fall from grace owed more to the vicissitudes of Irish politics than to any determination of Irish MPs to do right by the army, and irregularities at the barrack board continued. It was, however, the disbursement of army pay that excited most comment and which seems to have been subject to most abuses.

Eighteenth-century musketeer

Eighteenth-century drummer

Although until 1769 the army on the Irish establishment was limited to twelve thousand men, this figure must be regarded as 'ideal' and the reality was that soldiers in Ireland rarely numbered more than six thousand in the first half of the eighteenth century. Admittedly, four regiments served constantly abroad, but the remaining regiments were notorious for fictitious muster rolls, missing men, and nonexistent recruits. For example, in the 1760s some 1,350 'Warrant men' were listed as being in receipt of pay in the Irish army; this term was 'made use of for appropriating, under a fictitious name, to certain purposes . . . the pay of certain men, supposed to be in the Army, tho' in reality such men never existed'. The money was supposed to form a recruiting fund, but generally the colonel of the regiment seems to have pocketed it. Similarly, each captain could claim for a 'contingent man' in the foot regiments, while in the dragoons a 'hautboy' was allowed to each troop at a cost of around £180 per year. Once again these people were nonexistent, and the money appears to have gone to the colonel or to the officers. In short, at any one time up to 20 per cent of the effective men (that is, those returned as actually present) on the Irish establishment may not have existed and can be presumed to have enlisted 'under the Aerial Ensigns of the Invisible Legions'. As one bitterly hostile pamphleteer put it: 'Indeed this may not be the only country, that has thought itself sufficiently protected by invisible agents; but I believe the honour was reserved for Ireland of being the first to provide regimentals for this Light Infantry.'[17]

In the light of these irregularities it is perhaps surprising that attempts to keep the ranks free from either Irish Protestants (eligible for the cavalry only) or, especially, Irish Catholics seem to have been reasonably effective. The thinking behind the exclusion of Irish Protestants was that to enlist them would reduce their number in Ireland and thus weaken the 'Protestant interest'; furthermore, there was always the possibility that Irish Catholics would claim to be Protestants and thus gain entry to the ranks: better, therefore, to ban all Irish. (It would have been absurd to enlist Catholics, as one put it, to 'guard us from themselves'.[18]) The problem with this policy was that recruits were difficult to obtain (and retain), and since regiments on the Irish establishment had nearly two hundred men fewer than those in England, when an Irish regiment embarked for England or elsewhere, it had to recruit a large number of men in a hurry.[19]

This chronic shortfall in numbers was further compounded by the fact that a notice to embark for foreign parts was almost always the signal for wholesale desertion. Regiments generally made up their numbers by drafting soldiers from other regiments on the Irish establishment; but colonels were sometimes tempted to turn a blind eye to the enlistment of locals. On at least one occasion some officers took the extraordinary step of sending a parcel of Irish recruits to Scotland, bedecking them with plaid, and on their return to Ireland, attempting to pass them off as Scots. However, such practices were dangerous and, if caught, the culprits faced punishment: in 1728 a number of officers were suspended for attempting to enlist Irish recruits; and in 1756, Ensign Milo Baggot had forty-two recruits from his native Queen's County (now County Laois) disallowed, the lord lieutenant, the duke of Bedford, refusing 'to wink at practices of this sort'.[20] None the less, there is enough circumstantial evidence to suggest that there was an Irish Catholic presence in the British Army in the decades before the 1770s. In this respect it is surely significant that deserters had frequently 'Irish' names, and that in 1755 British regiments in Canada just arrived from Ireland were stated to be composed almost entirely of 'convicts and Irish Papists'.

What is certain is that as warfare in the middle decades of the eighteenth century became a labour intensive, as well as territorially extensive, pursuit, British ministers began to look again at those large numbers of Irish Catholics who, though clearly 'fit for service', lay under a prohibition. In 1762 an offer from the Catholic Lord Trimleston to raise three thousand Irish Catholic recruits for the king of Portugal's service at least got a sympathetic hearing from the British government before the Irish parliament threw it out. None the less, despite its rejection, Trimleston's proposal pointed the way forward, and from this time on the recruitment of Irish Catholics into the British Army proceeded apace, Lord Townshend commenting in 1770 that he was prepared 'to do the thing but avoid the name'.[21] With the provision of an oath of allegiance for Catholics in 1774, the way was clear to recruit them openly, if not entirely legally, into the ranks; however, Catholic officers could not be commissioned until 1793, and even then only into Irish regiments.

The marked absence of furore at the recruitment of Irish Catholics in large numbers into Irish regiments in the later decades of the eighteenth century can be seen as reflecting the maturing self-confidence of the Protestant nation. Admittedly, since the 1690s the confidence of the Protestant community in itself as constituting 'the whole people of Ireland' had been, much to the dismay of the English government, perhaps its most noticeable trait. The 'shipwreck' of the Catholic Irish at Aughrim had been so total as to preclude the possibility of a resurgence, and although Protestants could not rest entirely easy so long as the Pretender remained a threat, the penal laws against Catholics, the assumed permanence of English good will, and after 1714, the remoteness of a dynastic upheaval in England all combined to persuade Irish Protestants that the prospect of a Catholic revival was more of a 'bugaboo' than a real threat.[22] Accordingly, while Ireland undoubtedly had a large military establishment during the eighteenth century, this did not

Parade-ground scene by
Romeyn de Hooghe

reflect Protestant nervousness. It was rather a continuation under the Hanoverians of the old Stuart policy of 'losing regiments in Ireland', far away from 'the prying eyes of cheeseparers or of [English] backbenchers ever ready to invoke the "no standing army" issue'.[23] Even the construction of a large number of barracks throughout Ireland should be regarded as a product of the widespread aversion of the civilian population to billeting (this is what James's army was notorious for) rather than as the deployment of an army of occupation.[24]

Moreover, while there was clearly a much greater number of soldiers in Ireland than in England (even allowing for irregularities), it is by no means clear that their use differed from one country to the other. In both countries the army, in the absence of a police force, 'was the instrument of social coercion', and in putting down riots and aiding revenue officers, it appears to have been deployed in much the same fashion on both sides of the water.[25] Certainly there was no question that soldiers in Ireland could act without civilian authority. When the troops were ordered into west Connacht to put down the Houghers in 1711, they went 'with orders to act under the direction of specified local gentlemen'. Again, contrary to what has been frequently claimed, the army was by no means the first resort of the local gentry when confronting bandits, highwaymen or agrarian rebels. The local gentry were expected to maintain law and order themselves, and in general they did so. It was, for example, a mixture of locally recruited militia and volunteers that dealt with the remnants of Toryism in Cork in the early eighteenth century; and 'informally mustered forces' or posses were common elsewhere. In any case, army officers were reluctant to get involved in civilian matters, claiming, quite rightly, that their men had absolutely no training in these things.[26]

By the 1750s, Protestant confidence had clearly developed into something that could more accurately be described as Protestant nationalism; and a noticeable feature of this nationalism was both a willingness to engage in debate with England concerning the proper relationship between Ireland and England, and a refusal to accept the English view of that relationship. In this process of reappraisal the role of the army in Ireland did not escape scrutiny. The fact was that in English eyes the Protestants of Ireland constituted a sort of colonial garrison that owed not only its survival in 1690 to British arms but its continued existence thereafter; and the price to be paid for such protection was constitutional subordination, trade restrictions, a subordinate parliament, an acceptance that British priorities would

determine the disposal of Irish patronage – and a large military establishment. Needless to say, Irish Protestants rejected such an unflattering, unprofitable, and one-sided view of the Anglo-Irish relationship. They had expected to be partners in the Glorious Revolution but, so far from it, they found themselves practically excluded from the loaves and fishes of office. They even found themselves taken to task for complaining about the Woollen Act of 1699: 'This is not lookt upon as a modest or friendly behaviour, much less does it denote any sense of gratitude retain'd in a people that were so lately reliev'd by England.'[27]

Initially, prudence had determined that where a large standing army was concerned, Protestants should be circumspect in their criticism, but by the early 1730s, a vein of dissent can be detected and it was now Irish Protestants who complained about a lack of gratitude. One pamphleteer wrote in 1731:

> We have never had any one instance of a grateful return for the blood and treasure we have spent in the Protestant cause and in defense of their [English] liberties . . . we were never thank'd for venturing our lives and fortunes at the Revolution, for making so brave a stand at Londonderry and Inniskilling.[28]

By this date there were complaints that despite the large number of regiments on the Irish establishment, the number of Irish officers at a senior level was small (by 1769 it was claimed that out of forty-two colonels only seven were Irish), and there seems to have been some resentment at the ban on recruitment of Irish Protestants. The sending overseas of regiments paid for by Ireland was also objected to.

By the late 1730s there was some evidence to suggest that a standing army was seen as a threat to political liberty. The work of John Trenchard, the chief proponent of this thesis, was known in Ireland, and his Irish readers cannot but have been struck by his remark that 'an army kept in Ireland is more dangerous to us than [one kept] at home'.[29] Furthermore, the fact that there was no Irish mutiny act was a stated grievance of the small but influential patriot party that emerged in the Irish parliament in the 1750s; and the absence of a proper Irish militia was also a cause for concern. The arrival of Lord Townshend as lord lieutenant in 1767, charged with obtaining an augmentation of the army in Ireland, brought these grievances to a head and a veritable pamphlet war ensued from 1767 to 1770, in which the merits and demerits of Ireland's military establishment were discussed at length. It was only with the greatest difficulty that Townshend was able to gain approval for the proposed increase in the Irish army.[30] In short, Irish Protestants were by no means uncritical admirers of the army; nor were they wholly enamoured of a large military establishment. By the 1770s, when the Stuart threat had disappeared with the death of the Pretender, Irish Protestants had become so self-confident that they seized with alacrity on the opportunity offered by the Volunteer movement to provide their own defence force. The Protestant nation had come of age.

INTRODUCTION

1 The full title is *K. William or K. Lewis. Wherein is set forth the inevitable necessity these nations lie under, of submitting wholly to one or other of these kings*

2 'Mrs. Elizabeth Freke, her Diary, 1671 to 1714', *Cork Historical and Archaeological Society Journal*, 2nd series, vol. XVII (1911), p. 48

3 *Ireland's Lamentation* (London, 1689), p. 26

4 *County Louth Archaeological Society Journal*, vol. I, no. 2 (1905), pp. 56, 57; or A. Hewitson (ed.), *Diary of Sir Thomas Bellingham* (Preston, 1908)

5 *Report of the Commissioners Appointed by Parliament to Enquire into the Irish Forfeitures* (London and Dublin, 1700), p. 16

6 D. Dickson, C. Ó Gráda and S. Daultrey, 'Hearth tax, household size and Irish population change 1672–1821', *Proceedings of the Royal Irish Academy*, vol. LXXXII C (1982), p. 180

7 G. Story, *An Impartial History* (London, 1691), p. 76

CHAPTER I

1 A. van der Kuijl, *De Glorieuze Overtocht*, hereafter van der Kuijl, (Amsterdam, 1988), p. 22. This is not only the best account of the military and naval preparations in the Dutch Republic but also places them succinctly in their European context.

2 H. Nenner, 'The traces of shame in England's Glorious Revolution', *History*, vol. LXXIII, no. 238 (June 1988), p. 239

3 A. Lossky, 'Political ideas of William III', in *Political Ideas and Institutions in the Dutch Republic* (Los Angeles, 1985), pp. 43, 45–6

4 Each province of the Dutch Republic had its own governing body known as the States; each States was represented in the governing body of the whole republic – the States-General.

5 Lossky, 'Political ideas', p. 46; N. Japikse, *Prins Willem III*, 2 vols (Amsterdam, 1930), vol II, pp. 162–3

6 M.A.M. Franken, *Coenraad van Bueningen's politieke en diplomatieke aktiviteiten in de jaren 1667–1684* (Groningen, 1966), pp. 235–6, 254–5; D.J. Roorda, *Rond prins en patriciaat* (Weesp, 1984), pp. 128–9, 182–3; J.L. Price, 'William III, England and the balance of power in Europe', *Groniek*, vol. CI (1988), pp. 68–9; H.H. Rowen, *The Princes of Orange* (Cambridge, 1988), pp. 68, 134, 138–9; G.H. Kurtz, *Willem III en Amsterdam*, hereafter Kurtz, (Utrecht, 1928), pp. 147, 172, 177

7 Kurtz, pp. 67–8

8 H.P.H. Nusteling, 'The Netherlands and the Huguenot émigrés' in J.A.H. Bots and G.H.M. Posthumus Meyjes (eds), *La révocation de l'édit de Nantes et les Provinces-Unies 1685/The Revocation of the edict of Nantes and the Dutch Republic* (Amsterdam and Maarssen, 1986), pp. 22–4; R.D. Gwynn, *Huguenot Heritage* (London, 1985), p. 36, where the proportion of French exiles in 1700 is put at *c.* 5 per cent of London's population

9 Nusteling, 'The Netherlands and the Huguenot émigrés', p. 29

10 Kurtz, pp. 164–78; J. Solé, 'La diplomatie de Louis XIV et les protestants français refugiés aux Provinces-Unies (1678–1688)', *Bulletin de la Société de l'Histoire du Protestantisme Français*, vol. CXV (1969), pp. 629–39

11 *Edits, déclarations et arrests concernans la religion p. reformée 1662–1751* (Paris, 1885), pp. 270–1, 290–1; J.I. Israel, *Dutch Primacy in World Trade 1585–1740* (Oxford, 1989), pp. 341–2

12 Israel, *Dutch Primacy*, p. 342; van der Kuijl, pp. 20–1

13 Japikse, *Prins Willem*, vol. II, p. 248; N. Japikse (ed.), *Correspondentie van Willem III en van Hans Willem Bentinck*, 2 vols, (The Hague, 1927), vol. I, p. 45, Willem III to Bentinck, 25 August 1688; and p. 48, same to same, 29 August 1688

14 Israel, *Dutch Primacy*, p. 342

15 van der Kuijl, p. 21; Israel, *Dutch Primacy*, p. 342; G.N. Clark, *The Dutch Alliance and the War Against French Trade 1688–1697* (Manchester, 1923), pp. 4–6, 43

16 Japikse, *Prins Willem*, vol. II, p. 245; P.L. Muller, 'Een Brandenburgsche zending in Nederland in 1685', *Bijdragen voor vaderlandsche geschiedenis en oudheidkunde* (Zesde Deel, 1869), pp. 88, 107; Solé, 'La diplomatie de Louis XIV', p. 633; G. Symcox, 'Louis XIV and the outbreak of the Nine Years War', hereafter Symcox, in R. Hatton (ed.), *Louis XIV and Europe* (London, 1976), p. 191; J. Miller, *James II: A Study of Kingship* (London, 1978), pp. 163, 184–5, 189, 192, 194

17 Japikse, *Prins Willem*, p. 248; van der Kuijl, p. 21; Kurtz, p. 188

18 H. Manners Sutton (ed.), *The Lexington Papers* (London, 1851), p. 354 (Appendix: Extracts from 'The Journal of what passed in the time of Mr. Hop's abode at the Imperial Court at Vienna, as Envoy-Extraordinary from the High and Mighty States of Holland, from the 4th November 1688 to the 19th July 1689')

19 G. Burnet, *History of My Own Time*, 6 vols, (Oxford, 1823), vol. III, p. 229; van der Kuijl, p. 19; Clark, *The Dutch Alliance*, p. 9

20 C. Boutant, *L'Europe an grand tournant des années 1680*, hereafter Boutant, (Paris, 1985), pp. 699–862 for the most recent detailed account of the Cologne crisis; R. Fruin, *De Oorlog van 1672* (Groningen, 1972), pp. 39, 52, 123–5, 130; J. den Tex, *Onder vreemde heren* (Zutphen, 1982), pp. 14, 23–6, 86–7, 155, 158–9, 162, 167

21 Boutant, pp. 759, 764, 773, 782–3, 807; R. Fruin, 'Prins Willem III en zijn verhouding tot England', in P.J. Blok, P.L. Muller and S. Muller (eds), *Verspreide geschriften*, 10 vols, (The Hague, 1900–5), vol. V, pp. 169–71; Symcox, p. 193; *Mercure historique et politique*, vol. V (1688), pp. 703–4, 829, 843

22 Boutant, pp. 791–5, 802–3, 807–17, 827; Symcox, pp. 195–8; *Mercure*, vol. V (1688), pp. 941, 988

23 Boutant, pp. 764, 807–17; *Correspondentie van Willem III*, vol. I, p. 45, Willem III to Bentinck, 4 September 1688

24 van der Kuijl, p. 21

25 Symcox, pp. 179–83; R. Hatton, *Louis XIV and His World* (London, 1972), pp. 80–1; R. Hatton *Louis XIV and the Craft of Kingship* (Ohio, 1969), pp. 169–73

26 G.H. Jones, 'William III's diplomatic preparations for his expedition to England', *Durham University Journal*, vol. LXXIX (1987), p. 238

27 D. Ligou, *Le Protestantisme en France de 1598 à 1715* (Paris, 1968), p. 246

28 van der Kuijl, p. 18; Jones, 'William III's diplomatic preparations', pp. 242–3; Symcox, pp. 191, 195–7, 199–203, 210, 211; Boutant, pp. 765–8, 831, 833; W.A. Speck, *Reluctant Revolutionaries: Englishmen and the Revolution of 1688* (Oxford, 1988), p. 17; Miller, *James II*, pp. 192–4

29 Speck, *Reluctant Revolutionaries*, p. 77; Symcox, p. 203; Boutant, pp. 828–89

30 Japikse, *Prins Willem*, vol. II, p. 245; Roorda, *Rond prins en patriciaat*, pp. 136, 176–7

31 *Lexington Papers*, p. 328

32 *Lexington Papers*, pp. 329, 333

33 *Lexington Papers*, p. 354

34 P.J.A.N. Rietbergen, 'William III of Orange (1650–1702) between European politics and European Protestantism: the case of the Huguenots' in *La révocation de l'édit de Nantes*, pp. 35–50; *Lexington Papers*, pp. 330–2, 355–6; J.R. Jones, 'The road to 1688', *Groniek*, vol. CI (1988), pp. 56–8

35 *Lexington Papers*, p. 331

36 This is a main theme in five essays by M.A. Thomson to be found in R. Hatton and J.S. Bromley (eds), *William III and Louis XIV* (Liverpool, 1968): 'Louis XIV and William III, 1689–97' (pp. 24–48); 'Parliament and foreign policy, 1689–1714' (pp. 130–9); Louis XIV and the Grand Alliance, 1705–10' (pp. 190–212); 'The safeguarding of the Protestant succession, 1702–18' (pp. 237–51); 'Self-determination and collective security as factors in English and French foreign policy, 1689–1718' (pp. 271–86)

37 Japikse, *Prins Willem*, vol. II, p. 287

38 Quoted in J. Childs, '1688', *History*, vol. LXXIII, no. 239 (October 1988), p. 422

CHAPTER 2

1 C. Blount (?), 'An appeal from the country to the city', in *State Tracts*, 2 vols, (London, 1689–92), vol. I, pp. 401–2

2 H[istorical] M[anuscripts] C[ommission Reports], *Ormonde MSS*, new series, vol. V, p. 155

3 *See* C. Hibbard, *Charles I and the Popish Plot* (Chapel Hill, 1983)

4 J. Miller, *Popery and Politics in England, 1660–88* (Cambridge, 1973), pp. 9–12; A. Whiteman, 'The Compton Census of 1676', *British Academy Records of Social and Economic History*, vol. X (1986), pp. lxxix–lxxxi

5 HMC, *Dartmouth*, vol. I, p. 16

6 J. Lingard, *History of England*, 6th edn, 10 vols (London, 1855), vol. X, p. 203

7 C.J. Fox, *History of the Early Part of the Reign of King James II* (London, 1808), Appendix, p. cvi

8 J.P. Kenyon, *The Stuart Constitution*, 2nd edn (Cambridge, 1986), pp. 389–91

9 I have discussed this question in 'James II and toleration' in E. Cruickshanks (ed.), *By Force or by Default? The Revolution of 1688* (Edinburgh, 1989)

10 J. Gutch (ed.), *Collectanea Curiosa*, 2 vols (London, 1781), vol. I, pp. 339–40. *See also* G.V. Bennett, 'The Seven Bishops: a reconsideration' in

D. Baker (ed.), *Religious Motivation: Biographical and Sociological Problems for the Church Historian*, Studies in Church History (Oxford, 1978), vol. XV, pp. 267–87

11 *See* Miller, *Popery and Politics*, pp. 218–23

12 J.L. Garland, 'The Regiment of Macelligott, 1688–9', *Irish Sword*, vol. I (1949–53), pp. 121–7; British Library, Add. MS 29563, fo. 258; Archives des Affaires Etrangères, Correspondence Politique Angleterre, vol. 166, Barrillon to Louis XIV, 13–23 September 1688 and 24 September–4 October 1688

13 E.N. Williams, *The Eighteenth-century Constitution* (Cambridge, 1960), pp. 10–16

14 British Library, Add. MS 34487, fo. 30; J. Miller, 'Proto-Jacobitism? The Tories in the Revolution of 1688' in E. Cruickshanks and J. Black (eds), *The Jacobite Challenge* (Edinburgh, 1988), pp. 7–23

15 Dr Williams's Library, Morrice MS Q, pp. 359, 361; *Revolution Politicks* (London, 1733), book VIII, p. 18; Miller, *Popery and Politics*, pp. 259–61

16 HMC, *Dartmouth*, vol. I, p. 232; *see also* J. Miller, *Seeds of Liberty: 1688 and the Shaping of Modern Britain* (London, 1988), ch. 4

17 G. Burnet, *History of My Own Time*, 6 vols (Oxford, 1823), vol. III, pp. 372–4; S.B. Baxter, *William III* (London, 1966), pp. 244–5

18 A. Grey, *Debates in the House of Commons, 1667–94*, 10 vols (London, 1769), vol. IX, pp. 185, 276

19 Grey, *Debates*, vol. IX, p. 110; *also* vol. IX, pp. 35, 88–9, 96–7

20 H. Howitz, *Parliament, Policy and Politics in the Reign of William III* (Manchester, 1977), pp. 38–9; Grey, *Debates*, vol. IX, p. 473

21 Horwitz, *Parliament*, pp. 42–4, 53–4

CHAPTER 3

1 [W. King], *The State of the Protestants of Ireland under the late King James's Government* (London, 1691), pp. 12, 15

2 The classic Whig account is T.B. Macaulay, *The History of England from the Accession of James II*, 5 vols (London, 1849–61). For a useful treatment of the recent historiography of the 1688 Revolution *see* W.A. Speck, *Reluctant Revolutionaries: Englishmen and the Revolution of 1688* (Oxford, 1988), pp. 1–21

3 The most authoritative account of political developments in James II's reign is J.G. Simms, *Jacobite Ireland, 1685–91* (London, 1969); J. Miller, 'The earl of Tyrconnel and James II's Irish policy, 1685–1688', *Historical Journal*, vol. XX, no. 4 (1977), pp. 803–23 provides a definitive analysis of the way Tyrconnell came to dominate Irish policy; *see also* Miller, *James II: A Study in Kingship* (Hove, 1978), especially chs. 14 and 15

4 Simms, *Jacobite Ireland*, pp. 19–20, 25; Miller, 'Tyrconnel', p. 818

5 Simms, *Jacobite Ireland*, pp. 20–1. Lords justices were appointed to head the Government in the absence of a lord lieutenant or if the king were reluctant to appoint any one man as viceroy.

6 Simms, *Jacobite Ireland*, p. 33

7 Calendar of State Papers, Domestic, 1685, hereafter Cal.S.P.dom., p. 187; Miller, 'Tyrconnel', pp. 816–17

8 HMC, *Ormonde MSS*, new series, vol. VIII, p. 347

9 *See* letters from Irish Catholic clergy to James II printed in King, *State of the Protestants*, pp. 301–9

10 J. Miller, *Popery and Politics in England 1660–88* (Cambridge, 1973), pp. 223–4

11 *See* J. McGuire, 'Richard Talbot, earl of Tyrconnell (1603–91) and the Catholic counter-revolution' in C. Brady (ed.), *Worsted in the Game: Losers in Irish History* (Dublin, 1989), pp. 75, 79

12 Miller, 'Tyrconnel', p. 812

13 Simms, *Jacobite Ireland*, pp. 25–6, 35

14 Cal. S.P. dom., 1686–7, p. 405, Sunderland to lord deputy of Ireland, 5 April 1687

15 W. King printed the text of the Act of Attainder as an Appendix to the *State of the Protestants*, pp. 241–98

16 Quoted in Simms, *Jacobite Ireland*, p. 23

17 The significance of the Chester meeting is brought out in Miller, 'Tyrconnel', p. 41

18 Simms, *Jacobite Ireland*, p. 41

19 *See* M.E. Gilmore, 'Anthony Dopping and the Church of Ireland, 1685–1695' (unpublished MA thesis, Queen's University Belfast, 1988), p. 85

20 Cal. S.P. dom., 1686–7, pp. 79, 249, 351; S.W. Singer (ed.), *Clarendon Correspondence*, 2 vols, (London, 1828), vol. I, p. 576

21 Cal. S.P. dom., 1686–7, pp. 383, 415, 432; Simms, *Jacobite Ireland*, p. 43

22 Cal. S.P. dom., 1686–7, p. 353, The king to Dominick, lord primate of Ireland, 31 January 1687

23 P. Power (ed.), *A Bishop of the Penal Times* (Cork, 1932), p. 94, Archbishop John Brenan to Monsignor Cybo, 9 November 1687

24 Calendar of Clarendon state papers, vol. V, p. 687; R. Mant, *History of the Church of Ireland*, 2 vols, (London, 1840), vol. I, pp. 700–702

25 Miller, *James II*, p. 155

26 J.S. Clarke (ed.), *Life of James the Second*, 2 vols (London, 1816), vol. II, p. 621

27 Cal. S.P. dom., 1686–7, p. 442; Simms, *Jacobite Ireland*, p. 86; Simms, *The Jacobite Parliament of 1689* (Dundalk, 1966), p. 14

28 *See* J.R. Western, *Monarchy and Revolution: The English State in the 1680s* (London, 1972), pp. 112–55

29 This view was enshrined in the Declaration of Rights of the English convention parliament in 1689: 'the pretended power of dispensing with laws or the execution of laws by regal authority as it has been assumed and exercised of late is illegal'. *See* Speck, *Reluctant Revolutionaries*, p. 141

30 Simms, *Jacobite Ireland*, p. 36

31 J. Childs, *The Army, James II and the Glorious Revolution* (Manchester, 1980) pp. 78–9

32 Clarke, *Life of James the Second*, vol. II, pp. 636–8

CHAPTER 4

1 The best modern account is J.G. Simms, *Jacobite Ireland 1685–91* (London, 1969). Also worth consulting are T.B. Macaulay, *The History of England from the Accession of James II*, 5 vols (London, 1849–61); D.C. Boulger, *The Battle of the Boyne*, (London, 1911); and R.H. Murray, *Revolutionary Ireland and its Settlement* (London, 1911)

2 E.B. Powley, *The Naval Side of King William's War* (London, 1972), pp. 134–43

3 J. Childs, *The army, James II and the Glorious Revolution* (Manchester, 1980), pp. 56–79

4 J. Hogan (ed.), *Négociations de M. le comte d'Avaux en Irlande, 1689–90* (Dublin, 1934) and supplementary volume; L. Tate (ed.), 'Franco-Irish correspondence, December 1688–August 1691' in *Analecta Hibernica*, no. 21 (1959); S. Mulloy (ed.), *Franco-Irish Correspondence, December 1688–February 1692*, 3 vols (Dublin, 1983, 1984) detail Franco-Jacobite relations.

5 D. Stevenson, 'The Irish emergency coinages of James II, 1689–91', *British Numismatic Journal*, vol. XXXVI (1967), pp. 169–75

6 Mulloy, *Franco-Irish Correspondence*, vol. III, p. 181

7 J. Childs, *Nobles, Gentlemen and the Profession of Arms in Restoration Britain 1660–1688*, Society for Army Historical Research, special publication no. 13 (1987) has useful biographical details on a number of Irish (as well as British) officers who served abroad.

8 J. D'Alton, *King James's Irish Army List*, 2nd edn, 2 vols (Dublin, 1860), vol. II, p. 160

9 F.J. Reigler, 'Anglo-Irish catholics, the army of Ireland and the Jacobite war' (unpublished D.Ed. thesis, Temple University, Pennsylvania, 1983)

10 C.D. Milligan, *History of the Siege of Londonderry 1689* (Belfast, 1951) is a detailed, if partisan, account of the siege. *See also* J.G. Simms, 'The Siege of Derry', *Irish Sword*, vol. VI (1963–4), pp. 221–33. Rival contemporary accounts from the point of view of the besieged are G. Walker, *A True Account of the Siege of Londonderry* (London, 1689) and J. Mackenzie, *A Narrative of the Siege of Londonderry* (London, 1690)

11 T. Witherow (ed.), *Two Diaries of Derry in 1689* (Londonderry, 1888), p. 98

12 A. Hamilton, *A True Relation of the Actions of the Inniskilling Men* (London, 1690) and W. McCormick, *A Further Impartial Account of the Actions of the Inniskilling Men* (London, 1691) are the best contemporary accounts of the defence of Enniskillen.

13 J.A. Murphy, *Justin MacCarthy, Lord Mountcashel, Commander of the First Irish Brigade in France* (Cork, 1959), pp. 21–5

14 J. Childs, 'A patriot for whom? "For God and Honour": Marshal Schomberg', *History Today*, vol. XXXVIII (July 1988) is a good modern assessment of his career. For his lacklustre campaign in Ireland *see* J.G. Simms, 'Schomberg at Dundalk, 1689', *Irish Sword*, vol. X (1971–2), pp. 14–25

15 H. Murtagh, 'Huguenot involvement in the Irish Jacobite war, 1689–91' in C.E.J. Caldicott, H. Gough and J.-P. Pittion (eds), *The Huguenots and Ireland: Anatomy of an Emigration* (Dublin, 1987), p. 228

16 G. Story, *A True and Impartial History of the Most Material Occurrences in the Kingdom of Ireland During the Last Two Years* (London, 1691), p. 10

17 J.S. Clarke (ed.), *Life of James the Second*, 2 vols (London, 1816), vol. II, pp. 375–84

18 J.G. Simms, 'Sligo in the Jacobite war', *Irish Sword*, vol. VII (1965–6), pp. 37–44

19 K.P. Ferguson, 'The army in Ireland from the restoration to the Act of Union' (unpublished Ph.D. thesis, Trinity College Dublin 1980), p. 35 ff.; J. Childs, *The British Army of William III, 1698–1702* (Manchester, 1987).

20 K. Danaher and J.G. Simms (eds), *The Danish Force in Ireland, 1690–1691* (Dublin, 1962)

21 C. O'Kelly, *Macariae Excidium or the Destruction of Cyprus*, ed. J.C. O'Callaghan (Dublin, 1850),

p. 41. A similar picture is given in R.H. Murray (ed.), *The Journal of John Stevens* (Oxford, 1912), pp. 92–4

22 For the battle of the Boyne and the preceding manoeuvres see especially G.A. Hayes-McCoy, *Irish Battles: a Military History of Ireland* (London, 1969), pp. 214–37; J.G. Simms, 'Eyewitnesses of the Boyne', *Irish Sword*, vol. VI (1963–4), pp. 16–27; S. Mulloy, 'French eyewitnesses of the Boyne', *Irish Sword*, vol. XV (1982–3), pp. 105–11

23 H. Murtagh, 'The siege of Athlone, 1690', *Old Athlone Society Journal*, vol. I (1971), pp. 84–7

24 J.G. Simms, 'The siege of Limerick, 1690' in E. Rynne (ed.), *North Munster Studies: Essays in Commemoration of Monsignor Michael Moloney* (Limerick, 1967), pp. 308–14

25 J.T. Gilbert (ed.), *A Jacobite Narrative of the War in Ireland, 1688–91* (Shannon, 1971), p. 111 ff

26 J.G. Simms, 'Marlborough's siege of Cork, 1690', *Irish Sword*, vol. IX (1969–70), pp. 113–23

27 H. Murtagh, 'Connaught and the Jacobite war, 1688–91' (unpublished M. Litt. thesis, Trinity College Dublin, 1971), pp. 170–91

28 R. Parker, *Memoirs of the Military Transactions. . .from 1683 to 1718* (London, 1747), pp. 25–6

29 G. Story, *Impartial History*, pp. 152–3. Further details of their activities are provided in the same author's *A Continuation of the Impartial History of the Wars of Ireland* (London, 1693)

30 J.G. Simms, 'Williamite peace-tactics', *Irish Historical Studies*, vol. VIII (1953), pp. 303–23

31 H. Mangan, 'Sarsfield's defence of the Shannon, 1690–91', *Irish Sword*, vol. I (1949–53), pp. 24–32

32 H. Murtagh, 'The siege of Athlone, 1691', *Old Athlone Society Journal*, vol. I (1973), pp. 172–83

33 Hayes-McCoy, *Irish Battles*, pp. 238–72 is the best account of the battle. *See also* D. Murtagh, 'The battle of Aughrim' in G.A. Hayes-McCoy (ed.), *The Irish at War* (Cork, 1964), pp. 59–70

34 J. Jordan, 'The battle of Aughrim: two Danish sources', *Galway Archaeological Society Journal*, vol. XXIX (1954–5), pp. 6–7

35 H. Murtagh, 'Galway and the Jacobite war', *Irish Sword*, vol. XII (1975–6), pp. 1–14

36 *See* HMC, *Finch MSS*, vol. III

37 J.G. Simms, *The Treaty of Limerick* (Dundalk, 1961)

38 J.C. O'Callaghan, *History of the Irish Brigades in the Service of France* (Dublin, 1870) remains the best account.

CHAPTER 5

1 'Ulterior motive': by which a squadron or fleet was expected to adhere to its instructions and not – even after completing its task – take advantage of opportunities that arose; 'fleet in being': restraining, by threat of its existence, the activities of the enemy

2 The narrative has been largely based on E.B. Powley, *The Naval Side of King William's War* (London, 1972), which covers the period to June 1690. Thereafter other printed sources – such as the *Calendar of State Papers, 1688–91* and Historical Manuscripts Commission (HMC) publications – have been used, together with original documents from Admiralty records.

3 Warships were 'rated' by the number of guns they could carry: first-rates more than 90; second, 80–90; third, 60–80; fourth, 40–60; fifth, 30–40; sixth, fewer than 30. The rate of a ship also determined the pay of its officers.

4 HMC *Finch MSS* (1922), vol. II, p. 197, instructions to Herbert, 30 March 1689

5 Unfortunately no log survives for the *Greyhound*.

6 Log of *Deptford* (Admiralty papers, 51/4160); log of *Bonaventure* (Admiralty papers, 52/9)

7 No log survives for the relief. S. Martin-Leake, *Life of Sir John Leake*, 2 vols (London, 1920), vol. I, pp. 27–30 gives an account compiled from Leake's papers.

8 Log of *Antelope* (Admiralty papers, 51/4116)

9 *See* Powley, *Naval Side of King William's War*, ch. 10

10 HMC, *Finch MSS*, vol. II, p. 273, Shovell to Nottingham, 15 March 1690

11 Log of *Monck* (Admiralty papers, 52/72)

12 Instructions to Shovell, 3 July and 10 July 1690 (Admiralty papers, 2/6)

13 HMC, *Finch MSS*, vol. II, p. 287, Southwell to Nottingham

14 Instructions to Shovell, 16 August 1690 (Admiralty papers, 2/6); log of *Salamander* (Admiralty papers, 51/3963)

CHAPTER 6

1 L.G. Schwoerer, 'Propaganda in the revolution of 1688–89', *American Historical Review*, vol. LXXXII (1977), pp. 843–74 is a detailed survey of many aspects of this topic, to which the present essay is heavily indebted.

2 M. Goldie, 'The revolution of 1689 and the structure of political argument', *Bulletin of Research in the Humanities*, vol. LXXXIII (1980),

pp. 481–3 estimates the size of the market in England for pamphlets on the allegiance controversy of 1689 at 40,000–100,000

3 L.G. Schwoerer, *The Declaration of Rights 1689* (Baltimore, Maryland, 1981), pp. 105–16; P. Monod, 'Jacobitism and country principles in the reign of William III', *Historical Journal*, vol. XXX (1987), pp. 296–9

4 R. Munter, *The History of the Irish Newspaper 1685–1760* (Cambridge, 1967), pp. 13–14

5 J. Loftis, *The Politics of Drama in Augustan England* (Oxford, 1963), pp. 23–5

6 E. Hawkins, *Medallic Illustrations of the History of Great Britain and Ireland to the Death of George II*, A.W. Franks and H.A. Grieber (eds), 2 vols (London, 1885), vol. I, pp. 634–723

7 *Catalogue of Prints and Drawings in the British Museum. . .Political and Personal Satires*, hereafter *Cat. B.M. Satires*, 11 vols (London, 1870–1954), vol. II, pp. 6–15. I should like to thank Lindsay Stainton of the British Museum, Department of Prints and Drawings, for initial advice on the subject of seventeenth-century engraved prints, and for facilitating my research in the museum's collections

8 Hawkins, *Medallic Illustrations*, vol. I, pp. 632–4

9 Schwoerer, *Declaration of Rights*, pp. 115–16

10 *The Speech of the Right Reverend. . .Anthony, Bishop of Meath, when the Clergy Waited on His Majesty at His Camp near Dublin, July 7, 1690* (broadsheet, London 1690)

11 Lord Macaulay, *The History of England from the Accession of James II*, C.H. Firth (ed.), 6 vols (London, 1913–15), vol. III, p. 1137

12 Many of these news-sheets are preserved in the British Library, Department of Printed Books. Of particular relevance are the collections of broadsheets bound with the following call-numbers: 807. f. 36; 807. g. 21; 816. m. 23; 8122. i. 2. For an example of a news-sheet produced by the Jacobite presses in Dublin *see A Relation of What Passed in Connaught between His Majesty's Forces under the Command of Brigadier Sarsfield, and the Rebels. . .* (broadsheet [Dublin, 1689])

13 Hawkins, *Medallic Illustrations*, vol. I, pp. 627–32; *Cat. B.M. Satires*, vol. I, pp. 710–16

14 Hawkins, *Medallic Illustrations*, vol. I, pp. 647, 662

15 C.M. Hibbard, *Charles I and the Popish Plot* (Chapel Hill, 1983); J. Miller, *Popery and Politics in England 1660–88* (Cambridge, 1973); J.P. Kenyon, *The Popish Plot* (London, 1972), especially ch. 1

16 *Cat. B.M. Satires*, vol. I, p. 738

17 J.C.D. Clark, *English Society 1688–1832: Ideology, Social Structure and Political Practice during the Ancien Régime* (Cambridge, 1985), ch. 3

18 J.P. Kenyon, *Revolution Principles: The Politics of Party 1689–1720* (Cambridge, 1977), especially chs 2–4

19 On popular loyalism in London in the Restoration period *see* T. Harris, *London Crowds in the Reign of Charles II: Propaganda and Politics from the Restoration until the Exclusion Crisis* (Cambridge, 1987), especially ch. 6

20 Hawkins, *Medallic Illustrations*, vol. I, pp. 620–1, 630–2, 634–5; J. Vesey, *A Sermon Preach'd to the Protestants in and about the City of London. . .Octob. 23, 1689* (London, 1689), p. 16

21 This subject is discussed in P.K. Monod, 'For the king to enjoy his own again: Jacobite political culture in England, 1688–1788' (unpublished Ph.D. thesis, Yale University, 1985), pp. 90–6, 101–5. Dr. Monod's thesis is to be published shortly by Cambridge University Press.

22 *Cat. B.M. Satires*, vol. I, pp. 725, 740–1

23 G. Lord *et al* (eds), *Poems on Affairs of State*, 7 vols (New Haven, 1963–75), vol. V, p. 41

24 *A New Letter from London-Derry. . .* (broadsheet [London, 1689])

25 Hawkins, *Medallic Illustrations*, vol. I, pp. 634–5, 641, 650, 673, 697

26 *Cat. B.M. Satires*, vol. I, pp. 729–30

27 *Cat. B.M. Satires*, vol. II, p. 22. *See also* vol. I, p. 732 *and*, for examples of anti-papal satire in a different medium, W. Chappell and J.W. Ebsworth (eds), *The Roxburghe Ballads*, 8 vols (Hertford, 1869–97), vol. IV, pp. 313–14, 316–18

28 For what follows in this and the succeeding paragraph *see* D.W. Hayton, 'From barbarian to burlesque: English images of the Irish, c. 1660–1750', *Irish Economic and Social History*, vol. XV (1988), pp. 5–31

29 Dr William's Library, Morrice MS R, pp. 19–20, Roger Morrice's 'ent'ring book', 28 November 1689

30 *A Short View of the Methods Made Use of in Ireland for the Subversion and Destruction of the Protestants Religion and Interest. . .* (London, 1689), p. 30

31 G.C. Duggan, *The Stage Irishman: A History of the Irish Play and Stage Characters from the Earliest Times* (Dublin, 1937), p. 234 ff

32 *A Full and True Account of the Landing and Reception of the Late King James at Kinsale. . .* (broadsheet, London, 1689)

33 *His Grace the Duke of Schomberg's Character. . .* (broadsheet, London [1690])

34 J.G. Simms, *Jacobite Ireland 1685–91* (London, 1969), p. 154

35 *Cat. B.M. Satires*, vol. II, pp. 21–2

36 D.W. Hayton, 'Anglo-Irish attitudes: changing perceptions of national identity among the Protestant ascendancy in Ireland, *c.* 1690–1750', *Studies in Eighteenth-century Culture*, vol. XVII (1987), pp. 146–50; N. Canny, 'Identity formation in Ireland: the emergency of the Anglo-Irish' in N. Canny and A. Pagden (eds), *Colonial Identity in the Atlantic World* (Princeton, 1987), pp. 201–5

37 Hawkins, *Medallic Illustrations*, vol. I, pp. 714–17

38 Hawkins, *Medallic Illustrations*, vol. I, p. 720

CHAPTER 7

1 W. Petty, *The Political Anatomy of Ireland* (London, 1691), pp. 83, 116

2 *Calendar of State Papers, Domestic, 1689–90*, p. 832, 27 September 1690, 'There has been lately great quantities of English coins melted down and transported.'

3 [W. King], *The State of the Protestants of Ireland under the late King James's Government* (London, 1691), p. 94

4 Petty, *Political Anatomy*, p. 72; W. Petty, 'Treatise of Ireland' in *Economic Writings*, C.H. Hull (ed.), 2 vols (Cambridge, 1899), vol. I, p. 593. 'The Money, Plate, Jewels and Fine Furniture, which has been these last Two Years conveyed out of Ireland, or otherwise withdrawn from currant Uses, seems by a numerous Collection of Observations and Relations to be about ⅓ Part of the whole, or about 166 Thousand Pounds.'; p. 577

5 L.M. Cullen, *An Economic History of Ireland since 1660* (London, 1972), p. 22

6 J. Simon, *An Essay towards an Account of Irish Coins* (Dublin, 1749), pp. 56–8

7 Cullen, *Economic History*, p. 22

8 King, *State of the Protestants*, p. 97

9 Simon, *Essay*, pp. 151–3

10 Petty, 'Treatise on Taxes', *Economic Writings*, p. 85

11 Simon, *Essay*, p. 153

12 Simon, *Essay*, p. 157

13 W.H. Hardinge, 'A concluding memoir on the manuscript mapped and other townland surveys in Ireland', *Transactions of the Royal Irish Academy*, vol. XXIV, sect. C (1874), p. 309

14 Simon, *Essay*, pp. 156, 157

15 Simon, *Essay*, p. 59. It is hard to believe that the production of halfpennies for Ireland justified private investment in two full-scale presses. One explanation might be that the James machine was used for coining and the Duchess either for cutting blanks or flattening them. This is relevant to the discussion below.

16 J. Craig, *The Mint* (Cambridge, 1953), pp. 164–5

17 Hardinge, 'A concluding memoir', p. 313. The week in question is 1–8 March 1690

18 There is discussion of this point in M. Dolley and G. Rice, 'The mint of Limerick under James II' in *Small Change* (Numismatic Society of Ireland Occasional Papers 29–38, 1988), where the opposite view is put forward. *See also* note 15, above

19 Quoted in the Introduction to R.H. Murray (ed.), *The Journal of John Stevens* (Oxford, 1912), p. xlviii; G. Story, *A True and Impartial History of the Most Material Occurrences in the Kingdom of Ireland during the Last Two Years* (London, 1691), p. 94

20 Simon, *Essay*, pp. 160–2

21 Hardinge, 'A concluding memoir', p. 313. There is a slight discrepancy in the arithmetic, corrected here.

22 D. Stevenson, 'The Irish emergency coinages of James II 1689–91', *British Numismatic Journal*, vol. XXXVI (1967), pp. 174–5. This is the best survey and a good guide to the sources.

23 M. Dolley, 'Some reflections on the volume of the "Brass Money" of James II', *Seaby's Coin and Medal Bulletin* (December 1974), pp. 377–83 goes into the matter in some detail. The methodology used, however, does not seem to me to be satisfactory. Dolley's conclusion is that Story was correct in giving a total of £1,100,000.

Since the text of this article was written Father G. Rice has published 'The gun money of James II' in *Spink Numismatic Circular*, vol. XCVII, no. 7 (1989), pp. 224–6, which suggests a method of distinguishing between the products of the James and Duchess presses, starting from the premise that the latter was the machine used in Limerick. If 'Duchess' coins can be picked out, then it is possible the total production of brass money might be assessed on a firmer basis than at present.

24 *Calendar of State Papers, Domestic, 1689–90*, p. 373

25 A proclamation issued by William III at Dublin, 10 July 1690, reduced the brass money to scrap value. It was wholly demonetised from 26 February 1691 in areas not under Jacobite

control by a proclamation dated 23 February. Story, *Impartial History*, p. 54

26 Stevens, *Journal*, pp. 83, 102

27 Simon, *Essay*, pp. 57–8

28 S. Mulloy (ed.), *Franco-Irish Correspondence, December 1688–February 1692*, 3 vols (Dublin, 1983, 1984), vol. I, p. 134

29 *Franco-Irish Correspondence*, vol. I, p. 61, dated 17 July 1690, gives some inkling of the situation: 'when the King's [Louis XIV] troops disembarked the louis d'or was worth twenty to twenty-five shillings, today the exchange is so much increased that in Dublin one must give almost 60, which is a dozen of the copper crowns.'; *Franco-Irish Correspondence*, vol. I, p. 86

30 Stevens, *Journal*, pp. 164, 195

31 The 'St Patrick's halfpennies', issued in Dublin *c.* 1672, depict the saint holding up a shamrock, as does a trade token of similar date.

32 The last brass money coins are rare halfcrowns marked October 1690.

33 J. Gilbert (ed.), *A Jacobite Narrative of the War in Ireland 1688–91* (Dublin, 1892), p. 129

34 Simon, *Essay*, pp. 159–62

35 J.D. Bateson and M. Dolley. 'Some remarks on the "pewter" (tin) petty coinage of March/April 1690', *Irish Numismatics*, vol. IX (1976), pp. 44–9 discuss the pewter coins in some detail and give the results of a survey of surviving specimens.

36 Hardinge, 'A concluding memoir', p. 313

37 Dolley and Rice, 'The mint of Limerick', discuss the evidence for the numbers of coins struck at Limerick. I believe there are a number of reasons for suggesting a higher figure.

6 J.G. Simms, *The Williamite Confiscation in Ireland, 1690–1703* (London, 1956) is the indispensable source for any treatment of this subject. *See also* his more recent contribution to the *New History of Ireland*, vol. IV (Oxford, 1986), pp. 10–13.

7 Simms, *Williamite Confiscation*, p. 65

8 Simms, *Williamite Confiscation*, pp. 75–7

9 Simms, *Williamite Confiscation*, p. 160

10 Quoted in M. Lenox-Conyngham, *An Old Ulster House* (Dundalk, 1946), pp. 17–18

11 Quoted in Simms, *Williamite Confiscation*, p. 51

12 Quoted in Simms, *Williamite Confiscation*, p. 52

13 G. Burnet, *History of My Own Time*, 6 vols (Oxford, 1823), vol. IV, p. 430

14 *Report of the Commissioners Appointed by Parliament to Enquire into the Irish Forfeitures* (London and Dublin, 1700)

15 11 & 12 Will. III, c.2

16 PRONI, D1854

17 *A List of the Claims as They are Entered with the Trustees at Chichester House* (Dublin, 1701), no. 2699, p. 312

18 W.A. Maguire, 'The estate of Cuchonnacht Maguire of Tempo: a case history from the Williamite land settlement' (unpublished MS)

19 Indenture of 20 March 1702 between the trustees for the forfeitures and Agmondisham Vesey, Anne Vesey and Henrietta Vesey (De Vesci papers, Vesey of Lucan title deeds, PRONI transcript T3738/V/2

20 Simms, *Williamite Confiscation*, pp. 154–5

21 Simms, *Williamite Confiscation*, p. 160 and Appendix D

22 Miege, *Present State of Great Britain and Ireland*, p. 52

CHAPTER 8

1 *See* L.J. Arnold, 'The Irish court of claims of 1663', *Irish Historical Studies*, vol. XXIV, no. 96 (November 1985). As with the later Williamite court of claims, some of the commissioners were criticised for being far too favourable to Catholic claimants – 'friends of Teig, McRainsford, O'Beverley, McChurchill and O'Broderick'.

2 *State of the Papist and Protestant Proprieties in the kingdom of Ireland* (London, 1689)

3 G. Miege, *The Present State of Great Britain and Ireland*, 2nd edn (London, 1711), p. 51

4 W. Petty, *Economic Writings*, C.H. Hull (ed.), 2 vols (Cambridge, 1899), vol. II

5 *See* J.G. Simms, *The Jacobite Parliament of 1689* (Dundalk, 1966)

CHAPTER 9

1 *A Discourse Concerning Ireland and the Different Interests Thereof* (London, 1698), pp. 21–2

2 HMC, *Portland MSS* vol. III (1894), p. 479, James Bonnell to Robert Harley, 3 November 1691

3 The fullest account of William's attitude is W. Troost, *William III and the Treaty of Limerick (1691–1697)* (Leiden, 1983)

4 *See* J.I. McGuire, 'The Irish parliament of 1692', in T. Bartlett and D.W. Hayton (eds), *Penal Era and Golden Age* (Belfast, 1979)

5 J.G. Simms, 'The bishops' banishment act of 1697', (9 Will. III, c.1), *Irish Historical Studies*, vol. XVII, (1970–1), reprinted in *War and Politics in Ireland 1649–1730* (London, 1986). Apart from this and the other two articles by Simms cited

below (notes 8 and 10), there has been surprisingly little detailed study of the origins of the penal laws. M. Wall, *The Penal Laws* (Dundalk, 1961) deals solely with the laws against Catholic religious organisation, and devotes more space to their effects than to their origins. J.I. McGuire, 'Government attitudes to religious nonconformity in Ireland 1660–1719' in C.E.J. Caldicott, H. Gough and J.-P. Pittion (eds), *The Huguenots and Ireland: Anatomy of an Emigration* (Dublin, 1987) is a useful recent overview. P. Kelly, 'Lord Galway and the penal laws', in the same volume, demolishes the myth that the exiled Huguenot general pursued a private vendetta against Irish Catholics.

6 Troost, *William III and the Treaty of Limerick*, ch. 6; J.G. Simms, *The Treaty of Limerick* (Dundalk, 1961), reprinted in *War and Politics in Ireland*

7 Surrey Record Office, Guildford Muniment Room, Midleton MSS 1248/2, p. 73–5 ff., Alan Brodrick to St John Brodrick, 29 November 1702

8 J.G. Simms, 'The making of a penal law (2 Anne, c. 6) 1703–4', *Irish Historical Studies*, vol. XII (1960), reprinted in *War and Politics in Ireland*

9 The best introduction to Irish politics in the reign of Queen Anne is D.W. Hayton, *Ireland After the Glorious Revolution* (Belfast, 1976). *See also* Hayton, 'The beginnings of the undertaker system' in Bartlett and Hayton (eds), *Penal Era and Golden Age*, pp. 43–8. The extent to which the Tories did in fact seek to restore the Stuarts is still fiercely debated by English historians. For a brief review of the controversy *see* the new Introduction to G. Holmes, *British Politics in the Age of Anne*, rev. edn. (London, 1987), pp. xxix–xxxvii

10 J.G. Simms, 'Irish Catholics and the parliamentary franchise', *Irish Historical Studies*, vol. XII (1960), reprinted in *War and Politics in Ireland*

11 J.C. Beckett, *Protestant Dissent in Ireland 1687–1780* (London, 1948) is still the standard account of policy towards Irish Presbyterians.

12 Trinity College Dublin, MS 750/5, p. 192, King to William Wake, archbishop of Canterbury, 1 August 1719

13 The general view is that no such result was intended. For an alternative interpretation *see* S.J. Connolly, 'Religion and history', *Irish Economic and Social History*, vol. X (1979)

14 D. Dickson, *New Foundations: Ireland 1660–1800* (Dublin, 1987), p. 121. On the general question of the economic and social effects of penal legislation *see* L.M. Cullen, 'Catholics under the penal laws', *Eighteenth-century Ireland*, vol. I (1986)

15 J.G. Simms, *The Williamite Confiscation in Ireland, 1690–1703* (London, 1956). Arthur Young's estimate – a throwaway comment in the course of making a quite separate point – should not be taken too literally.

16 The first use of the term, for some time believed to date from 1792, has now been traced back to 1782: W.J. McCormack, 'Vision and revision in the study of eighteenth-century Irish parliamentary rhetoric', *Eighteenth-century Ireland*, vol. II (1987), pp. 15–33. For the ambiguities of the term, and its changing meaning over time, *see* the same author's *Ascendancy and Tradition: Anglo-Irish Literary History from 1789 to 1939* (Oxford, 1985), pp. 69–89

17 F. O'Ferrall, *Catholic Emancipation: Daniel O'Connell and the Birth of Irish Democracy 1820–1830* (Dublin, 1985)

CHAPTER 10

1 As described by John Trenchard, *An History of Standing Armies in England* (London, 1739), p. 9

2 J.A. Houlding, *Fit for Service: The Training of the British Army, 1715–1795* (Oxford, 1981), p. 52; K.P. Ferguson, 'The army in Ireland from the Restoration to the Act of Union' (unpublished Ph.D. thesis, Trinity College Dublin, 1980), p. 17

3 J. Childs, *The British Army of William III, 1689–1702* (Manchester, 1987), p. 94; J.P. Reid, *In a Defiant Stand: The Conditions of Law in Massachusetts Bay, the Irish Comparison and the Coming of the American Revolution* (Philadelphia, 1978), p. 114

4 T.W. Copeland (ed.), *The Correspondence of Edmund Burke*, 10 vols, (Cambridge, 1958–78), vol. I, p. 343, Burke to Charles O'Hara, 20 February 1766

5 R.W. Jackson, 'Queen Anne's Irish Army Establishment in 1704', *Irish Sword*, vol. I (1949–53), pp. 134–5; Houlding, *Fit for Service*, p. 52 and map; F.G. James, *Ireland in the Empire 1688–1770* (Cambridge, Mass., 1973), p. 178

6 Quoted in J.L. McCracken, 'The social structure and social life, 1714–60' in T.W. Moody and W.E. Vaughan (eds), *A New History of Ireland*, (Oxford, 1986), vol. IV, p. 83

7 'Irish remarks or observations on discipline' by [Lt.-Col. Caroline Frederick Scott], *c.* 1750, Royal Archives, Windsor, Cumberland Papers, Box 44,

no. 99. I acknowledge the kind permission of Her Majesty the Queen to quote from the Cumberland papers. Houlding, *Fit for Service*, p. 56

8 'Irish Remarks'; J.R. Fennell, 'The army in Ireland at the time of the Seven Years War' (unpublished MA thesis, University College Dublin, 1983), p. 24; McCracken, 'Social structure', p. 51

9 Houlding, *Fit for Service*, pp. 115–6

10 Quoted in James, *Ireland in the Empire*, p. 178; Derby Borough Library, Catton Collection (Ireland), vol. XXXVI, Thomas Waite to Sir Robt. Wilmot, 12 March 1763

11 Houlding, *Fit for Service*, p. 107

12 'Irish Remarks'

13 For 'soldier-baiting' in England *see* A. Hayter, *The Army and the Crowd in mid-Georgian England* (London, 1978), p. 21; PRO Home Office Papers, 100/14/93, Lord Sydney to the duke of Rutland, 4 September 1784

14 D.B.L., Catton Coll. (Ire.), p. xli, Waite to Wilmot, 22 February 1766; *see also* the list of incidents in James, *Ireland in the Empire*, p. 180

15 PRO, HO 100/6/137, Nugent Temple to Townshend, 20 March 1783; on desertion *see also* T. Bartlett, 'Some reflections on indiscipline and disaffection in the French and Irish armies in the age of the French Revolution' in H. Gough (ed.), *Ireland and France in the Age of the French Revolution* (Dublin, forthcoming)

16 Fennell, 'The army in Ireland', p. 25

17 *Consideration upon the Augmentation of the Army* (Dublin, 1768), pp. 27–30

18 R. Cox, *Aphorisms Relating to the Kingdom of Ireland* (Dublin, 1689) cited in Ferguson, 'Army in Ireland', p. 18

19 For the problems caused by drafting *see* J.W. Shy, *Towards Lexington: the Role of the British Army in the Coming of the American Revolution* (Princeton, 1965), pp. 274–6

20 McCracken, 'Social structure', p. 82; James, *Ireland in the Empire*, p. 179; Fennell, 'The army in Ireland', p. 41; PRONI, T2915/3/32, Bedford to Richmond, 19 November 1757

21 McCracken, 'Social structure', p. 82; PRONI transcript T3759, Pembroke Calendar of Papers, William Fitzwilliam to Lord Fitzwilliam, 27 September 1755; on Trimleston's offer *see* Calendar of Home Office Papers, vol. I, p. 173, Halifax to earl of Egremont, 13 April 1762; PRO, Chatham papers, 30/8/84/103, note by Townshend, *c.* 27 December 1770

22 *See* T. Bartlett, 'The Protestant nation' in G. Ó Tuathaigh (ed.), *The Long Relationship* (forthcoming)

23 Houlding, *Fit for Service*, p. 6

24 *See* [W. King], *State of the Protestants of Ireland. . .* (Dublin, 1691), p. 155

25 On this point *see* the important articles by S.J. Connolly: 'The Houghers: agrarian protest in early eighteenth-century Ireland' in C.H. Philpin (ed.), *Nationalism and Popular Protest in Ireland* (Cambridge, 1987), pp. 139–62; 'Violence and order in the eighteenth century' in P. O'Flanagan *et al* (eds), *Rural Ireland: Modernisation and Change* (Cork, 1987), pp. 42–62; and 'Albion's fatal twigs: justice and law in the eighteenth century' in R. Mitchison and P. Roebuck (eds), *Economy and Society in Ireland and Scotland, 1500–1939* (Edinburgh, 1988), pp. 117–25

26 Connolly, 'Houghers', p. 146; J. O'Donovan, 'The militia in Munster 1715–78' in G. O'Brien (ed.), *Parliament, Politics and People: Essays in Eighteenth-century Irish History* (Dublin, 1989), pp. 31–47

27 S. Clement, *An Answer to Mr. Molyneux* (London, 1698)

28 *Some Remarks on the Conduct of the Parliament of England as Far as it Relates to the Woollen Manufacture* (London, 1731), pp. 11–12

29 Trenchard, *Standing Armies*, p. 45; *see also* the roughly contemporaneous but anonymous pamphlet entitled, *Proposals for raising a Standing Army of Wax* (Dublin, ?1736)

30 T. Bartlett, 'The augmentation of the army in Ireland, 1767–69', *English Historical Review*, vol. CCCLXXX (July 1981), pp. 540–59

SELECT BIBLIOGRAPHY

Baxter, S.B. *William III* (London, 1966)

Beckett, J.C. *Protestant Dissent in Ireland, 1687–1780* (London, 1948)

Carswell, J. *The Descent on England* (London, 1969)

Childs, J. *The Army, James II and the Glorious Revolution*
   (Manchester, 1980)
   The British Army of William III, 1689–1702 (Manchester, 1987)

Danaher, K., and J.G. Simms (eds). *The Danish Force in Ireland, 1690–1691* (Dublin, 1962)

Dickson, D. *New Foundations: Ireland 1660–1800* (Dublin, 1987),
   chs 1 and 2

Ehrman, J. *The Navy in the War of William III 1689–97*
   (Cambridge, 1953)

Ellis, P.B. *The Boyne Water* (London, 1976; reprinted Belfast, 1989)

Foster, R.F. *Modern Ireland, 1600–1972* (London, 1988), chs 6 and 7

Gilbert, J.T. (ed.). *A Jacobite Narrative of the War in Ireland 1689–91*
   (Dublin, 1892; reprinted Shannon, 1971)

Hamilton, E. *William's Mary* (London, 1972)

Hatton, R. (ed.). *Louis XIV and Europe* (London, 1976)

Hatton, R. and J.S. Bromley (eds). *William III and Louis XIV. Essays
   1680–1720 by and for Mark A. Thomson* (Liverpool, 1968)

Hayes-McCoy, G.A. *Irish Battles: A Military History of Ireland*
   (London, 1969)

Macaulay, T.B. *History of England* (5 vols, London, 1849–61)

Macrory, P. *The Siege of Derry* (London, 1980)

Miller, J. *Popery and Politics in England 1660–88* (Cambridge, 1973)
   The Life and Times of William and Mary (London, 1974)
   James II: A Study in kingship (Hove, 1978)

Petrie, C. *The Jacobite Movement: The First Phase, 1688–1716*
   (London, 1948)
   The Great Tyrconnel (Cork, 1972)

Powley, E.B. *The Naval Side of King William's War* (London, 1972)

Robb, N.A. *William of Orange, A Personal Portrait* (2 vols, London,
   1962 and 1966)

Simms, J.G. *The Williamite Confiscation in Ireland, 1690–1703*
   (London, 1956)
   Jacobite Ireland, 1685–91 (London, 1969)
   War and Politics in Ireland 1649–1730 (London, 1986)
   See also his contributions to *The New History of Ireland*, vol. III,
   ch. 19, and vol. IV, ch. 1 (Oxford, 1976 and 1986)

Speck, W.A. *Reluctant Revolutionaries: Englishmen and the Revolution of
   1688* (Oxford, 1988)

van der Zee, H. and B. *William and Mary* (London, 1973)

Wall, M. *The Penal Laws* (Dundalk, 1961)

Wolf, J.B. *Louis XIV* (London, 1968)

THE CONTRIBUTORS

THOMAS BARTLETT, a graduate of Queen's University Belfast (at whose Institute of Irish Studies he is the current Senior Research Fellow), lectures in history at University College Galway. He co-edited (with David Hayton) *Penal Era and Golden Age: Essays in Irish History 1691–1800* (1979), is joint editor (with S.J. Connolly) of the journal *Irish Economic and Social History*, and has written on various aspects of the political, constitutional and social history of Ireland in the eighteenth century.

S.J. CONNOLLY is a graduate of the University of Ulster, where he has taught since 1981 and is now Reader in History. He is the author of *Priests and People in Pre-Famine Ireland* (1982); *Religion and Society in Nineteenth-Century Ireland* (1985); and of several chapters in *Ireland Under the Union 1800–1870* (vol. v of *The New History of Ireland*). His most recent work, *Religion, Law and Power: The Making of Protestant Ireland 1660–1760*, is to be published shortly by Oxford University Press. He is joint editor (with Thomas Bartlett) of the journal *Irish Economic and Social History*.

G.C. GIBBS, a graduate of Liverpool University, lectured for many years at Birkbeck College and is now Reader Emeritus in History at the University of London. He is the author of numerous articles and essays on British foreign policy in the early eighteenth century and on the Huguenots in England and Holland. He is currently co-ordinating the British contribution to an international research project on Huguenot refugees in Europe, 1680–1715, and is also working on a biography of William and Mary.

DAVID HAYTON is a graduate of Manchester University and Oxford (where his doctoral thesis dealt with the government of Ireland under Queen Anne). He is now working on the 1690–1715 volumes of the *History of Parliament*. He has written numerous articles on Anglo-Irish politics in the late seventeenth and early eighteenth centuries and co-edited (with Thomas Bartlett) *Penal Era and Golden Age: Essays in Irish History 1691–1800* (1979).

ROBERT HESLIP is a graduate of Queen's University Belfast. He is Assistant Keeper and Curator of Numismatics in the Department of Local History at the Ulster Museum. He is the author of a number of articles on Irish coinage and has a particular interest in the use of coins and medals as historical evidence.

JAMES MCGUIRE, a graduate of the National University of Ireland, is Senior Lecturer in Modern Irish History at University College Dublin, and author of a number of articles on the political and religious history of Ireland in the later seventeenth century. He was co-editor of *Parliament and Community* (1983) and is currently joint editor of the journal *Irish Historical Studies*.

W.A. MAGUIRE is a graduate of St Andrews University and Queen's University Belfast. Since 1980 he has been Keeper of Local History at the Ulster Museum. His publications include *The Downshire Estates in Ireland, 1801–1845* (1982); (ed.) *Letters of a Great Irish Landlord* (1974); *Living like a Lord* (1982), a biography of the second marquis of Donegall; and a number of articles on the history of Irish landownership.

JOHN MILLER was educated at Jesus College, Cambridge, and was a Fellow of Gonville and Caius College before joining the staff of Queen Mary (now Queen Mary and Westfield) College, London, where he holds a personal chair. He is a leading authority on later seventeenth-century English history. His publications include *Popery and Politics in England, 1660–88* (1973); *The Life and Times of William and Mary* (1974); *James II: A Study in Kingship* (1978; reprinted 1989), and numerous articles. He is currently working on a biography of Charles II.

HARMAN MURTAGH, a graduate of Trinity College Dublin and the National University of Ireland, lectures in law at the Regional Technical College, Athlone. He is editor of the *Irish Sword*, the journal of the Military History Society of Ireland, and an authority on Irish military history in the late seventeenth century. He has lectured and written extensively on the Jacobite war.

A.W.H. PEARSALL graduated from Cambridge after serving in the Royal Navy. Until 1985 he worked in the National Maritime Museum, Greenwich, as Custodian of Manuscripts and latterly as Historian. He is the author of a number of articles and papers on aspects of naval history.

INDEX